ALL OF US

ALL OF US

AMERICANS TALK ABOUT
THE MEANING OF DEATH

Patricia Anderson

Delacorte ▓ Press

Published by
Delacorte Press
Bantam Doubleday Dell Publishing Group, Inc.
1540 Broadway
New York, New York 10036

Library of Congress Cataloging in Publication Data
All of us : Americans talk about the meaning of death / [edited] by Patricia Anderson.
p.   cm.
Includes bibliographical references.
ISBN 0-385-31278-4 (hardcover)
1. Death—Psychological aspects. 2. Bereavement—Psychological aspects. I. Anderson, Patricia (Patricia June)
BF789.D4A45   1996
155.9′37—dc20   96-472   CIP

Manufactured in the United States of America

Published simultaneously in Canada

September 1996

10   9   8   7   6   5   4   3   2   1

BVG

Dedicated to the memory of
DIANE CLEAVER
whose sudden death reminded a
whole lot of people about
the truly ephemeral and
precious nature of our lives.

And to my beloved mother-in-law
EUGENIA SHIFRIN
who lived an extra twenty years
for this child who needed her so.

CONTENTS

ALL OF US

"I sensed a relationship between attitudes toward death in their most general and common expression, and variations in the awareness of self and other, the sense of individual destiny and of the collective destiny of the race."

. . . PHILIPPE ARIÈS

"Tell me how you die and I will tell you who you are."

. . . MEXICAN FOLK ADAGE

A NOTE TO READERS

In setting out to do this book my original aim was to canvass as wide a variety of experience as possible—rich and poor, black and white, young and old. In the fields of medicine, the social services, the sciences and arts, I identified individuals who, I felt, had something interesting to say on the subject. They in turn directed me to other people they felt might have something valuable to contribute; and they, in turn, suggested others. The project simply grew and grew. I wound up with a great surfeit of material, reinforcing my original finding—we have a lot to say on the subject of death.

After talking with more than two hundred people and taping 110 interviews, I came to realize that the true story wasn't in a list of predetermined quotas but in the voice of each individual, sharing fear and uncertainty as well as inspiration. While not every demographic category is represented, I believe many universal experiences are.

The book is shaped to show the mosaic of our culture, our relationship to tradition and ritual, and the development of current conventions. Thus some voices appear more than once as their experience is appropriate.

The chronology in this book traces the origins and development of what has come to be the dominant cultural model for death in the United States at the end of the twentieth century. As such, it focuses on the evolution of Western Christianity and scientific rationalism as it has influenced that attitude. It is not a geographical chronology but rather a chronology of ideas that have traveled from one geographical region to another.

I have used the term "West" in its conventionally vague sense, which is to say the cultural ethos developed from the traditional "Western" historical canon and currently epitomized in the United States. Conversely, I have chosen not to use the terms "B.C." and "A.D." but the alternative "B.C.E." (Before the Common Era) and "C.E." (Common Era), because they are commensurate with the longer time frame I am presenting.

Our view of history is constantly revised as we make new discoveries, modify prejudices, and change the point from which our view is taken. Those revisions are, in and of themselves, worth much discussion and consideration. In this chronology, however, I have omitted that discussion and glossed over many developments that would be seen as important by any measure in order to present a quick and, I hope, informative look backward.

THE GREATEST MYSTERY OF ALL

One hundred thousand years ago Paleolithic people gathered together some bones and shells and created the first ritual in human history. It was a death ritual. Last week I stood on a beach with my family, raised a glass in tribute, and scattered seashells into the ocean. It was a death ritual.

The toast was in the name of my mother-in-law, who had died seven days before, the shells her personal collection of mementos gathered from the places she had loved. We honored her name, drank to her spirit, and symbolically released our attachment to her, giving those lovely delicate shells and polished stones over to the sea, over to impermanence incarnate in the wind and the waves.

During the week since Eugenia died we had definitely done some crying but we had spent most of our time meeting the myriad requirements that arise in the aftermath of a contemporary life. In addition to dealing with the phone company, the post office, the bank, and the government, we found ourselves writing letters, packing boxes, and consoling others. Taking care of her business was, in a way, like taking care of her.

Now, on the beach, a finality began to sink in. She was really and completely gone. Death had come to us in her place, interrupting the assumption of future, reminding us of our fragility. It was a rainy day but we ignored the gathering storm, huddling together on the sand long after the shells and the champagne were gone. We needed one another. We needed time to stop and pay attention to death.

Personally I'd always found death interesting, strictly from a theoretical standpoint of course. The difficult aspects of bodily disintegration frightened me as much as they do anybody, but the *idea* of death was amazing. All is impermanent. We are impermanent. How do we deal with that? It's so bloody big.

Now I thought about those early beings, perhaps gathered on a beach like this, thousands of years ago. What did they do when their mother died? Who was the first among them to raise a voice in the face of death? Were they lumbering, perplexed and goofy, trying vainly to revive a dead mate, like cartoon apes, whimpering and confused? Were they touching and tragic, lifting their arms in anguished pleading to an incomprehensible sky? Or were they noble beyond our awareness, so merged with the cyclical nature of life and death that they possessed a great understanding of reality, an understanding we have lost and forgotten. Was death easier for them? Or harder?

No one really knows what these people were doing when they first found a ritual voice. Scholars are sure only that it was around the event of death. It's believed that early humans thought of death as an external phenomenon, something visited upon them by the gods or by magic. That's what death looked like then. It was mysterious and it was often sudden and it was everywhere. There was very little "natural" death from aging because everyone died from wounds or bites or falling out of trees or into pits, usually early in life.

Agrarian societies planted seeds, watched them grow, flower, and die, then sprout up again next spring. They saw babies grow, flower, and die, then more babies born and dying, everything born and dying over and over with the seasons of the earth, the whole world born and dying.

In the East this cyclical view prevailed, as in ancient Taoist China, where death was seen as an integral aspect of nature's laws, themselves the universal principles guiding reality. As such, death was accepted with a kind of joy. In Vedic India death was viewed as just one more experience in the continuous cycle of experience making up the wheel of life and death, leading to the next birth in the succession of birth, death, and rebirth in the world.

In the West, things took a different turn. Judeo-Christian culture developed a linear view wherein death was seen as the final end of material existence and the beginning of an immortality defined by punishment and reward.

But whether you lived in the East or the West, death was in your face. Until the nineteenth century, one-third of the people on the planet died before they were three years old, one-half before reaching the age of eight. Everyone saw death happen frequently, and both the event and our sense of it were integrated into daily life.

Over the last millennium, our beliefs about death have evolved slowly, influenced by cultural change in general. But for all that time we lived *with* death, not *in spite of* death, and while it wasn't a very pretty proposition, it was not denied.

Then suddenly, about fifty years ago in the West, a dramatic transformation occurred. Economic, social, religious, and demographic changes, combined with advances in technological medicine and public health initiatives, made death seem to disappear. The average life span soared and we stopped seeing people die. For the first time in history, a human child could grow to full adulthood without experiencing the death of anyone close to him or her.

More than that, death's status changed. Science seemed to hold the potential to eliminate it. No longer an acknowledged certainty, death became a possibly curable disorder. This was not one more attitudinal step along a continuum of change, but a seismic shift, a radical reconsideration of our very destiny.

Within the space of a few generations, we took advantage of this opportunity to ignore death. It was a relief. How wonderful to enjoy longer, healthier lives. How wonderful to give birth and know our children would likely outlive us. How liberating to come out from under the omnipresent death of the past. But this gift came with a catch. As we lost our familiarity with death, we also lost our sense of how to deal with it. As sacred and secular protocol diminished, we lost our ritual voice and, most grievously, we started to ignore the dying, leaving them in the hands of institutions devoted to cure and bereft of care. Death became shameful, and the dying a painful reminder of human fallibility.

This was such a revolutionary change from most of human history that social observers, historians, and others could not help but notice it. In the 1960s Geoffrey Gorer wrote of the "pornography of death," in the 1970s Philippe Ariès wrote of the "brutality" of this social revolution and Elisabeth Kübler-Ross and others spoke out against what came to be called "the death taboo." In a world where death was shameful it was no longer safe to die.

Twenty-five years later it has become commonplace to call America a death-denying culture. Problems generated by the proscription of death have become too difficult to ignore. Ethical and moral dilemmas surface over questions of rights and dignity, lawsuits are instigated, euthanasia legislation is proposed, a suicide manual becomes a best seller. The taboo is so effective, it has created a massive backlog of need for information and comfort about death. As this accumulation of unanswered need grows greater and greater it spills over the inhibition the taboo has set in place, like water over a dam. Today many people have realized there is something wrong with how we die.

While researching a book on a related subject, I was surprised to hear how people talked about death. Interviews would become sidetracked as I listened, fascinated, to the most remarkable experiences, opinions, and reflections. I talked at some length with sociologist John Riley, who did the first major national survey of attitudes toward death in the early sixties. He described his initial meeting with interviewers from the National Opinion Research Center at the University of Chicago, all of whom said to him: "People will not talk about that." "They'll run away." "We'll have doors slammed in our faces."

Dr. Riley convinced them to give it a go and developed a beginning protocol. They went off to do pretesting and to conduct the initial interviews. Ten days later, when they met again, Dr. Riley told me, "As soon as I walked in the room I realized that something had happened, I could tell from their expressions. They all had one thing to tell me. They said their respondents in one way or another had *thanked* them for the opportunity to talk about death, had expressed gratitude for the chance to talk about it. We went on to complete the survey, which provided the original data base for much of the work that followed, but I always felt the most important point coming out of that research was that first reaction—the revelation that people would talk about it, that some people even *wanted* to talk about it."

I found myself having the same experience, and I realized that this isn't just another social issue. This is everybody's future, big time. I started asking people: "What do you really believe about death?" "How do you comfort yourself in the face of death?" "How do you answer your children's questions about it?" "What do you think happens when we die?" I began to wish I could get us all in one big room to talk about this thing together. It was clear we have much to tell each other.

As the end of the millennium nears and the baby-boomers reach midlife—confronting AIDS, aging, and their own mortality—there is a new urgency to this consideration. The wake-up call may be the death of a parent or lover, the loss of a job, or the realization that expectation is no longer open-ended; but whatever triggers that glimpse into the future, a lot of people are looking warily ahead to the lonely, mortified kind of dying we have created by default and wondering if there isn't a better way to do it. Could death be different than it is for most people now? Could death be better? Do we have the potential for a completely new understanding of death and dying?

Personally, I've always wanted to feel okay about death. Mostly I've wanted not to be afraid of it, but the conventional platitudes have never worked for me. I remember my beloved father-in-law saying, "Basically I think, death, this is not good. From the point of view of a living person, this is not a good thing. People talk about death being a part of life . . . that's a crock. It's not a *part* of life, it's the *opposite* of life. I say to them, 'It's *death* you schmuck, not life, death!' Try being dead and say, 'Hey, it's just a part of life. Go ahead . . . try.' "

He succumbed to Lou Gehrig's disease in 1991. His lungs failing, he wanted no respirator, no further treatment, nothing. "When it's time, it's time," he said, ". . . and it's time."

All of us die. It's the one sure thing you and I have in common. Maybe we are the two most dissimilar people in the entire world, maybe we couldn't agree on anything if given a hundred years, maybe we would hate each other on sight. It doesn't matter. We have an absolutely irrevocable bond, you and I. In this we are the same. We are going to die.

Sitting on the beach with my family, I looked at the gray sky and the rough ocean and I thought of Eugenia, who had died a gentle death with her family by her side. I thought of all the different kinds of death that have happened and will happen and I wondered what my own death will be like. I felt that longing for safety that lurks in the core of each one of us, the longing for love and care, the longing to know it will be okay.

Suddenly I had an overwhelming sense of being part of something, something so old it had no name, a vast unbroken line of longing that stretched back a hundred thousand years. As my fear and sadness joined with all the fear and sadness in that ancient lineage, I felt released from the terrible wish that it were different. I think my heart surrendered to death for a moment, surrendered to everything, just the way it is, with no exception, no qualification—as if there were nothing to count on but my need for compassion, and Death said, "Get it?"

I stood up and took a deep breath. I had one last handful of shells, a few especially delicate pieces I'd been hesitant to give up. I found myself walking across the sand, then faster, finally running toward the water. With a cry I threw them, *flew* them into the sea and there, in their split-second arc against the sky, I saw the secret of safety hidden in the middle of death. No matter who you are, no matter what you believe, no matter, no matter, no matter what— there truly *is* something bigger than all of us.

FLEUR GREEN
Age: 48
Psychotherapist

༄

About twenty years ago I had a dream. In the dream, I'm lying in a hospital bed and I feel pretty sick. A doctor comes in and he's very officious. He goes to the end of my bed, picks up the chart, looks at it, puts the chart down and comes around to the bedside. He looks at me and says, in a very matter-of-fact voice, "There's nothing we can do. You are going to die." I sit bolt upright in bed, filled with indignation, and I say, "How *dare* you say that to me, I'm an American!"

Now during that time I was doing encounter groups a lot and the message in all of those groups was, "You are powerful." "You can achieve whatever you want to achieve." "You are in control of your life."

On a certain level that idea is ego-strengthening and it's important. But of course, at a much deeper level, it's just not true. You can't control everything and you can't do whatever you want to do. Life and death are huge, much bigger than we are. If you ask me, humans have about as much chance of grasping the totality of life as blue jays have of grasping long division. You can exercise a lot of choice about your experience, but to imagine you are choosing the totality of your life is silly. More than that, it makes death a big problem, like if you die you didn't get it right. That's awful.

MARTA ARQÜELLO
Age: 35
Project Director
University of California Center for the
Study of Latino Health

❦

I see a lot of cultural disorientation, and I don't mean in the Latino or immigrant community. I mean in the dominant culture, in the white culture. This country isn't anchored to anything. It's become unmoored. And as I was thinking about death, and that whole thing of our denial and death becoming more separated, more sanitized in the dominant culture, I was wondering, maybe there's a link between that sense of being unanchored and that denial. Because in a way, death is what anchors life at some level.

I was thinking about AIDS as this allegorical thing. Sometimes you hear people say that AIDS may have been the best thing that ever happened to them because they finally found meaning in their life. Now that's really horrible. The obscenity of a culture that does that, where you can't see that you have power to do things and affect people and love one another and live a meaningful life until you're confronted with this virus that's going to kill you, slowly. I mean, AIDS *is* allegorical—we are all infected so you'd better just do it now.

Hmmm. "Just do it." They'll probably make a commercial out of it. Death will be commodified too.

HELEN TWORKOV
Age: 52
Editor, *Tricycle: The Buddhist Review*

❧

When I was growing up there was the sense that everything bad in life was going to be made better. For smallpox they came up with a smallpox vaccine. For polio they developed a polio vaccine. If the Soviet Union had atomic bombs they came up with hydrogen bombs, bigger bombs, better bombs, bombs for every problem. Whatever was wrong, something would fix it, we would be protected. The Nazis had just killed six million Jews but this would never happen again. It was the fifties and the prevailing assumption was that the world was evolving toward a better place, a natural progression that would inevitably bring improvement and better things.

Of course, as a child you have no sense of history, so from my seven-year-old view everything *was* going to get better. And, because death was something bad and associated with illness, and all these diseases were being overcome by the Western medical establishment, it seemed that if you lived long enough, you could outlive death, you could be cured of death. They were going to solve all problems, including this little problem that you had to die.

Children were discouraged from knowing much about death or experiencing it or even going to funerals. I remember it was very common, when I was a child, for kids not to go to their grandparents' funerals. The conventional wisdom was that children were too young, you protected them from knowing about this fact of life. Again, it was a "problem."

Now, compared to other cultures, this is weird. Throughout history, in any real community, someone you knew would die every couple of years, either on your block or your road or in your family or your church. And you would know about it and participate in some ritual around it. The whole process of dying and death and funerals was an accepted part of everyone's life, including the children's lives. Now it's possible to go for ten, twenty, thirty years without going to a funeral. Even with AIDS killing so many people who are in their twenties. That's really aberrant. In what kind of society do you go to a funeral for the first time in your life when you're twenty-five?

I have a very close friend, we are both Zen students. His brother had been quite ill and we knew he was dying. About two days before the brother died, my friend called me and started asking questions about what to do at the time of death and what arrangements could be made for a ritual or ceremony that would be meaningful.

This is not all that unusual. For any American who has any feeling whatsoever about the death process, whether you are on a religious path or not, you find yourself suddenly faced with having to invent a ritual for dying. Any meaningful ritual, around both the death and the funeral, has to be invented. The available ritual, the one that you buy from a funeral business, is empty and impersonal. If you want something that actually has to do with anything, or anybody, you have to invent it. On the spot.

And it's such a crazy American situation, because suddenly you have to take into account all these different factors. Like, maybe the wife is Jewish and the brother is a Zen student, and the dead person was a Ramakrishna follower, and the children don't want to hear about any of it. And everyone has their own idea about what should happen and what the service should be like and who should perform it and what should be done. It's like a three-ring circus, where everyone is doing something different in the middle of the event of this person's death.

In America, we can't default to the cultural heritage because we don't have one, as far as I can figure out. All we have is materialism and denial. There's nothing for us to fall back on. We may default to an *older* ritual. Maybe Jews will go back to something that was more traditional, or Catholics will go back to something that was more traditional. God knows what the Buddhists will do. I mean, it'll be light years before anyone is going to give us permission to have our bodies laid out on a hilltop and eaten by birds, a Tibetan Buddhist practice called "Sky Burial," which is certainly how I'd like to go.

The point is, it's hard to do this in a way that really resonates with meaning for the people involved. And although some people seem to be considering death a little bit more than they used to, the society in general continues to make it very difficult to actually acknowledge it in any meaningful way. In this small town where I've spent a lot of time, you're no longer allowed to bury somebody on your own land. It's become illegal, even though, if you walk in the woods, you'll find little cemeteries everywhere, places where there were large farms and family members were buried outside the kitchen window. You'll find these little clumps that are all covered over. But now, it's illegal to bury somebody on your own property. Not that everyone wants to do that, but the point is, each family has to keep reinventing some new ritualized way of going through their grief.

My father died about ten years ago. I helped take care of him for three months before he died. My mother was very anxious around my father as he was dying. She was very uncomfortable with death and she was holding on to him as well. She was just very, very anxious. He actually couldn't stand having her in the room during those last weeks. Even in a kind of semi-coma, he would withdraw from her anxiety. You could see it. So I knew I could bring something to that situation which might be helpful.

My father had bone cancer and there was a lot of pain, on and off, but in some ways it was a wonderful death. We took care of him at home and he died there. We never put him into a hospital or a nursing home. We were able to do that because the family was there, my sister and her husband came. We learned how to administer morphine, IV needles, oxygen tents, we had a hospital bed. At the end we had nursing help. I think if you don't have a certain amount of help it would become too difficult, but we were able to manage it.

After my father died I would have preferred that his body not be moved and that I be allowed to sit zazen in the room with him for three days and three nights. Zazen is simply sitting in meditation.

The Jewish custom is to bury people right away. However, as it happened, my father couldn't be buried for three days because he died over Labor Day weekend. He died on a Friday night and the next day was the Sabbath and you're not supposed to have a Jewish funeral on the Sabbath. Then, on Sunday, the Provincetown Cemetery was closed because it was a holiday weekend. They couldn't get anybody to open it up or dig the grave, so they didn't bury him until the following Monday.

In many cultures it's considered best to wait three days before disposing of the body in whatever way, burial, cremation, or whatever. And I would have to say, from my experience of being with people who have died, it would take a couple of days for you to feel that they're totally gone, totally dead.

All you have to do is be with someone who has died. Even if you refuse to revert to religious terms, and you don't want to talk about consciousness, you can still make a simple observation. It's not a black-and-white situation, it's not like he or she is alive in one second then there's this death rattle and they're dead. It simply doesn't work that way. When you're with someone who is dying you can feel that energy leaking out over a period of months or weeks or days, however long their death takes. And after they stop breathing, there is still something, for a while.

So you have to begin to question, "What else is going on in the body?" "What does the body contain?" "What else is it housing besides this breath?" Because it's so clear that there's a life there after the breath stops. At some point you say the person is dead, but you don't say that right away. It takes a little time.

I asked to sit with my father but it made my mother too anxious to have his body in the house. I don't think her concern had anything to do with Jewish tradition. I think for her there was just a lot of personal anxiety about death and dying and dead bodies and she didn't have any comfort with it.

Finally, she compromised on my behalf. She let me sit with him all of that first night and didn't call the funeral home until the next morning. I went with my father's body to the funeral home and I sat with him there.

WES NISKER
Age: 50
Writer and Broadcast Journalist

❧

When people die, I think a lot of families return to older ways, to their traditional forms of burial and rites of passage. Although more and more I hear about people requesting cremation rather than burial, and more and more I hear people say "Please celebrate," writing in their wills "I want a party," "I want a wake." But of course that's traditional too.

In this country people are taking certain elements of different traditions and mixing and matching. Here we have a polyglot mythology of all the world's cultures. It's beautiful and very rich, but sometimes a bit confusing.

I think part of what the whole "New Age" is about is trying to find new ways of relating to the mysteries, finding or creating rituals that will bring wonder back into our lives. Because ritual is really a way of honoring something that we don't understand.

I attended a men's movement retreat a couple of years ago, in Mendocino, California, with Robert Bly and James Hillman, and we performed a West African grieving ritual. One of Robert Bly's themes is that we don't know how to grieve.

People took their loss, symbolic or real, and wrote it down on a piece of paper and placed it, with some cherished objects, in a designated sacred ground. Then we went to the other side of a field, several hundred yards away from the sacred place. There was drumming and singing and then people would run or dance or walk to the sacred ground across this large field, and the movement somehow activated the grief. It was almost as if we were mining our own grief.

This ritual worked quite well. I'm fairly skeptical, and often I find it hard to let myself go into a ritual, but this one really grabbed me. I found myself grieving for my parents who had died in the years previous. I suddenly realized how little grieving I had done at the time. I had done some but there was a real core of grief that hadn't been touched. By digging up the grief I found my emotional self again, and that opened me up to a new intimacy with the world.

Maybe our ways of letting go are just too stifling. There is a kind of shame that goes with weeping in public or grieving too much— we are required to be "civilized" and not make too big a show.

At the men's retreat, because we were grieving in a group, the grief went from being a personal thing to also being a community grief. Several people I talked to felt this. The ritual evoked a universal kind of sadness, and that changed the quality of the event. It became archetypal and there was a potency to it that went beyond solitary grieving.

As evolved as we may think we are, we humans still feel deeply lost. Something like this ritual reminds you that you're human and when you remember that you're human you're connecting to everyone else. It's not bound by a particular culture. It's a species consciousness that emerges.

People need to go through all the stages of anger and grief. They have to actually move through them because if they don't, or if they're cut off from their sadness, it stays there and poisons them. That's why we need the rituals, whether they are old or new ones. We have always needed rituals to help us deal with the hard stuff.

I went to a funeral recently that was profound. It was a Catholic funeral in a Catholic church. The symbolism, the expression, the feeling, the acceptance, were very moving. Very moving. I think the Catholic Church is much closer to an acceptance of death than other churches, than the Protestant churches, certainly.

Now I'm not a Catholic, I'm an Episcopalian, but the Catholic Church certainly offers hope, hope in the face of deep bitterness. You acknowledge that it's bitter. If you didn't have bitterness you wouldn't need hope.

This funeral was for a man who had died suddenly of a heart attack at age fifty-nine. He was a vital man, the former publisher of the *Times Herald*, where I used to work. His coffin appeared in the back of the church, the priest came down from the front to greet him and sprinkle on the holy water. The flag of the church was placed on the coffin which was then brought into the sanctuary and there were the Eucharist and varied eulogies. Then the American flag was put on the coffin, the flag of Ireland, which he loved, and also a special flag that had been made for him at the request of his family. Finally, when the coffin was taken back down the aisle, a bagpipe player appeared from the back of the church playing "Amazing Grace."

At the cemetery they had the bagpipes again. The American flag was folded by two sailors (Tom had served in the Navy). A trumpet played "Taps." It was haunting, very beautiful.

Now, all of this symbolism was quite powerful, and so many people since then have said that it was very important to them. They were moved by it.

You see, his death was a surprise. He wasn't in his eighties or at the end of a long illness or anything. The death was a sudden shock to people and we needed something, some ritual to help us absorb the shock. And all the things I have described to you are very simple; they are very obvious. They used to be done as a matter of course. Today though, we have drained away the essential juices from our death ritual and therefore from our hearts. With serious consequences.

For a long time we have had an amazing faith in science. Now I believe in science, but not as the one true way. Certainly not the only way. Today I think we're seeing a rebellion against science as the only way, in New Age thinking and the like, and thank God for it. It seems there's some kind of shift toward more faith in a nonmaterialist or a nonscientific approach to things. Look at the best-seller list. *Care of the Soul, Women Who Run with the Wolves;* these are not books you would expect to see on the best-seller list.

We have here a great welling up of belief that I think churches have not yet figured out how to tap. Certainly in the Bible Belt, church attendance is doing very well from what I understand, but in the more mainline churches, not so well, not so well as they would like. Which just shows that they are not reaching people. They're not reaching the belief that is there, ready to be reached. I'm sure they're making efforts to adapt to contemporary needs but they're adapting in the wrong way. They don't understand that people need symbolism. People need ritual. If they need to discuss the environment, they can go to the Sierra Club. If they need marital counseling they can go to a marriage counselor. I'm all for the church providing comfort, of course, with personal troubles and counseling, but I think they'd better be careful about becoming too modern in the empty way, which is to say, draining the church of its essential symbolism and ritual.

I think we've had a devastating loss of symbolism, and if you lose symbols, then you also lose the mystery those symbols are meant to represent. So it's a horrible loss of mystery. A denial of mystery. There has to be a way to acknowledge mystery and to bring the mysterious into everyday life. That's what ritual does, and that's what must happen.

When I was about ten or eleven years old, both my grandparents died, my father's parents. They died just two years apart. Those were the first funerals that I remember going to, and they made a great impression on me. I was not frightened, I was fascinated. These were serious religious services and I found them very satisfying, the ritual and all. You see, they *should* be satisfying. Not in the way a lovely apple tart is satisfying, of course, but deeply satisfying in that there is some sense of rightness with the universe, that this pain has some purpose, some context.

Now this is the South and, traditionally, people take the rituals of death very seriously in the South. It is customary to call, to take food, to write letters and send flowers and all of that, to acknowledge the death.

However, even here it's changing. For example, it's now quite common to have a private burial, just for the family, before a memorial service. With the funeral I was telling you about, they considered the burial equally important. His wife went to the trouble to have the trumpeter and the bagpipe player also there at the graveyard. That was not an afterthought, it was not something tacked on later, it was the culmination of what we had experienced that morning.

To some extent I think this might be about ethnic communities as well. What I was seeing last week was very Irish, very Irish Catholic. It may be that those cities and regions that have retained more distinct ethnic communities have retained more of the old ways of dealing with death. Because remember, these traditions involve strong religious ties. There is a wonderful book called *Protestant, Catholic and Jew,* written by Will Herberg several years ago, in which he said the American faith is in America. It's not faith in a religious tradition at all, it's faith in America. And he cited a quotation from President Eisenhower, who said, I don't know what these people are, they may be Protestants, Catholics, Jews, I don't care what they are, they're Americans.

Well you see, that's very American. And it is American to give no thought to religion as any kind of qualifier. The American faith is in America. Nonetheless, it was also very revealing—I don't care what they are—as if it didn't matter. But religious and ethnic traditions matter very much. They have a purpose in everyday life. It's not just a way of holding on to the past, it's a way of helping you to deal with the difficulties of life, like death. And this is something we're going to have to come to terms with in America.

Of course, we do have a pluralistic society, which is terribly important. There's a book by Richard Hofstadter, *America at 1750,* in which he said that freedom of religion came about because it was absolutely necessary. They had Anglicans in Virginia, they had Catholics and Jews in Maryland, they had Baptists in Rhode Island, they had Methodists in Georgia, they had Puritans in Massachusetts— they had to have freedom of religion. And this was mostly unheard of at the time. At the time you had the established Catholic Church in France and the established Anglican Church in England and so forth, and the Founding Fathers were very wise in coming up with freedom of religion in order to accommodate all these groups.

Well, that has become more and more necessary, as we know, as we follow our constitutional law. But in order to honor pluralism, we have essentially *eliminated* all these religions. And there's all the difference in the world between respect for different religious cultures and the insistence that they all vanish.

You see, we're supporting our multiculturalism by saying there shall be no culture, and that's too thin, it's too thin. It's not deep enough. It takes away the old ways we've developed, over so many years, to help us face the big things, like death.

I was talking to a cancer specialist the other day and he said that in his practice, he finds people are not so much fearful of death as they are fearful of what will happen between now and death. In other words, the last illness, the difficulty of it.

. . . But you know, as I'm thinking about it I realize that that can't really be true. I'm sure people say that but I don't think it's really true. It has to be that we have displaced the fear of death to the fear of illness. Not that anybody wants to go through a terrible illness, but I think it's still repressed. I think we are fearful of death and just don't want to admit it. I think I probably am. It is quite possible that I deeply repress my fear of death. It's one thing to fear the illness, but we see the illness. We *see* it. We don't see death.

Now, my friend who planned her husband's funeral last week, she saw death, because she came home, went to sleep as usual and when she woke up the next morning her husband was dead beside her, in the bed. So she saw it. But most of us don't. And you don't come to grips with what you don't see. Why bother?

JED MATTES
Age: 41
Literary Agent

❧

This happened to someone I know. She was visiting a friend of hers in the hospital and it was a shared room. There was another woman in the other bed and at one point this other woman said something. My friend looked over toward the bed and the woman there spoke again. It sounded like she was asking for something. So she went over to see what was wanted and what the woman said was, "Please hold me, I'm dying." My friend put her arms around her shoulders and she died.

Now this woman didn't say, "Get a nurse" or "Hurry" or "Help me," or any of that. She just said, "Please hold me, I'm dying." She knew she was dying and she was completely alone, no one was there with her. There was hustle and bustle in the hospital and there was her roommate and there was this visitor and they were talking to each other, and she was dying.

Frankly I marvel at this woman's ability to be clear about what she wanted and needed. The way illness is dealt with today causes the whole process of death to be very remote from most people. How do you know what you want as you're dying, if you haven't given it a moment's thought—ever? For me of course, as a gay man in New York in the eighties and nineties, my entire world is surrounded by people dying. It's not in the least remote and I've been required to give it quite a lot of thought.

Being surrounded by AIDS has jump-started the process that seems to happen more naturally in one's sixties, or seventies. It's jump-started it not only for the person with AIDS who is dealing with his or her imminent death, it's also done so for people like me. I'm forty-one years old and I'm healthy and I sometimes look at three dinner guests in my home and realize that the likelihood is that all three of them will be dead in a few years. Now that is going to impact me and others like me (and there are a lot of people like me), who are maintaining and developing ongoing friendships and relationships with a certain knowledge that they will survive this person by as much as decades.

You are faced with this weird juggling game of having and needing friendships that you value so much, and also knowing that you cannot depend upon those friendships being there into the future. It stimulates you into thinking, "Well, what *is* it all about?" You have to question all sorts of things that you didn't have to look at before, because an awareness of death is right in your face. You *can't* ignore it.

There is another element to dealing with this that's very hard to get across. Having a life that is inundated with death, with the death of *young* people, having that perspective, and at the same time being in a larger world that is essentially unaware of it. This is simply surreal. It's even more surreal than AIDS itself.

Death is, in some fashion, a part of every hour of my day, every day of the year. It has been for the last ten years and it's going to be for the next ten years. It has every trauma and tragedy of Dresden, but the world at large doesn't recognize the trauma—as if the Second World War is going on but nobody else notices.

Sometimes it creates the sense that I'm literally on another planet. And the more amazing thing beyond that is—we all are coping. Having laid out for you how peculiar it is, the fact is that I am getting on with my life. In the middle of this absolute devastation, work gets done, the rent gets paid, the laundry gets done, Christmas presents are bought, movies are gone to. Life goes on. Life goes on even for me, and I'm in the middle of it.

Given the antiseptic, impersonal nature of death in our culture, where we essentially absent someone into a clinical situation and their death becomes the responsibility of this large complex, I think we are dealing with it pretty well. An anthropologist might find some kind of tribal phenomena going on in the gay community. We are taking care of one another.

You find people clustering, people taking shifts, people feeling a sense of responsibility, and also a desire to help. It's a loving thing to do. It gives you some sense of empowerment. Here's this disease that we all feel so helplessly powerless about, and here's a way to have some impact on one manifestation of it. Someone is dying and I can make him more comfortable.

Although I'm wary of making assumptions and generalizations about the gay community, I do think that this is happening as people are experiencing friends dying over and over again. We just get into gear and we've got experience doing it, and we do it a lot better now than we did five years ago.

If you think of the woman I told you about: She's in the hospital, she gets a card or two, maybe a phone call, but basically, she's alone. Compare that with someone who has a group of people making sure that every day he gets three visitors, and someone spends each night there and people are real alert to what is going on with him all the time—I don't think there's any comparison. By actually *doing* it, we've become more expert at it.

RON SHORT
Age: 49
Playwright

❧

I grew up in Pine Mountain between Kentucky and Virginia. Here everything is divided by mountains, one side to the other. It's part of the Appalachian chain, that whole distinct group that runs up and down the east coast—Smoky Mountains, Cumberland Mountains and all.

It's an incredible place, just extraordinarily beautiful. I think it's paradise. And there's so much history here. These are the oldest standing mountains in the world—850 million years old. We have more species of trees here in one holler than they have in all of Europe. There's a little plant up here in the mountains that was the final link in proving Darwin's theory of natural selection—galax—there's a town named after it. But more than anything else, the mountains are just a powerful force in your life. When you look at that beauty every day, it slowly seeps into your very being. The mountains become a part of who you are.

Here, death is a very personal thing. People accept it and take it onto themselves as a part of living. Nursing homes are fairly new up here, it's only in the last twenty years or so they started putting older people in nursing homes and having them die in hospitals. Used to be people died at home.

Now there's some people would say, "Well that's 'cause there weren't any hospitals," and that's true, but nevertheless, there was another side to it. The care of elderly people, or anyone who got sick or hurt, was a part of taking care of family and seeing to them all the way to the end, to the very end. So taking care of the dying was not a burden, it wasn't martyrdom or sacrifice, it was part of your respect for family and it continued all the way through their death and their burial.

After people had died they were prepared for burial, often right inside the house, kept very close, and often buried in the backyard, or up on the hill in back of the house. You can see evidence of that in every little place, just drive down any back road and you'll see small cemetery plots up behind the house. Those are family plots.

And every year, most families had a memorial service, a family memorial service. I'm not talking about Memorial Day, the national holiday, which some people around here call Decoration Day. The family memorial day is a designated day for each family, a time set aside when the community would come to the family graveyard and there's preaching and singing and remembrance.

I grew up with that, and again it's changing, but in my family there is still a family memorial service. On my father's side it's the third Saturday and Sunday in July and on my mother's side it's the first weekend in August. At one time it was a great community gathering, a ritual of the highest order, exploring the traditions of family and community. People came from all around. In the olden days I remember some of the old guys would even ride horses in, so there would be trucks and horses.

On the top of the hill there was a little pole shed made out of cedar poles, with a tin roof and rough seats and a little preaching stand, a platform where the preachers and the baptized members of the church would sit. And they would tell stories about my great-grandfather and my great-grandmother and my grandma and grandpa. They'd talk about their lives and they don't hesitate to tell personal stories about people who have died. They were remembered, brought into the sermon, brought into the living testament of life.

Something like that is evidence of your place in this world, because it gives you clear evidence of your connection not only to present family but to the past as well. It acknowledges that death exists and that it's our job to keep our relationship to people who have gone, so our lives have meaning, so we have our history.

It is a celebration of our life now and of what went before, but it is also certainly mourning. There is a kind of purging of all the emotions. People don't hold back or try to hold back the emotions. In fact it is an event where there is a celebration of public mourning for the family. I often think of scenes of tribal people wailing, it's very much akin to that. Some people find it just too emotional. They find it, I think, in some ways, coarse, for mourning to be that public. It's intense for people who aren't used to it, and even with some people who have grown up here. There's a kind of sentiment about it, a feeling that there's no reason for all that carrying on.

Well, I believe there's *every* reason for that carrying on. Somebody you knew and loved is gone, and I can't think of anything more appropriate than to publicly mourn that loss, acknowledging the importance of that person and of your caring about them.

I don't know of anything that says more about us as a culture, as a people, than the way we treat dying, and how we see ourselves in relationship to somebody else's death, whether it's family or friend.

Here there was great respect for that. People sat up with the dead here. Of course, it was out of fear sometimes too, because in the early days, without doctors around to declare people dead for sure, there was always these old stories, stories of somebody rising up. So I think that was part of it too, just to make sure. *"Three days dead before they put you down."*

So maybe it grew out of that worry, but it was definitely bigger than that. It was an opportunity for the community and family to come together and to declare themselves in some kind of alliance around that person's importance and that family's importance and also their own importance—to ensure that when the time come, there was an acknowledgment of their own death.

I can't think of anything worse than dying alone. And unknown. Here there is the sense that death is eased by being in the company of people you love. You see yourself being missed. You see yourself being cared about and you know that people are going to remember you.

My grandmother died in the hospital. It was the first time she'd ever been in one. Hospitals are foreign environments, and my family— they're not backward but they're not people who are confident in those kinds of institutional situations so it's very hard for them to be aggressive in addressing nurses and doctors. I was a medic in Vietnam and I've had more experience with hospitals on top of that, so I tried to help. I spent a lot of time with her. I was with her when she died. The hardest part about it was that the very last thing she asked me was to take her home. That was the hardest thing. They kept telling the family, you can't take her home. "She's too sick, she has to have IVs, she needs a respirator," and all that. Well it didn't make any difference in the long run, she was going to die anyway. The dying was easy compared to the guilt. I said at the time, never again would that happen if there was anything I could do about it.

I've seen people die. It's hard. It's never an easy thing to do. I've seen people die of terrible wounds, but there's this thing I've seen happen, like they know what's going on even though the medical world around them says they're out of their heads, they're not themselves, they're talking crazy. I think there's an understanding of what is happening no matter what the situation. In my grandma's case there was such clarity of thought, and when the last thought on your mind is "I want to be home," then that must be the most important thing there is.

Like I said, I flew medevac in Vietnam and I saw guys who were terribly wounded, and they wanted to go home. It wasn't just the pain, they wanted to go home because they thought they might die. It's like the mountains, back to that. If you look at this landscape every day it becomes a part of who you are. What you fix your eyes upon becomes a part of how you see yourself. So how can you see yourself in the hospital—a place that is so totally foreign to the nourishment of the soulful self.

I understand that we didn't have the IVs and we didn't have a respirator. I understand all of that. But I said to the family, it seems to me that this other may have been more valuable than the respirator. That's my way of thinking on it.

It's hard. The management of family is hard anymore. The simple things of getting the supper on the table, feeding and clothing the family, it's all hard, much less dealing with death in the family. Each person has to make the judgment for themselves and maybe it's not as important for some people, but I guess you can tell that for me, place is critical to your identity. Those little graveyards up on top of the hill, managed from generation to generation—they're a way for people to see themselves, a way of knowing who we are. That's why it's important, important enough to maintain the rituals which keep the tradition alive.

A few years back, I was going up the hill with my father and mother, going up the hill to the graveyard in Dickenson County where we used to live. They're getting old and my father was resting, and he said to me, "You know, one of these days you're going to be coming up here alone." And it wasn't that he was telling me that he was going to die. He knows I know that. What he meant was it was time for me to take the responsibility for the identity that he'd carried all his life.

I've always been able to go there as a child because that's what I've always been in that place. My parents were there, my aunts were there, my grandma—and so I was a child in that place. At that moment I realized I had become an adult. I had to take responsibility not only for showing up, I had to be responsible for its full meaning. I had to figure out whether I can keep the tradition alive in my family, and for my community.

REBECCA WALKER
Age: 26
Writer and Activist

❧

In African culture and African-American culture there is a general encouragement to face death directly. When I was about eight or nine years old, my mother said, "Go get a pen and paper, you're going to write my will," then she had me write not only the will but the funeral plans. She has always talked to me about how she wants things to be taken care of. She wants to be on a hillside, down the road from the house, wrapped up in some beautiful cloth.

Now on the one hand this made me feel very grown up and responsible that she had asked me to do this. I felt she trusted me, like this was a wonderful honor in a certain way, but then I also had a nagging fear that it meant that my mother was just about to die, as if she had one foot off the planet and one foot on the planet. That made me terribly insecure about her presence here.

I would say to her, "Mom, I really don't want you to die," and she would say, "Rebecca, I will always be with you. I will *always* be with you." And I feel that she will always be with me. She always *is* with me. And it was a way to start understanding that.

Also, it wove death into my life in a way that made it a little less alien. Here she was dealing with it and I was dealing with it; it was not a foreign thing. It became something very much between us. I think that there's an attempt there to overcome fear and to tap into the power of fearlessness, to face a core truth that you can't avoid. So even if I did go through some insecurity about it, it helped me.

My first actual experience of death was when my grandfather died. I was only three or four and I don't really remember it very well but people in my family tell me about all of us going down to Georgia for his funeral. I've heard stories about my aunts, crying and throwing themselves on his casket, and I have images of a very tradi-tional, southern, black Baptist funeral, with the procession and the green grass and the old white church. My mother's family comes from that tradition of singing at funerals, of outdoor-sunshine funerals, bringing everyone together to remember the person, to see that the person lives through the offspring.

The first time I really personally felt the loss of death was about four and a half years ago. Ivory, a man who had become a kind of uncle figure in my life, the person who had given me my first job, died of AIDS. He had known he was HIV-positive for five years and not told anyone. When I learned he was dying he was already in the hospital, already hooked up to the machines and the IVs and everything. I remember going to the hospital and finding only a small part of him there. It was hard, having to talk to him about what was happening to him and hearing him tell me. He gave me this set of charms and said, "Make a bracelet out of these and give it to your children and tell them stories about me." I was devastated. I didn't expect to lose him.

When I found out he was sick I was leaving on a trip to Africa so I didn't get a chance to stay with him until he died. But when I was in Egypt I wrote him a letter saying, "I love you and I miss you and here I am in Egypt." I didn't know how to get it to him so I sent it to my mother and asked her to take it to him. Some time later I had a dream where he came to me and said,

"I got your letter, I love you very much. I'm going to go on now. Everything is fine. I'll see you."

After I had this dream I called my mother and found that she had not given him the letter. I said, "But I had a dream that he got it." And she said, "Well that means he got it. He died last night."

I've had that experience a number of times, the experience of awareness as someone dies. There's some bond, some connection that I've felt, of people going through a different kind of space. I think there's a real strong communication that happens between us and them as they're making that transition away from us.

∞

I was brought up in the house of my grandparents in Chile. When I was around four or five my grandmother died. My grandfather mourned her for the rest of his life. He dressed in black and painted the furniture in his room black. The radio was forbidden, desserts, flowers, music were forbidden. That house had been illuminated by my grandmother's spirit and when she died, it died with her. I spent my childhood in a place of mourning.

I did not see my grandmother dead and I do not remember the funeral at all. I don't recall what I was told but I do remember the loss, the fact that she was not there. I did not ask many questions because it was a very painful thing for my grandfather. What I did was—I invented a ghost that lived in the curtains in the living room.

The living room had very heavy velvet curtains in a sort of red wine color. They never moved them, probably because they were full of dust, and I had the idea that the spirit of my grandmother lived in the curtains. So I would pin little messages for her inside the curtain. Then later I thought that her spirit lived in a small silver mirror that had been hers and, for many years, I always carried it with me. So I created a protective spirit, a benevolent angel that was my grandmother.

I come from a Catholic environment where children were told that the person had gone to heaven, and that was it. But there was no real explanation of what death was about, or birth for that matter. Life was taken for granted, it wasn't questioned, and death as well. It seemed totally unavoidable and it wasn't questioned.

I was scared of death like I was scared of horror movies, the living dead, zombies. But I was also scared of many other things. I was scared of the devil, afraid he would appear in the mirrors at night. I was scared of rats, I was scared of the gypsies. I was scared of so many things. My childhood was a time of terror, of unanswered questions, of loneliness, of no explanations, of darkness. My real life began when I had some control, when I no longer had to depend on adults for answers or for protection.

The first contact I had with the morbid, real way of seeing something dead was also when I was very young. They would kill the little kittens. We had many cats at home and, at the time, no one did the operation to neuter them, so every six months we had ten or twelve new kittens and the cook would drown them in water. They would tell the kids to get out when they did it, but we spied. We knew what was going on and we saw the dead kittens but there was no real explanation, they were just dead because they were a nuisance. They killed the puppies too, so we saw a lot of that.

Then, much later, when I was around twenty-six years old, I saw a dead human body for the first time. I was doing a television program. A man had had a heart attack and died in the street and his papers, his documents, said that he was called Allende, and the person who picked up the body in the ambulance related that name with the name of the person who had the TV program. I ended up in the morgue identifying a body that I could not really identify because I had never seen him before. But it was my father. My stepfather came and he told me it was, so I took a good look at him. That's the only image I have of my father, already dead in the morgue. That was the first time I was close to a dead human body. Much later, during the military coup, I saw many people die, but that was the first time.

When I came to this country I was surprised at how easily people keep death out of their lives here. As if it can be Disney World all the time.

ARTHUR TSUCHIYA
Age: 45
Senior Policy Advisor
Office of Policy, Research, and Technology
National Endowment for the Arts

❦

Generally speaking, the members of my family were not religious people but they understood the social function of religious practice. They would join a Protestant church wherever we lived. We moved a few times when I was a kid and they would check out different Methodist or Presbyterian churches and then settle on one. It took me a while to figure out that what they were really doing was looking for a minister who would give sermons that were socially motivated, concerned with social justice and equality, that kind of thing.

Which was good but, unfortunately, it meant that when someone in my family would die, I would have to go to those sorts of generic Protestant funerals that are so depressing. It's that dismal standard American funeral with open-casket viewing, or whatever you call that process, very somber and constrained, no one really talks much and there's no allowance for humor or for really celebrating the person's life or anything like that. For the most part, that would be the procedure. In my father's case, he was a scientist; there was a pragmatic side to him and he didn't think having an open casket was desirable or necessary. He wanted to be cremated.

He died in 1984, at the end of a long illness. One organ after another failed and finally his kidneys went and he was put on dialysis. I was living in New York at the time and flew back to Minneapolis to find there was no chance of his recovery. I was the person in the family who made the decision to take him off life-support systems and to bring him home. We decided to try to nurse him ourselves, with the help of a hospice program. So we did that.

My father was born in this country, of immigrant Japanese parents. My mother's family had been living here when my grandmother became pregnant. They went back to Japan for about a year and it was during that year that my mother was born, and then they came back to the U.S. when my mother was very young.

They lived in the Midwest where there were very, very few Japanese Americans in the twenties. My mother's father had an import store in a prime location in downtown Minneapolis. When the Depression came along, business was bad everywhere. On top of that, a boycott of Japanese goods was promoted as Japan became more aggressive and imperialistic. This was before Pearl Harbor but there was already a general anti-Japanese feeling that turned into an organized boycott. So although my grandfather had been a fairly successful merchant earlier, the combination of the Depression and the boycott did his business in.

My grandfather maintained a journal from around 1917 until the early 1960s. He wrote daily entries, always in English. Each entry would give the date and the temperature. Parts of it are very sad, especially during those Depression years. The date would be February something, the temperature would be twenty below zero and the entry would read: "No customers today." It was such a difficult life during that time, incredibly bleak.

You can infer from reading the journals that there was a lot of fear during the Second World War about being considered an untrustworthy alien. He talked about the visits that he would get from representatives of the federal government and the kinds of questions they would ask. I think that had something to do with his keeping these journals in English, although around the house he always spoke Japanese to my grandmother.

My mother and father were totally assimilated but of course they grew up with that broader kind of racism that was always there and then, during the war in particular, they felt a need to demonstrate that they were loyal Americans. Neither of them impressed my sister or myself with a lot of information about Japanese culture. I think most of the Japaneseness that I've picked up was unspoken and just sort of absorbed. It's body language, tonality of voice, other things that slipped through that were not conscious. But all the verbal lan-

guage, all the deliberate stuff was really about trying to be mainstream American.

As my father had gotten older, he had become much more interested in his Japaneseness and less inhibited about expressing his interest in things Japanese. He went to Japan a couple of times, started
wearing a Japanese robe, that sort of thing. Toward the very end of
his life what he really wanted to eat was a kind of Japanese egg
custard, and my mother knew how to make this. I don't remember
ever eating it as a kid but at this point it was something that she made
daily for him. My mother was not able to care much for my father
although she would cook. My sister, Marilyn, came back to help as
well. Marilyn and my father were estranged. There was a lot of
conflict between the two of them and I think she really hated him in
a lot of ways, but she did come back, she came back dutifully.
Marilyn was pregnant with her third child and when my father saw
that he was extremely delighted. I think that made Marilyn feel even
worse because she didn't agree with the traditional idea that her
worth lay in having babies.

The moment when he actually died seemed very natural. You
could see it coming. He had been less and less conscious. His periods
of wakefulness and alertness were fewer and further between. There
had been times when he had seemed more comfortable with a cool
damp towel placed on his forehead and my ex-wife Nancy, who was
among the people caring for him, had just been putting a fresh towel
on and he kind of shook his head as if he didn't want it there. My
mother and my sister and Nancy and I were in the room with him. It
was quiet. His breathing became more rapid and then there was a
kind of wheeze and then it stopped and you couldn't hear him
breathing anymore. We all were silent for a while and meditative,
and then we looked around and sort of indicated to one another that
we weren't sure, really, whether he was dead or not. It was a funny
moment, an almost humorous moment of confusion about that because his eyes were still open. I got down very close to him and I
couldn't hear any breathing. I felt for his pulse and I couldn't feel
anything. I closed his eyes and it was over.

My mother died just this past year. I'd had a difficult relationship with her for the last couple of decades, from before my father died. She had pretty much checked out of being actively interested in me or in my family. Marilyn was much closer to her than I was.

When my aunt called to say my mother was ill, I realized she was indicating that there was a possibility my mother could die but she couched everything in very euphemistic terms and that, combined with my own psychological filter, complicated by the fact that I was dealing with a lot of intense stuff at work that was very important to me—well, it all gave me a rationale for not dropping everything and going right then. This time it was my sister who talked to the doctor and got the real story and went back to Minneapolis. As it happened, Marilyn was with my mother when she died, quietly and peacefully.

I am aware that my aunt felt I was coldhearted, that I wasn't very responsible or a good son because I didn't get there until after my mother had died. But I don't really feel guilty because I don't think there was anything I could have added and I know that Marilyn was very caring and did as much as anyone could have done. Actually I feel okay about it.

You know, I had always assumed that Marilyn regretted not being able to come to a happier feeling toward my father before he died. He and I talked through stuff and I felt I'd cleared the decks with him. But Marilyn didn't want to, didn't see a need to, and didn't. I just assumed she had a lot of stuff left. But now I understand that she probably *was* fine with the way that happened. She's always said that she was okay with it, I just didn't believe her.

But now, the way I feel today about my mother's death, I don't feel like there was unfinished business. That's surprising. I knew there would be some sense of relief once she died just because there was always this tension and so on, but I feel like something's completed. And also there's a kind of symmetry now in that both my parents are dead. I don't know how to describe it, it just seems . . . completed.

The day after the memorial service we took her cremains in a little wooden box to the cemetery. It was a small group, just me, my cousin, my sister and her husband and kids. Each of us said a few things and the younger children had daffodils that they laid down next to the little box. I thought it was touching how Sarah, the child Marilyn had been pregnant with when my father was dying, was now here, laying a flower on my mother's grave.

There had been a big snowstorm several days before although it was warm that day. We're standing around this small hole that had been dug in the plot and, at a certain point, Marilyn realized that we were standing right next to my father's grave. She said "Oh, we need to clean this off," and bent down to brush the snow off the marker set in the ground. At that moment it felt as if a resolution took place in terms of all four of us—my mother, my father, my sister, and me. I was so grateful to her for doing that. To my mind it was a gesture that acknowledged my father, it was what my mother would have seen as the proper thing, and somehow it bridged a perceived gulf between the four of us.

You never really know what's going to get to you or trigger your feelings. There's something in me that is sorry for my parents because they were so secular in their approach but I haven't addressed that side of things for myself. Most of the various funeral services I've attended haven't really helped me deal with loss or death. I haven't found the appropriate way to acknowledge these big events. Meaningful ritual is hard to come by. For me, at that moment, when Marilyn actually bent down in the snow and cleaned off that marker, it was like a ritual gesture and it had great meaning. It tied us all together in some final way. I found myself filled with tears.

WESTERN IDEAS ABOUT DEATH CHRONOLOGY PART 1

⌒∽⌒

From the beginning of our history, death is the first event we consecrate in the genesis of ritual more than 100,000 years ago.

c. 100,000
B.C.E.

We stop leaving our dead in the underbrush, throwing them off a cliff, or eating them, and take to burying them in the earth, along with tools, shells, bone and ivory ornaments. Concepts and beliefs about death begin to form.

c. 30,000
B.C.E.

We paint pictures on the walls of caves and adorn the dead with red ochre tints before they are ceremonially buried.

c. 10,000
B.C.E.

Prehistoric peoples live in a world where most newborns die in infancy, most children die before they are grown, and those who make it to adulthood generally die before the age of fifty. Like animals in a televised nature program, we kill and are killed, or die from injuries. The mundane experience of a natural death is rare.

The event of death itself is perceived as an external phenomenon to be resisted with the magical assistance of the gods or the spirits in nature.

Paleo-Indian peoples populate the North American continent, developing a wide variety of languages and practices but maintaining a shared cosomology in which concepts about death, nature, and place are essentially integrated.

It is, however, in the ancient Near East where we find the origins of ideas about death that will come to be dominant in Western European culture and eventually in the United States.

3000–2000 B.C.E.	Ancient Mesopotamian texts describe an underground "netherworld" where people go when they die.
	Egyptians develop mummification and other preservation methods because they believe it is necessary to maintain the body to ensure a good life in the realm of the dead.
	The idea of judgment after death makes its first appearance in Western history in the Pyramid and Coffin Texts, now known as The Egyptian Book of the Dead.
1500–500 B.C.E.	Hebrew texts describe death as the punishment imposed upon the human race for disobeying the Creator.
	Homeric Greeks develop the Western concept of the soul. As more people begin to think of spirit as separate from the physical body it opens the way for the practice of cremation.
	Followers of the Persian prophet Zoroaster believe the body itself will be resurrected intact into paradise.
	Socrates drinks poison in the face of execution, creating a model for honorable suicide. Fifty years later,

Artistole declares suicide unlawful on the grounds that it deprives the community of the services of the individual. We begin a debate that will continue to the present day.

100 B.C.E.– 100 C.E.

Virgil describes the afterdeath state as "The Abode of Sleep." The idea of death as sleep persists, in one form or another, throughout most of Western history.

The Sadducees, a Jewish sect of this period, propose that life ends at death, and originate the slogan "Let us eat and drink, for tomorrow we die." However, most everybody else, Jews and gentiles alike, not only assume they survive death but believe the dead to be active participants in this world. It is common to contact the dead for advice and make offerings for their well-being.

By the beginning of the Common Era we have developed a variety of ideas about death and the concept of life after death, including notions of judgment, punishment, and reward.

ᗧ

When I was young, about six or younger, we had goldfish and they seemed always to be dying. Instead of flushing the goldfish down the toilet I asked to have them given to me. I developed an elaborate burial ritual for these fish. One of my uncles used a shredded tobacco called Prince Joe which came in a narrow tin can, a kind of oval can with a flip-top lid, and he always gave these tins to me when they were empty. So I had this magnificent casket for the fish. I would have an elaborate ceremony then bury the fish and then, on a regular basis, I would dig it up to see what had happened to it. Then I'd rebury it and I'd wait a little while, a week or so, and dig it up again, until finally there was nothing but corruption and bones. Now you might think this was weird, but I just wanted to know what happened, what *really* happened to something when it died.

The mystery of death is astounding really. Think about our ancestors trying to cope with it, trying to get the right ritual or the right dance or the right arrangement of stones together to honor their dead. I remember reading about some archeological dig in China which went back, I don't know, a very long time, and what they found was a gravesite with multiple skulls, painted with layers and layers of red ochre. It was obvious that the skulls had been revered and cared for and that this was an early manifestation of ritualistic ancestor worship; that need to keep our foremothers and forefathers with us, caring for them even after they had died, maintaining the skulls. I mean, when you think of the head, of the disembodied head, it's where we see, where we smell, where we taste, talk, everything is there. This was a ritualistic way of communicating beyond death, connected to what they had learned, connected to who they knew.

We've lost the mystery of that, because we live in a very artificial way now, disconnected from organic growth where everything begins in darkness, the seed pushed into the wet darkness of the unknown, which becomes something wholly other, wholly different from how it starts out. It turns into something that is impossible to see in the seed itself. And when you think of every leaf and every seed that each tree and each plant produces, and all of it dying and going into the ground, the soil, the earth made up of the death of countless millions of leaves and millions of earthworms and insects and millions of this and millions of that—all grinding together, creating the loam, and out of that comes new life.

We are surrounded by death. It's not part of the shadowland, it isn't; it's part of the daylight. And there is nothing fearsome about death if you are immersed in that organic rhythm. We flee from death because we're disassociated from natural cycles.

Today we go to the supermarket to get our celery and our carrots. Large numbers of people live in block towers, surrounded by asphalt and concrete where they completely lose sight of the growth of organic life, the biological diversity of life. Living in those conditions, people can wind up with a great fear of the natural cycle, which can turn into a great fear of aging, where you have these horrible surgeries performed, so-called plastic surgery, people literally cutting and carving themselves up to try and stop the natural process. Then, when we see someone who looks natural, they look frightful to us. We become afraid of the elderly, literally *afraid* of the natural thing, the real thing.

In truth, death is a daily reality. Every day is born out of the day that has died, and so on ad infinitum. But in this simple reality lies something that I think most people simply can't deal with: the idea that not only has the day died, but that we have died, one day of us has died, in this limited life span we have. It's what one of the Psalms says, every blade of grass is numbered, and every day the grass withers and the leaves fade.

I was born and raised in a Catholic family. In fact, I was a Benedictine nun for fourteen years and I'm still a Catholic now. I believe the soul is eternal and the body does what all matter does, it falls back into *materia,* and *materia* is the body of the Divine Mother.

I believe our spirits keep on moving through time. I believe in reincarnation. There's nothing in Catholicism that says the line between alpha and omega can't have a circle around it. Nature teaches me that reality is cyclic.

Faith in divine revelation through the Word means less and less to me because for me, more and more, the divine revelation is all of nature; it doesn't come to me through theological teachings, and it doesn't come to me through savior figures, it comes to me through the real world. Now, I don't mean in any way to imply I don't believe in and honor the savior figures and the holy people throughout time, but the mystery of death and resurrection and immortality doesn't begin with Jesus Christ. To really understand Christianity, you've got to immerse yourself in the Egyptian mysteries.

I was in Egypt recently. This was a civilization where for thousands of years the Divine manifested in animals, a place where the animals were worshiped as divine, honored, paid tribute. That's an amazing fact when you think about it, an amazing statement about the ancient recognition of the power of the natural world. But we seem to be trying to ignore that power. Maybe it's because we're afraid of death, and separating from the natural world makes us feel like we can separate ourselves from death. But of course it doesn't work that way, not at all.

TOMAS YBARRA-FRAUSTO
Age: 52
Program Director
The Rockefeller Foundation

༄

I was at a celebration for *El Día de Los Muertos* (the Day of the Dead), at the Native American Community House this year, and it was a wonderful experience because, as one of the people there said, "We have roots here now because our dead are buried here." The tradition of the Day of the Dead has now seeped into New York with the coming of tens of thousands of Mexicans. When you bury your dead in a place then you have roots in that place.

It was a wonderful event with all the traditional things. The music and the *ofrenda,* which are little altars made by hand with flowers, pictures, and mementos, the special *pan de muerto,* the bread, the traditional foods, and the little skulls made out of sugar, the little skeletons.

Some of the kids had added tapes and CDs on the altars, or wrapped a little skeleton with a bandanna the way that street kids wear. It was a kind of intergenerational dialogue as the young learned the traditions from the past but changed the tradition by adding elements from their own experience, reflecting the current reality of children who are already more American or are becoming Americanized.

People ate and drank and danced and listened to music, and then there was a ceremonial ritual about coming together. It was the beginning of a new context and a putting together, a remembering and a remaking. It was an homage to ancestors and it took place in an urban New York reality.

I am from San Antonio, Texas. My great-grandfather and my grandfather and my father and myself were all born in the United

States. In these old, settled communities which are made up of fifth-generation Americans, a kind of Mexican worldview is still maintained in which death and life are two parts of the same continuum. Death is a threshold. This notion comes from ancient pre-Columbian worldviews that the people have kept alive in their folklore.

For the Day of the Dead we would always go to the cemetery, where we cleaned and decorated the graves. There are particular customs for doing this. For example, the graves of little children, they're called *angelitos,* or little angels, usually have a little box underneath the cross, and in this box they place the child's favorite toy. It can be a doll or a little car or whatever. When you go to the cemetery you look at all these little toys, and if you're a child yourself this is kind of interesting and you ask, "Why is this here?" And your mother would say, "Well, because this little angel went to heaven and he's going to be playing with a toy like this. And this is to remind us here of the afterlife." So with the decoration of a grave a child becomes integrated into this whole system of beliefs about dying.

There are many, many customs and traditions and tales dealing with death. For instance, it is said that, when someone dies, there is a point when the dead person sits up, *se siente muerto,* and throws out a ball from their body and this ball is composed of all the wants that that person did not realize in his life. So if it's a little tiny ball then you know this is a good person. He died a good death. He had his wishes fulfilled. He did not die unfulfilled. If the ball is big, then the person was someone who was very retentive, did not show emotion, did not express himself. He died badly because he died taking with him all these unfulfilled desires. As children, whenever we went to a wake we tried to stay up all night to see if this would happen.

So what you're learning is that this is a culture that's affective, this is a culture based on sentiment and on fulfillment of desire. You express your feeling by hugging or touching or telling the person what you have to say. This is a culture that values real connections with people, relationships and communion with other beings or with things.

Death and dying in popular lore has a very dense meaning. It's about how you lived; it's about a cultural belief that life is meant to be lived to the fullest, and death will reflect that legacy.

ALAN MOYLE
Age: 43
Filmmaker

⁓

The artist who lives next door has a Day of the Dead party every year and she insists that everybody treat it with some respect, so I learned that from her. Her name is Carla, she's Latin, her father was a famous Mexican actor. At these parties you have to bring a present for the dead people, and there's something cool about that. You pay your respects to everybody who has died that year. It's a big thing here in L.A.

There's a store here that sells Day of the Dead paraphernalia. The symbolism is so strong that they make a living all year long, and they're not selling to Mexican people, they're selling to people who want to decorate their houses, because no matter what your budget is there's something cool there.

In a way it's like designer places selling crosses, it's a hip thing. But it's something else too. People need it in some way. White people need it.

I think people feel really bad because there are no families any-more. I'm married to a Latin woman. Now *these* people know how to keep family together. They have get-togethers at the track, with everyone bringing food. Can you believe completely hokey situa-tions in parks where the family gets together and they all hug? Really important.

My wife's mother died when Diana was twelve. We go to her gravesite on her birthday, out in a Mexican neighborhood. You should see the Mexicans at Christmas or Easter, in the graveyard. They show up and really party and have a good time and hang out. They decorate the graves with flowers, bring Christmas trees, you see mariachi bands, you see families getting together, there's not a grim face in sight. It's terrific.

I especially like to go down to the little children's grave area and you see families there, youngsters attending the graves of little kids that died and all the beautiful expressions and they bring them cards and toys and food and soda and no one steals them, you know.

It's so great. They include the dead in on the whole thing. The family goes and has a little party with the dead person. And they're not sitting around saying, "Ah man, Jose, we miss you." They're there to have a hang-out and Jose's *there*. It's sweet, it's fucking sweet.

I think everyone feels bad because they don't have any families and because they don't have any religion and because television creates the cult of celebrities that have everything and we don't. The comparison cults, the cargo cults created by television make a shitty atmosphere for everyone because it's everyone sitting at home watching someone else live. Watching someone else's stuff, stuff, stuff. I mean, I can see why everyone's upset and pissed off. It's not *their* stuff. And it's not real. That's why the Day of the Dead thing is valuable. There's something *real* underneath it. With all the altars and the little skeletons and sugar things, death is underneath it.

I had never made an altar before, myself, not for a dead friend. But when River [Phoenix] died, I wanted to do something, so I made an altar for him. The things I put on the altar were anything I could find that made me feel like I was saying something . . . they weren't the traditional things. Like I put this little wedding bride and groom, which had nothing to do with River, had all to do with me, and I put it on the altar, I don't know why. . . . And the son of the artist who lives one house over from Carla, had made an Egyptian sarcophagus out of plasticine, with a dead body, so I put that on the altar as well. And pictures of River, candles, flowers, and a few little odds and ends, rosewater and a little bell that looks like an Aleister Crowley bell. Hey, instant ritual.

It was fun doing it. It was my way of saying, "Okay River, here's a little scene." I was thinking, if he was watching me do this, he'd think "Oh cool, that's nice," you know? And then at one point I got down on my knees and prayed for a minute but it didn't feel right. In fact it didn't feel half as real or as right as when I was putting it all together. I was humming, buzzing a little bit and then when I was

finished and I sat down and stared at it . . . it was a little anticli-
mactic. Process is the thing. I'll probably just throw it out now.

Now the earthquake here in L.A. was an event that had a little death
thing around it. Some people said they thought they were going to
die. I didn't for a second think I was going to die, but of course I
wasn't in a real dangerous situation. I wasn't on top of a high-rise. I
was in the back of my loft, which is a one-story wood structure.
Actually, if the building had fallen in, we *could've* died, but I didn't
think about that at the time. We were in bed, and the back door is
five feet from the edge of the bed and so we ran to the back door.

There *was* a horrifying roar which was unlike any other earthquake I've ever been in. It sounded like some huge beast roaring, the
sound was totally terrifying. At the same time I was preoccupied
with trying to get the back door open. I couldn't get it open, 'cause
it was jammed, so I was thinking "Why can't I get the door open?"
and "Isn't this amazing?" and "We're probably gonna be okay now
because we're up against a wall." I was also thinking, "What the fuck
is that *sound*?"

No, I didn't think about dying but a lot of people shat their
drawers, I understand. A lot of people said, "I've been in a lot of
earthquakes but this time I thought I was going to die." There *was*
something about this one, it had a personality that way, its own vibe,
so to speak.

Down the street from us there is a family with two little boys and
their building was in far worse shape. It was a two-story brick building and it was all twisted and you could see through the walls. You
could hear their cries inside. We shouted their names and we could
hear them call back. We couldn't hear what they were saying but we
could hear that they were in there. And it was very very dark. All the
lights were out. And they were stuck in there. So suddenly we had a
bigger mission, you know? Their drama put our little broken-plate
drama into perspective.

I go through the rap of telling everybody how sad and horrible it
was, but frankly, between me and you, I'm glad it happened. I'm
sorry some people died, but first of all, thousands died in Mexico's

earthquake and fifty died here so, get a life L.A., right? In L.A. a minor inconvenience is a major tragedy. Every time there's a heavy rainstorm it's a big news event. People can't get to work at their usual commute hour and it's treated as news. In the East weather is a reminder that there are forces out there that are bigger than us. Here they expect it to be the same all the time, it's just background for them. There's no *Other* out here.

I love weather, I love huge weather. I once went to Long Island to *be* in a hurricane. I drove out there 'cause I knew one was coming. Now you could call that a death wish or you could just call it a desire for action, an interest in feeling that other thing, you know what I mean? The Other. And hopefully it's bigger than you and hopefully it's exciting. Even a good rainstorm reminds me that nature's alive and well and we don't live in the TV. So when the earthquake came, secretly I was thrilled. It bonded people, there was action, there were things happening, life, death, dismay. Action. Life and death are the same thing. Action is what counts.

We did bond. The whole fucking city bonded. That's a beautiful thing right? The earthquake is like, "Hey, here's a beautiful bonding thing for you guys." "This is to show you could die any minute, so get it together." It's definitely a visitation by God no matter what you think of God. Here he is in all his terrible otherness, in all his terrible unknowness. Even if you have a vision of a good God, then this is him on a very bad day, right? So it's great that way, it makes everybody small the same way. I loved it. It's this mutually terrible thing and you can't blame anyone, it's too big for that.

People were holding hands in the street. The next night we had dinner with neighbors we've been polite to, they were just downright appreciated good neighbors. But after the earthquake we had a dinner with them where everybody talked about themselves on deeper levels and we shared all this stuff . . . it was great. This all happened naturally. I guess everyone felt glad to be alive.

You know, it's possible that people really get off on death. I mean, they're definitely fascinated with it, right? They get a buzz going whenever it happens near them, they stare at accidents and all that. Maybe they avoid talking about it because everyone else avoids it, you know what I mean? Everyone thinks they shouldn't admit it but inside they're just plain *hypnotized* by it. Personally I love the subject of death, I love talking about it. And facing death is . . . energizing. If it doesn't kill you, it'll wake you up.

FRANK SNEPP
Age: 50
Journalist
Officer, Central Intelligence Agency, Retired

℘

The first time I encountered death at very close range was about two months after my arrival in Vietnam in 1969. I was in a bar on the outskirts of Saigon. It was the first time I'd gone anywhere without carrying a weapon with me. I was just sitting at the bar having a beer and there were some bar girls around and all of a sudden two people came bursting through the door firing. Everybody around me fell. The bar girl to my left took a round through her stomach and she fell up against me, bleeding profusely. The bottles along the bar all exploded, just as they do in western movies. I stood there, in the middle of this havoc, and for a split second I felt as though I was invulnerable. I grabbed the girl and carried her up some steps in the back of the bar. The space was very confined. How I made it without being shot, I don't know. The death toll in the place was high, some ten-odd people were killed that night.

Anyway, I'd swung this girl over my shoulder and stumbled into an upstairs room and there were lots of other people already there, no lights, the press of bodies, there was terror everywhere. I sort of crouched down beside the door and a few minutes later one of the gunmen came bursting into the room. Since the lights were out there was no firing, at least for a moment anyway, and I recall very vividly sort of lunging out the door, almost under his elbow, into the hallway, still somehow holding this bleeding woman, and she whispered to me, "Your friend is in there."

I didn't know what she was talking about. I had no friend that I knew of in there, no friend had been in the bar, simply people I had seen. I put the girl down, went back into the room and sure enough, there was an American in there, wrestling with the gunman.

In that instant something very strange happened. My memory

is—it sort of veers between extreme clarity and extreme vagueness when it comes to that night and it's vague on this particular episode, but basically, we beat the guy to death.

I have replayed this scene many times in my mind and I ask myself, "What happened downstairs?" "Why wasn't I shot?" "Must be I'm invulnerable, only a silver bullet could get me." That's one of the lessons you draw from something like this, as absurd as it sounds.

The second lesson I drew from this was—I was not a brave person but I was a person capable, in extreme circumstances, of turning off my feelings, not only my feelings about my own safety but my feelings about hurting another human being. It's something that a combat soldier could undoubtedly tell you all about. I was initiated, if you will, into some kind of blood rite that particular night. I often thought about it during my subsequent years in Vietnam. It was a seminal experience in my life because it made death extremely real for me yet not real, or rather, not close, not *proximate*.

If you were in Vietnam for as long as I was, you saw all sorts of terrible things. I was there for about five and a half years, during some of the worst years and until the last minute, and what happens in that kind of situation is—death begins to permeate your thinking and your existence.

If you're in the CIA something else happens as well. Because you command so much knowledge, you begin to rise above any sense of mortality, you develop a sense that information will out, that the power of the mind will keep death in abeyance. It becomes a game. You think, if only you keep this piece of information in mind, then you'll be safe.

The Agency is an elite club and that adds to your sense of immortality. You are the elite of the elite and nothing can touch you. As one former CIA agent put it, it's like being part of a religious cult and, as with all cults, it carries a sense of its own perfection and imperviousness to the slings and arrows of fortune. You can get away with a lot and that's how you begin to think of yourself . . . as someone who can get away with a lot, as some kind of god. And like a god you begin to feel death can't touch you in return, and I was lucky enough that it didn't.

I had some close scrapes. Somebody threw a hand grenade at my car and it bounced off. As a result I'm partially deaf in one ear, but had it gone through the window I wouldn't be here. And there were other close brushes. I picked up a little shrapnel here and there, but so what already? So what already? Nothing really touched me, no one had the silver bullet. I keep going back to the experience in the bar I told you about because there was one moment there when I said to myself, "They can't do it, they can't get me."

As everyone will tell you who's been in a war, you become insensitive to suffering and to death, because if you dwelled on it too long you simply couldn't function. A lot of people develop a real attachment to totems, especially weapons as totems. I remember I used to load up my car and my briefcase with every manner of weapon you can imagine. I had a hand grenade in my briefcase, a submachine gun in the boot of my car, I carried a forty-five, I had a Browning automatic, all sorts of pistols, I kept a carbine under my bed. And it's ironic that these instruments of death become your sureties *against* death—I don't mean in a practical way, I mean in an emotional way. You spend a lot of time polishing the weapon, or stroking the totem if you will, because you come to believe that they will keep you safe so long as you keep them safe. It goes way back to the ancient myths and the idea of totem in the first place, as something that magically protected you. It becomes part of your armor, your emotional armor.

Shortly after the episode in the bar, I began wearing a Montagnard bracelet which I still wear today. It's quite simple, made of brass, probably fashioned from some cannon shell. I wore it through so many bad experiences that I came to believe that it kept me alive, that if I ever took it off I would die. To this day, whenever it breaks I very quickly have it mended because it's become part of my own sense of . . . I won't say *immortality* . . . but . . . prolonged mortality. It is definitely, as far as I can see, a contributor, a stay in my life, it helps hold things together and enables me to keep away the dark thoughts of death that might become overwhelming for some people.

Some of my colleagues became very morose and incapable of separating themselves from thoughts of death. It was true of GIs much more so than CIA agents, in part because the GIs were thrown constantly into the surreal environment of combat, whereas we were able to hold that at arm's length oftentimes. Also, CIA agents were there a long time and the duration of one's exposure to constant death inevitably—what can one say—it *polishes* the surface, or buffs the surface, so that you no longer think of death as anything but just another fact of life, the way eating is a fact of life, happening every day. It becomes a pal.

One of the most stunning things I remember, and I remember it very vividly, was my first experience of somebody being shot very close to me. You look into someone's face and they're animated and they're alive just as you are, and the next minute they're dead. Making the transition, in your own mind, being able to accept that this animate object is suddenly an inanimate one, is a major leap. Woe to the man or woman who is forced to make that leap so often that it no longer affects him or her. I haven't reached that state but I can tell you it happened to others more than I like to recall. This thing that used to be a human being becomes an inanimate object, something that is unrelated to you. You treat it as a piece of meat.

I was particularly struck in Vietnam by the difference between the Judeo-Christian view of death and the Vietnamese or Buddhist approach to death. The Vietnamese view death as a terribly romantic consideration. No love story in Vietnam was ever free of a tragic death at the end. It's not for nothing that the Zeffirelli version of Romeo and Juliet, the movie, was *hugely* popular during the last years of the war and played in all the movie theaters in Vietnam, and in fact was very popular all over Asia. The Romeo and Juliet story is quintessentially Asian and very very Vietnamese. The idea of dying for your love, of sacrificing yourself for a higher purpose, was very much a part of the Vietnamese ethos. It spoke to something not only deeply Buddhist in the Vietnamese character but something that went way beyond any kind of formal religion. It was somehow part of the Vietnamese experience. It's why the Viet Cong could *hurl* themselves against barbed wire in their rubber sandals and their black pajamas, knowing that they were facing overwhelming fire power. Because there was always the notion that death was a transcendent experience, that you somehow redeemed the banality of your life through a sacrificial death.

That's something the Americans never understood. If one is looking for an explanation as to why we didn't carry the day in Vietnam, it's because we didn't understand that. We never realized that there was no zero-sum game for the Vietnamese, that they would suffer casualty after casualty without limit. This will sound peculiar to antiwar protesters, but the Vietnamese leaders had no sense of the moral boundaries of physical sacrifice that affected and shaped the thinking of American policy-makers.

By way of explaining this point, I recall one particular period in Vietnam, late in 1969, when we policy makers were debating whether or not to bomb the dikes in Hanoi. There was a thesis that this would bring the war to—at least a standstill, because the casualties would be astronomical. I think the projection was that two million North Vietnamese would die as a result of the attacks or as a result of subsequent famine, because breaking the dikes would destroy the rice crops.

Well. The Americans decided not to do it because the prospect of inflicting so many casualties was simply too much. This was all outlined in the intelligence estimates. I submit to you that the Vietnamese, on the other hand, would have had no such qualms. This is not an ideological viewpoint, it's simply a fact of life. General Giap, the Vietnamese commander in chief, admitted at war's end that every *year* he'd been willing to sacrifice a hundred thousand men, sixty to a hundred thousand men. They were sent down the Ho Chi Minh Trail system and chewed up. That's a different view of death, or of the value of human life if you flip it over, very different from the one that animated Americans in Vietnam.

I won't presume to go too far down this road but I do think that this was quintessentially Vietnamese, even if they weren't devout Buddhists, even if they were Catholic for instance. I believe that, because of their history and because of the suffering they had endured almost without cease, they had turned into souls very similar to the kind of soul I became. The longer you are in a situation where there is constant death, the more you simply accept it. More than that, you felt improved by it—that's the only way to say it—*perfected* by it.

I'm not saying I think the Vietnamese went into battle with trumpets blaring and with hearts throbbing looking for a knight's death or a chivalric experience. I think a lot of westerners did that, and particularly Americans who grew up in the South, who were nurtured on those tales of great heroism at Gettysburg—Pickett's charge and what have you.

I was brought up that way. I was part of the warrior tradition of the South. Dying in battle was a positive, it was the way you became a knight. You either won the battle or you were brought home on your escutcheon. That's what was expected of you. And if you didn't triumph or you didn't die, you weren't a man, you weren't a southerner, you weren't worthy of that tradition.

No Vietnamese I knew felt that he was becoming a better warrior by thrusting himself into the jaws of death, I think he felt that he was playing out a fate. There's a slightly different glint through the prism there.

In any event, the southern tradition was very significant in shaping my views, not only of life but also of death. I can think of no greater glory than being part of Pickett's charge. I know that will sound slightly antique, but that's the way it is and I have constantly—having been brought up a southerner—conducted myself with a view to completing Pickett's charge. In other words, always charging into the cannon's maw.

I was brought up mainly by my grandmother, who was very much into the southern warrior tradition. I spent Sunday afternoons listening to Confederate war songs on the Victrola, as she would call it. My formative experiences were permeated with songs and banners and heroic visions. She would remind me that one of my forebears, a colonel in the Confederacy whose name was John White Golay, and who was at Pickett's charge, died standing on a cannon with his hat on his sword saying, "They've got me boys but they haven't got us all."

Now if you're a little boy and you're brought up with that vision, death doesn't hold horror, it holds something else—a challenge. This was the greatest act, dying this way, and I think a lot of southern boys were brought up with that notion.

Of course I'm talking about white southern boys. I mean, if you were brought up in the South, the notion that blacks might have a similar, or even dissimilar sense, just didn't register. The fact of the matter is, the thing I'm talking about is almost exclusively white Anglo-Saxon madness. It comes down to us from the Celts and the Saxons and so on. It goes right back to King Arthur and the Round Table and that tradition is very real in the South. It's an ancient tradition that touches on this idea that death can have the effect of perfecting you, of improving you in some way.

And it *was* my experience that death, or the exposure to death, can actually hone your sensibility. And it's not just exposure, it's involvement. I want to emphasize involvement, because I wasn't simply a bystander, I was, in various small and large ways, a contributor to people's deaths. I had collected intelligence that enabled people to kill, I'd been involved in operations that resulted in people's deaths and I had killed people—directly. I was a callow youth at the time, I didn't think of my role as an instrument of death if you will . . . I was a CIA officer. I was a professional, just as a combat soldier is a professional. He doesn't think of himself as an instrument of death, or she doesn't.

It is only with the curse of middle age that you begin to think in these philosophical terms. Now I have a *tremendous* sense of remorse about the pain and suffering that I've inflicted, but it took quite a while to become reflective about it all—in a way that was anything but protective. I can honestly say, never in those days did I rethink the morality of my contribution to so many deaths.

And I don't think I'm the only person who ever had that experience. There's that scene in the movie *The Best Years of Our Lives,* I think it's Dana Andrews walking among the B-29 carcasses and he's thinking something like, these were the best years of our lives . . .

raining death down on people, let's be honest about it. And that was true of my experiences in Vietnam. Because inflicting death, after all, is godlike, and as terrible as it sounds, that's what happens to you in war.

I mean, there was an aspect to my Vietnam experience which was very Hemingwayesque. I'll never forget, I was in a Porter aircraft which was a CIA plane and I was winging my way down to the foot of South Vietnam and we began taking ground fire and all of a sudden holes burst in the wings where ground fire had connected. And instead of being frightened I had this exhilarating feeling and I remember saying to myself: "Isn't this the greatest? This is it, *this is the edge of everything*!" Now that's something that people don't admit to themselves oftentimes, but the proximity of death, when you can just reach your hand out and touch it, that can be exhilarating, and it can be terribly romantic, in a Western way, not a Vietnamese way but a Western way. You are simply on a high, and there is nothing like it that will ever come again.

I left Vietnam with the last CIA contingent off the roof of the embassy. When I came back to the United States I couldn't find anybody to talk to. Some would say this was post-traumatic stress syndrome or delayed stress syndrome. Whatever it was, I carried with me a sense of—apartness. And the only people I could identify with were those who had been through Vietnam, who had experienced that . . . that "transfiguration." Only they seemed good enough, or bad enough, to be part of my life. It took a long time to move out of that sense of apartness. Because I had the feeling that nobody had been brushed by death or by great events which were often suffused with death, as I had.

It wasn't a sense of superiority, it was a sense of detachment, it was . . . thinking back on it, it was a terrifying attitude because I think probably anything would have been possible. Somebody could have said, "Let's go off to another war," and I would have done it. Because death had ceased to have a sinister aspect to it, it had ceased to be fearful. I hate to say this because it sounds so melodramatic, but

I had looked it in the face and accepted my involvement in it so profoundly that I was utterly changed.

I was so detached from everybody else that I simply couldn't have survived very long. I wrote a book which was my exorcism, as a way of ridding myself of some of the ghosts. Actually it was an experience very similar to that of the character in *The Pawnbroker* when he takes a paper spike and he rams his hand on the paper spike, and he's trying to make himself feel. This is somebody who'd been through much more terrible experiences than mine, in the Holocaust, but I wrote the book in the same spirit. I kept saying to myself, "I've *got* to feel something." "I've *got* to understand what happened here and I've got to make myself respond to this experience emotionally as well as intellectually and vice versa."

Well the reentry was a gradual process, it didn't just happen with one event or another. But it happened. I'm more sympathetic of people who are facing death, whereas I wasn't before. I mean if you were dying of cancer I would have said, "Eh, forget it." But I think that now I can accept other people's fear. I can understand it and I am no longer dismissive of it. Even if I think the person is misguided about death, as I do with many people who are very religious and who approach death from a religious standpoint. Instead of being contemptuous of them I can be sympathetic, I can be compassionate. I suppose that's a passage.

How did it happen? I guess if there are twenty other people in the raft, you've got to accommodate yourself to them. And that's what happens when you come out of a war zone. Strange to say, but, in a way, the world is more limited and you have to accommodate yourself to people who haven't had your experiences. So that reality just batters away at your preconceptions and you begin to soften I suppose. That was the passage.

Basically I just don't think about death anymore, or not very profoundly anyway, it's not a preoccupation. Maybe I'm still suffering from some of the residue of that sense of immortality that came into being in Vietnam but I'm not sure of that at all. I mean, the silver bullet is gonna come sooner rather than later and it's not frightening, it's not sobering, it's not anything.

My mother died about two years ago and I did not feel any compulsion toward tears. I have found it impossible to feel any sadness whatsoever. Now somebody could say, "Boy, is that guy screwed up." And my sisters would say "Well, you didn't accept your mother's death." But I did accept it. That's the whole point. I *accepted* it. The fact of the matter is—it's no big deal. I can ask myself, "Where is the sense of tragedy?" It's not there. I've seen too much of it already.

As I said, the warrior tradition is *very* profound in my life. I can't think of anyone in my family who was particularly concerned about death. Even if the fear was there, very few of my family members would have acknowledged it. That would have been seen as weakness and weakness was not tolerated.

In the matter of religion, I can recall my father going to church and his being very taken with this Christian vision of salvation. To me it didn't ring true, I was contemptuous of it. If you are rigorous, about belief and reality, and if you can't just "have faith," what happens is you finally hit a wall. The wall is death and religion is like those totems. Of course, religion is full of totems but more than that, like the myths, it's designed to ease what you cannot accept, to armor you against the terror or the terrors. In the case of religion, I think the armor is simply too thick, you can't move in all that armor. You have to go into so much denial that it becomes absurdly limiting, you have to go much too far, emotionally and intellectually, so I was contemptuous of it.

Not that I don't understand the desire to believe in something that way. After all, the great injustice in life is death. You put all this currency into developing yourself, you spend all this time educating yourself and suddenly it's snuffed out. If you begin thinking about the injustice of it, it'll drive you mad. This is an age-old quandary.

But I think if you're looking for answers or for solace by turning to the Judeo-Christian tradition, you're gonna wind up terrifying yourself because you will finally have to accept it on faith, which of course is what Christianity says. But that requires negation which is, itself, a kind of death, an intellectual death. Denial is another word for it, self-denial and denial. I think that's what organized religion requires of you, at least what the Judeo-Christian ethic requires of you, that you shut yourself down. I don't see why people should do that, you should *expand,* you should pursue your questions. *That's* life, *that's* living. Otherwise you are already constricted. You die before your time.

> *If God is good he is not God,*
> *If God is God he is not good,*
> *Take the even take the odd,*
> *I would not sleep here if I could,*
> *except for the little green leaves on the wood*
> *and the wind on the water . . .*

That's Archibald MacLeish and it sums up what I realized at one point in my life: You've got to go one of two ways, you've got to take everything on faith or take nothing at all. And if you're arrogant enough to try to approach life intellectually you can't take everything on faith, so what you finally say is—the world and man and woman are all part of a machine that just keeps clicking on. And if you adopt this somewhat bastardized Spinozan view of life and death then you are prepared to go into a war zone, you are prepared for the kind of evolution in thinking that I went through. You are prepared to die in the warrior tradition.

HOBIE DAVIS
Age: 47
Sculptor and Carpenter

ℒ

When I was nineteen I got my draft notice. It was Vietnam and it was a time when they got every nineteen-year-old that could be got. So I went around to see if I could enlist and get some kind of training that would help or something. Now, when I look back, I was just . . . well, I don't want to get into a psychological characterization of myself . . . it just seemed like that was the thing that was happening at that time.

I had a charge on my record, illegal possession and consumption of alcohol, so the Navy, the Air Force and the Coast Guard wouldn't take me, especially with me having just got my draft notice. So I went to the army. I like machines so I said, "I'd like to fly a helicopter, man." Now this is before the whole helicopter thing got so intense. To me they just seemed like interesting machines and I thought I might as well learn about them.

The guy there was your basic lying recruiter and he said, "Well why don't you try out as a mechanic first and then, when you prove yourself as a mechanic, we'll let you be a pilot." Which is really *not* the way it happens at all, but I was set up like that.

Then they sent me to the wrong school. I was supposed to be a prop and rotor repairman but they sent me to a single-engine, fixed-wing school. I didn't know they'd screwed up until I got to the school, on the East Coast, in Virginia, and by that time it had become very clear that you didn't want to have *anything* to do with helicopters unless you were nuts, or a real warrior-type and you wanted to get into the blood and action and all that. I could have said, "You didn't give me the right school, you gotta give me the right school," but I didn't say anything at all. I just kept quiet.

They sent the wrong orders to get me to Vietnam and by the time they'd figured *that* out I was at a different army base in Ala-

bama, working as a lifeguard because I could swim. I wound up in
Special Services, where the entertainers go, and the people who
requisition basketballs, stuff like that. Next thing I know I'm handing
out archery equipment and horseshoes at Long Binh Post about
eighteen miles outside of Saigon.

Vietnam was considered a no-front-line-type war, where the
enemy owned it during the night and we owned it during the day.
The general ratio was nine support troops for every man in the field.
I was one of the nine. Long Binh Post was the second largest supply
post in the country, a huge place, you'd never know everybody
there, it was so big. So I'm buried in support. I had very little actual
contact with people beyond my little scene. The few field troops that
I saw were usually in these half-tracks, these big personnel carriers or
armored vehicles that carry troops so they can't be shot. These guys
definitely had an aura about them, a hardness that . . . looked different. I wasn't part of that scene.

I spent most of my time just trying to amuse myself. They sent us
one thousand charcoal barbecue grills and a rototiller by mistake, so I
sculpted and contoured all these little hills around the supply hut
where I passed stuff out. I built a suntan salon on top of a metal
shipping container disguised as a big sign for the rec area. It was like
that. It was just learning about reality—you're on your own in this
life so what are you gonna do with it? I was working on that.

There was a group of guys who were making money, having a
good time. They had black market things going and they were ready
to leave, stay in Vietnam, go to Cambodia, whatever, depending on
how the thing went down. In the meantime, a riot in the post
military prison, which was known as L.B.J. (Long Bin Jail), revealed
the scale of racial prejudice in our army in Vietnam. A whole lot of
racial things had come down. Anytime they wanted to get rid of a
black person, it seems like they could find some marijuana on him
and throw him in L.B.J. The inmates were protesting the abuse of
one of the prisoners—the MPs had set dogs on this guy and almost
killed him. So they burned the place down. And the rest of us had to
take up loaded weapons with fixed bayonets and guard these people
in our own army, who were still trying to protest. Among the hun-

dreds of American prisoners we corralled, I saw only one or two
white faces, it was all black GIs, and anyone who wanted to stay
honest and straight with this protest thing, they sent them to Leaven-
worth for the rest of their tour of duty. The sum of this experience
caused a sickness in me that was the death of my patriotic feelings
and my respect for this country for a long time.

The first time I saw someone die was in Saigon. We would go
into the city from time to time, for a holiday. On this particular trip
the ARVNs, the Vietnamese regular army, were coming through.
There was this big machine-gun nest sort of thing in Saigon, built up
with sandbags all around it and a big guard station with U.S. Army
MPs everywhere. Three of the ARVNs had commandeered one of
those little pedicabs and one of their buddies was laying on it, completely limp and covered with blood and they were trying to get the
military police to help them find a hospital for their friend. The MPs
were just totally ignoring them and were not going to help them at
all. These are American MPs and there was just this total "we-don't-
care" vibe . . . as though the ARVNs weren't really people.

In the army we had all these old sergeants from Korea. They
brought in the lingo, the "Mama-san," "Papa-san" thing from Korea
and along with that the whole attitude that these people weren't
really worth anything. And that's the way they treated those folks
and a lot of American kids unconsciously picked that up. There was
just so much racism of all kinds. It was a kind of socialization process,
you know?

I was nineteen and looking out at this strange world, having
grown up in Seattle where nothing ever happened except rain. And
I'm seeing this guy dying, or maybe he's dead already. He was lying
there motionless, totally red with his own blood. It looked like death
to me. And no one would help them. That was like a hit, it really
affected me.

When you got leave to go into Saigon, the big thing to do was to
go to prostitutes in town, to these special massage places where they
would walk on your back and stuff like that, and then go and eat in
these old French restaurants on top of small hotels and have a big

steak dinner and look out over the city and the stars. About once a month or so we'd go in and do that.

On one of these excursions we were riding in this "Deucenahaf," this two-and-a-half-ton flatbed truck. There were three or four guys in the cab and I was the only one in the back on the flatbed. The streets of Saigon are a whole teeming world filled with pedicabs, bicycles, tiny motorcycles, scooters, every kind of vehicle. Often you'd see a couple riding these scooter things, the man driving and the woman riding sidesaddle on the back. There are no real stoplights and very little traffic control of any kind, just a few Vietnamese policemen, these thin little guys dressed in white and wearing white hats. Everybody called them white mice, because they were so tiny I guess. When larger streets turned into smaller streets all the traffic would merge in together and everyone had to maneuver and kind of find their own way.

We were driving into one of these merges and there was this couple on a scooter that got forced closer and closer to us, and then finally the edge of our flatbed caught the woman's shoulder and flipped her off the bike and under these gigantic dual wheels of our truck and we rode over her. I'm yelling at the people in the cab that we had just run over this person, "Stop! Stop! Stop!" And the driver just sped up.

One really angry Vietnamese in the crowd chased us on his scooter and finally got ahead of us and got to the white mice and had them stop us. So here we are in the middle of Saigon, completely surrounded by Vietnamese people, talking and waiting for our MPs, our police, to come and try to straighten this thing out. And it was like my stomach was just gone or something. I had looked into the expression on this woman's face as she went under these wheels. The hugh heavy wheels just crushed her. She was so small . . . they're such a tiny people.

Come to find out later that this guy who was driving this truck had bad eyesight and had killed someone already before, and he was just getting as far from the scene as he could so that he could make up a better story and try to lose himself in the crowd, all that sort of thing. . . .

It was weird, to be with these guys, not really well acquainted with these GIs or anything, and to feel like I was taking on their responsibility, the responsibility for *our* actions, and feeling bad because we didn't stop, didn't help, but not knowing what to do.

As I look back on it from more than twenty years, I can see my callow youth, my immature values and my inability to walk alone and choose what I felt to be true and right, no matter what was going on with everybody else.

Since then I've been through a lot of things. Some major acid tripping. I learned a lot from that. That's how I hooked up with God actually. I have a strong Christian faith that works for me. But back then I didn't have that, and I sure didn't know anything about death. It was surreal, with so many people getting wiped out. I was there but I was an innocent. . . .

CITYKIDS

DARNEICE	MANAN	ANDREW	CARLOS
Age: 16	Age: 17	Age: 18	Age: 19

JUDY	EDWARD	WILLIAM
Age: 16	Age: 19	Age: 16

❧

DARNEICE: Right now it seems like a lot of people have been dying, and that's brought the reality of it to me—kids getting shot around my neighborhood.

At first I was sad. When the first people I knew died, I was crying a lot. But now, you know, I'm hanging around the neighborhood and I hear, "Blah-de-blah got shot last night," and I say, "Oh, really?" I stopped crying. Now it's more like "Oh, yeah."

You can't keep crying. I think I got used to it. It's mostly people I grew up with. You know, you grow up and separate. All we did was say "Hi," or hang out with each other every once in a while. I wouldn't call them or anything like that, I'd just hang out with them. Now we can't.

Sometimes you can still see the blood on the street where they were. It depends on where they got it. Sometimes I wonder if I heard it, when they got killed, if those were the gunshots I heard last night. Maybe I saw them the day before they died, or the day they died. That's usually what I think of—the last time I saw them or where they got shot or what happened.

Now that death has been brought to me I feel like I'm going to die. Before I never thought it could touch me, not that kind of getting killed or getting hurt. Now I'm scared of cars, I'm scared of everything. Now I feel like I could die at any minute. Anything could kill me.

MANAN: Everybody is scared. If you hear that somebody got shot, you think it could be me, 'cause most of the time it's stray

bullets that are killing kids so, yeah, you do get frightened. I try to be
more alert and aware of where I'm going, to make sure that nothing's going on that's shady or anything, 'cause you have to be very
careful. But nobody's safe, 'cause you can get killed easy. Once you
walk out the door you never know what might happen.

PA: *What do you think happens when we die?*

MANAN: Oh I believe there's a God, definitely, and there's
heaven and hell, all that stuff. I believe in that. I believe in it strongly.
And with death and everything? I'm scared of it and I'm not scared
of it. I mean, it feels like somebody's watching over me. I do ask,
"Dear Lord, watch over me," when I go to school or wherever, just
in case, 'cause you never know. One day you miss praying, that
could be the day the bullet hits you or the car hits you.

DARNEICE: I don't think I'm scared of death at all. I'm just afraid
of getting there, I'm afraid of the pain of getting there. I'm not sure
what happens after you die. I kinda think when you die you're just
dead. I mean that's it. You die and it's a black hole. You go to sleep
and you just never come back and you disappear, like you never
came.

I don't think about religion 'cause it doesn't make a lot of sense
to me. They said you have to wait till Judgment Day. So what does
the person do until Judgment Day? They just lay there until the end
of time? I don't know about that. And then when the body's corroded, what happens?

JUDY: I never heard about waiting until Judgment Day.

DARNEICE: I was told about Judgment Day. They decide who
goes to heaven and who goes to hell.

MANAN: Okay, look. In the Bible it does tell about Judgment
Day and it says the Christians that die are going to be put in waiting
until Jesus comes to take his people. Until then the people will not
be physically in their bodies but they're in, it's like a spiritual body,
and they will be waiting for heaven and hell and all that.

DARNEICE: So where's that? Where's heaven and where's hell?

MANAN: They're spiritual places, there's no real location. People
usually say heaven's up and hell's down but there's no real, physical
location.

DARNEICE: But people have been up there and they've been down there and they haven't found heaven or hell.

MANAN: It's a spiritual place, you can't go there physically. You want it to be what you can see and touch?

DARNEICE: Yeah. And besides, think about it, heaven and hell? That's not fair. Look at all the people in the world, how many are there?

PA: Over five billion.

DARNEICE: Five billion people in the world. There are about twenty million different beliefs about what the truth is and if you have the wrong belief you're going to go to *hell*? You just happen to be in the wrong place or have the wrong belief? It's not fair. It doesn't make any sense. I'm sorry, it just doesn't make any sense.

Sometimes I think these ideas are like a safety net, you know what I mean? Religion could be a way of comforting people about their fear of death. Or to control people, so they say there's this or that waiting for you. I don't know, it's very hard for me to swallow.

JUDY: I could see why people would think that religion doesn't make sense but also the scientific theory that there was a bunch of molecules and chemicals and they slammed together and created everything . . . now that's also weird. So who created the chemicals? It's like *everything* is confusing. I've learned not to theorize about it but to just believe it.

ANDREW: I haven't totally formed a theory about all this yet but one of my most recent thoughts is that the whole thing about death and going to heaven is a great big punch line. Life is the joke and death is the punch line because you just die and that's it, you know? That's it. You thought you were going somewhere but you're not. You're down in the ground, the joke's on you, screw you.

It just doesn't make sense to me that you'd go somewhere and be happy, or go somewhere and burn. If I were to believe in a conception of heaven and hell I would say where we are right now is hell because it can't get much worse than the planet we're living on. Having to worry about getting killed every time you walk out the door, who's going to mug you next, stuff like that—and once you've served your time down here, as it were, then you go on to heaven or hell? I don't think so.

We think that we're the first part of a two-stage type of thing where first we're here and then we go to heaven. It's theoretically possible that we're already in heaven or we're already in hell from wherever we were before, and we just don't know it because we don't know if such a thing as past lives exists. We don't know what that is or what that means.

JUDY: You mean like when we were born, that was a death from the other life, or something?

ANDREW: Yeah, and we don't remember anything from before. We don't know that we died when we come back.

EDWARD: Something like *Quantum Leap* maybe, we just leap from one body into another body or something . . .

DARNEICE: I'm praying for reincarnation, that's what I'm hoping for, 'cause I don't want to just die and have nothing. That would mess up my life right now.

WILLIAM: I sort of believe in reincarnation. Maybe I was George Washington or something, but it's like everyone was saying, you just don't know. I come from a family that is very religious. I'm Catholic but I don't really share that. I mean, I *do* agree with most of what religion says, but some things I really disagree with. Some of the things that they say are evil I just don't believe are evil. Like they say, "Homosexuality is evil," and I'm like "Okay, sure, I'm going to hell now, right?" So I just think to myself, "Whatever I believe is right, that's what's right." Because I believe strongly in what I believe in. So that's what I think about my religion.

DARNEICE: They're not teaching kids about death. Not really. In my opinion, kids are not learning the finality of death. Death is it. You cannot come back to what you've left, okay? You can't. You watch a cartoon, somebody gets shot, somebody falls off a cliff and they come right back. It doesn't happen.

ANDREW: Darneice . . . cartoons are not real.

DARNEICE: Sure, you know it's not real, or you come to a point where you know it's not real. But little tiny kids don't know. Kids do stupid stuff 'cause it's put into their head. They saw it happen so the idea stays in their head, even though it's not real. You know what I mean?

EDWARD: I did a report on this last semester for English class and I think what everybody in society should do today is: Every parent should watch TV with their kids and explain the difference between what's real and what isn't . . . what's death and what's . . . I'm trying to find the right word . . . you know, just TV . . .

JUDY: I think everyone's afraid of traumatizing their children or something. They don't want to say anything that will influence them in a bad way. But also, little kids wouldn't understand it anyway, I don't think they can understand the concept of death.

Little kids are born without racism and without any premeditations about anyone or anything. They're just there to learn and I think everybody's afraid of what to teach them first. A lot of people are saying maybe sex education should start in kindergarten and other people are saying "No, 'cause that would put ideas in my child's head." I think that's why they don't approach death because they're afraid if they teach it the wrong way it will hurt their child.

MANAN: Yeah, but with cartoons it's all in fun. It's a joke.

DARNEICE: I don't care, you cannot get smashed by a fifteen-ton thing as a joke, it's not funny. I don't think it should be funny that somebody gets their head blown off or their beak blown to the other side of their face or their feathers burned off. People are going to laugh and stuff, I know, people are going to laugh but . . . if you show it over and over to little kids who don't know anything . . .

JUDY: Some parents don't know how to explain to their kids. I remember I was watching the news when I was six or seven with my mom and there was some rape story on. I didn't know what they were talking about. I thought they said "rake," and so I was asking, "What'd they take a rake and like *scrape* someone?" I was like, "Mom, what's rape? What's rape?" And so she told me in the technical terms, "It's forcibly having sexual intercourse," and I was like "What?" "What's that?" And she didn't want to answer. She was reading a book and she just pretended like she didn't hear me.

But you know, everybody stiffens up and no one knows how to explain it, whether it's about sex or about death. If people were able to figure out a way to explain it, a way that would be understood, I think it would be good. But we don't have a way to do that.

DARNEICE: Yeah . . . can you imagine? "Well honey, if you really got shot with that gun there would be blood and brains spattered all over the scenery."

PA: What do you think would be a good kind of death?

DARNEICE: I want it to be on the news. I want my body to be hung up somewhere . . .

MANAN: Hung up?

DARNEICE: Adorned beautifully . . .

MANAN: What do you mean?

DARNEICE: If I'm gonna die I want somebody to kill me, right? 'Cause I want it to be on the news. And I want to be all dressed up, because if I'm gonna be this way for eternity I wanna look good, okay? I don't want to be dressed afterwards because if they dress me afterwards it's not gonna be the same. I want to choose my clothes and be dressed the way I want. I want to die pretty. And then I want somebody to hang me on the side of a building or on a gate or something like that . . .

[*Everybody is laughing*]

No really, I'm serious. I had a dream about this. If I'm going to be on the news I want to look good. I want a picture.

MANAN: But you won't see it so what's the point?

JUDY: I want a party.

MANAN: My mom said the same thing, she wants balloons and everything. She said she's had a good life, she's lived the way she wants to live, so she wants it to be like a festival, a celebration of her life. Balloons and people having fun.

ANDREW: I want to die like Jackie Onassis died. It was big in the news, everybody heard about it but it was so refined and calm and no one was crazy and yes, there were hundreds of cameras but they were, you know, held back. It was nice, the way it happened. Thousands of people knew about it but they weren't clamoring all over, it wasn't a paparazzi event, it was just a nice, refined funeral and that's it. That's a nice way to die if you're someone like her.

JUDY: I would like to die peacefully, in my sleep or something. If

I had to die in a more active way, I would like to die while fighting for something I believed in. Not like in battle but for a good cause, if it could help something, if it wasn't just a meaningless death. I don't want to die from a stray bullet in the street, I don't want to die from an accident, from a plane crashing. I want it to be either incredibly peaceful or with a purpose.

DARNEICE: If you die in battle, you don't feel it because the adrenaline is pumping. I know people that got shot, they didn't even know they got shot because of the action, the shock or whatever. So that's better. Or sedated. I want to be sedated or in action . . .

JUDY: I want to be cremated because I heard somewhere that some year in the future there's not going to be enough living space because of all the cemeteries. So I'm going to make it easier on the world.

WILLIAM: I'm not sure what a good death would be. I don't really want to die but I don't think I would want immortality. Everyone else is going to die and you'd just be left there. A dream death would be . . . I would have to be happy, like reach total happiness. I want to die from happiness.

MANAN: I think it would be important to resolve any problems that I have with people. And then die in my bed, in my sleep, after prayer or something.

DARNEICE: Are you serious?

MANAN: Yeah. I don't want to get shot or burned up or strung up.

DARNEICE: Don't you want to be on the news?

MANAN: No. I'd rather just be in my bed, on my pillow, with socks on my feet and just, you know, die.

DARNEICE: I want it to be on the news in every country. I want people to write books about my death. Gosh, yeah, I want to be famous for *something*.

EDWARD: To get to that point you got to be like Michael Jackson or Elvis Presley or somebody . . .

DARNEICE: No, I would get it by dying in such a weird way. If my body's on the side of a building, hung up and decorated, they're going to wonder how it got there. People are going to come out, before it gets corroded. And then I want it cremated and then I want somebody to plant a beautiful flowering plant and put my ashes in it. I just thought of that right now. Put me in a plant.

JUDY: I think I'd like that too. 'Cause then in a way you're still living.

EDWARD: I just want to be in my bed and be asleep.

DARNEICE: It's not peaceful, dying in your sleep. When they say somebody died in their sleep it doesn't mean they were sleeping when they died. Let me tell you what happens. It goes like this. They're sleeping, right? And when somebody comes and checks on them they're in their bed and it looks like they're sleeping, but they didn't die like that.

ANDREW: Not necessarily.

DARNEICE: No really. You're sleeping, right? And then you wake up and then you go into some kind of convulsion or choking and then you go back down and you're dead, and when they find you it looks like you were sleeping.

JUDY: Your body can just slow down. I mean your heartbeat can slow down, your brain movements and breathing can slow down, just get slower and slower and slower . . .

MANAN: If you die in your sleep you just die in your sleep, period.

DARNEICE: No, it's like some sort of convulsion.

ANDREW: Not always, not necessarily.

DARNEICE: Yes it is.

JUDY: I'm not going to think that. I'm not going to think . . .

DARNEICE: Okay, you go on, you people sleep.

ANDREW: When people are in comas and die, they don't wake up out of the coma and die. They stay in the coma until they're dead.

DARNEICE: There's a shiver or something . . . they do something.

ANDREW: There might be a jerk or something 'cause when you die you excrete waste from your body, after you're dead.

CARLOS: You what?

DARNEICE: Yeah you do. And then your nails grow and your hair grows . . . death releases things, things release . . .

CARLOS: Repeat that again? When you die *you what?*

ANDREW: Your body flushes out . . .

DARNEICE: You urinate on yourself and everything. It's because your muscles release.

CARLOS: Wow, I never knew that.

EDWARD and others: Is that true?

PA: Well, sometimes, in some cases, but not always. It varies quite a lot in different circumstances. Death can be messy. With violence there's that kind of messiness. And sometimes, at the end of an illness, the body is deteriorating and you don't necessarily have complete control over it anymore. Of course, after the body dies, you don't have any control over it.

Lots of people I've talked to think there is a part of themselves that will separate from the body as they are dying. They feel that the part of them that is aware—some call it a soul or a spirit, some don't have a name for it—that part of them will be moving away already. They think that when the body starts to deteriorate like that, they're not really there anymore.

JUDY: Lots of people feel that way.

MANAN: The body is like a shell.

EDWARD: Like a shell.

DARNEICE: Well . . . maybe.

WESTERN IDEAS ABOUT DEATH
CHRONOLOGY PART 2

✑

Throughout the ancient Near East, a strict separation is maintained between burial places and population centers. Although the dead are honored, they are buried outside the villages, towns, and cities because it is feared their spirits might emerge from sleep and cause trouble for the living. Every night is Halloween.

c. 100 C.E.   Across the widespread Roman Empire, many cults and forms of worship proliferate, including one devoted to Yahweh of Jerusalem and his son, Jesus. Known as Christians, these disciples believe that martyrdom is the highest expression of their faith and many kill themselves to demonstrate the strength of their devotion.

Saint Augustine condemns suicide in order to ensure the future of Christianity.

c. 400   Like the old Zoroastrian belief, the new religion teaches that the bodies of the dead will be physically resurrected and so the dead must be protected until they arise. Burial near the tomb of a martyr is said to provide such protection.

Eventually the belief in bodily resurrection leads to secular laws calling for dismemberment and mutilation to penalize criminals in the afterlife as well as here on earth.

c. 500   As Christianity spreads, the church edifice itself is declared to be sacred ground and bodies are interred within it to provide protection for the dead. Political favorites win coveted spots indoors. For the rank and file, the churchyard eventually becomes an extension of holy ground.

The prohibition against burial inside the city is lifted, and by the twelfth century only social outcasts are buried in the fields or, as it is later referred to, "the dump."

Christian monks and missionaries travel to the British Isles of Beowulf, the Celts and Druids, and the Anglo-Saxon kings who worship Thor the Thunderer and Odin, God of Magic and Poetry. There they are invited to present their beliefs to chieftans who gather together, saying:
"The present life of Man seems like to the swift flight of a sparrow through the room wherein you sit at supper in winter. The sparrow, whilst he is within, is safe from the wintry storm; but after a short space he immediately vanishes out of your sight. . . . So this life of Man appears for a short space, but of what went before, or what is to follow, we are utterly ignorant. If, therefore, this new doctrine contains something more certain, it seems justly to deserve to be followed."★

1000–   The Legends of King Arthur depict a ritual prepara-
1100   tion for death that becomes the ideal. When a knight

★ W. P. Hall, R. G. Albion, and J. B. Pope, *A History of England and the Empire-Commonwealth* (London: Blaisdell Publishing Co., 1965), p. 12.

is about to die he is supposed to lie with his head facing east toward Jerusalem, ask forgiveness from those he has harmed, pray to God for grace, receive the rites of absolution, and wait calmly for death to come.

The "average guy" is also expected to know when death is imminent. He will observe the signs and portents, as well as his own condition, and will inform his family saying, "Now is the time."

Death is a public experience. When the priest brings the last sacrament, passersby join the procession to the deathbed (which is surrounded by friends and family, including children) to pay their respects and join in the ritual.

By the end of the first millennium of the Christian calendar, death in Western Europe has become uniformly ritualized under the auspices of the Roman Church, and the dead, sleeping under the protection of that church, are no longer such a fearsome concern to the living.

LEE DAVIS
Age: 50
Teacher

⟡

There is a long-standing Christian tradition in my family. My great-grandfather was a farmer-preacher in Tennessee. His name was Granville Lee. In those days you didn't get paid for preaching, you just did it because you had the call. So he'd go out and plow his fields and then come home and work on his sermons.

My dad was an ordained Baptist minister. The Second World War started just as he completed seminary and he went into the Navy because he figured he was going to be needed where men were dying. That gave him a really different perspective than if he had been a small-town preacher in Kentucky. He got a wider worldview and so did I. We moved at least once and often several times a year.

Being a minister was my dad's job but it was also his calling. It was definitely something that pervaded all through our lives. When I was growing up you never knew who he was going to bring home for dinner. Sometimes you'd wake up and there'd be a stranger sleeping on the living room sofa because somebody'd had a fight with their wife or husband or whatever and needed a place to stay, so my dad would take them in. He would help out, he loved people.

I was taught that when you die you go to heaven, and there's a kind of weighing of what you did on earth. In heaven you are yourself, but also there's this shape that you become, as the result of your attitudes, your actions. All that you have done and been in this physical life creates who you become in the life after death. It's almost like the way you were on earth is the mold for who you become. I didn't have any problem believing that there was a life after death because it seemed to me that human beings were too amazing to just disappear into nothing.

In the 1960s I went to the University of California at Berkeley and it was very uncool to be a Christian there. For a very long time I was hoping that I wouldn't have to be a Christian.

You see, I always knew God was really important to me, that I wanted to find an answer to the puzzle. I wanted to understand reality and the meaning of life and death, things beyond the tangible. But I was hoping that Buddhism or Hinduism or vegetarianism or *something* cool would work for me. So for a long time I was a spiritual seeker in a lot of those different ways. I sat at the Zendo and I chanted and I ate only kidney beans or whatever, but at one point . . . well, I just wound up back where I'd started.

Actually, one of the things that led me back to it was reading Jung's autobiography. He talks about how each family seems to have questions and how one person in the family will get to a certain point on it and then they pass it on to the next generation and then *they* work on this question or issue and then they pass it on to *their* kids, etc. I started wondering, "What are my family questions?" And as I looked, on both sides of my family, it was clear they definitely were dealing with Christianity.

So I realized that I needed to take a closer look. I could discard it or accept it, whichever, but my decision would be based on a really good look at it to see if it was real. Not bypassing or accepting out of hand, either way, but really to investigate it and see if it worked.

I had reached a point in my life where I was alone a lot. My two-year-old son and I moved out into the country. I tried to get in touch with God, in any way I could, and question him about this Bible and this stuff that he had set down in that particular way. I came to a realization for myself that it *did* work for me, it *was* real. Christianity was a way that I could understand reality.

When you're baptized into the Christian Church, or when you accept Christ, you die to your old way of doing things and symbolically start life again. You're immersed under the water, which is a symbol of death, and then you come up again and it's like you begin again. The idea behind this is: You're beginning a new way of being alive, not serving yourself but trying to learn how to serve God and your fellow men and women. Then, on a daily basis, you are actually trying to die to yourself. You have decided not to let your ego push you around but to learn how to love your neighbor as yourself. Putting another person ahead of yourself is a kind of mini-death.

In the Bible it says we're to number our days. I didn't understand what that meant until I got to be middle-aged, because when you're twenty it's easy to think you're going to live forever. But finally you realize, "Hey, I've got *x* number of more productive years and then I've got some years in which I'll be alive but maybe I don't want to be working eight–ten hours a day." You start to see your life go through certain periods or phases and to think about that. You start to number your days, to say, "It doesn't just go on and on and on, and you're not always going to have all this energy and all this strength and all this beauty and all the problems you have to deal with, so number your days. Think about what's important for to-day."

It's hard not to fear death because our spirits have become so intertwined with our bodies and it seems like very few people are able to get out of their bodies without some kind of pain or anguish. None of us like to feel pain. It's a difficult transition. I *like* my body, it's become a friend to me, it'll be difficult to leave it behind. But my hope is there's another God-made body waiting for me that's at least as wonderful as this one.

To tell the truth, for me, growing older is a lot scarier than dying. We treat our old people so badly. At the very time when you need the beauty of nature, with serenity and peace and birds singing and sunshine around you, we shut them up in these harshly lit, concrete bunkers with other old people half out of their minds, or terrible smells or bad cooking. It must be hell. To me that's much scarier than dying—to grow old, poor and abandoned. But it helps keep death out of sight. It helps us pretend it doesn't happen.

We don't know anything about death anymore. It's like child-birth. For a long time nobody had seen a child be born except doctors and nurses in the hospital. Then people started having child-birth at home again and now, among some people anyway, it's a bit more common. Dying at home is beginning to happen again too.

But still, a lot of people don't have much awareness of the beginnings and the ends of life.

I'm glad I was around when my grandmother died. I didn't actually see her at the moment she died but I was in the house at the time. I saw her decline, I saw her dying . . . and I heard her.

See, I think death has a sound. I'm one of those people who learned to sing before I learned to talk and I tend to think of things in terms of their sound. To me, in this way, death has a sound—a very particular sound I heard when my grandmother died.

I was six or seven, running around in this big dark old southern house. It was real hot outside and real cool inside. I would hear these sounds come floating out of her room, kind of soft and high-pitched. It wasn't so much crying as it seemed like little songs. It was striking to me as a child because it didn't sound like *her*. She was a large, firm, decisive woman in life but as she was dying even her way of talking had become different. Her voice had become high and light, almost childlike. It was as if, now that she was leaving her body, she was letting go of this strong persona she had had in life and was becoming a child again. She had a lot of cancer in her at that point and I'm sure she was taking drugs for the pain but it didn't sound like she was crying out or raving or anything. It sounded like singing. They were like little songs. It seemed to me like the sound of death.

NOAH
Age: 12
Elementary School Student

❧

I would say I have a kind of wondering attitude toward death, wondering what goes on after, if anything. I'd like to believe there's a heaven and there's an afterlife but, to tell you the truth, I don't really know for sure. Sometimes I wish I could experience it and see what it's like but then come back and fulfill my life, you know, just so some of the mist would be cleared.

Like in that movie, *Flatliners*. I thought that was really interesting. Where people experimented with death. They would let them die and go into their death process, then, before it's too late and they're stuck in there, they put those two things on them and give them a shock and they're back. Every time they went under they kept confronting their little fears, the things they were afraid of about death, and they figured stuff out, and it all came together at the end and they really began to live once they had gotten past their fears.

In America, people's view of death often comes from movies or TV shows. Like there's a movie, *Defending Your Life,* where you go up to this kind of heaven place and eat all you want and not gain an ounce. People would love to think of it that way, or like you're floating around on a cloud and angels are passing by and if you do these things and years of waiting go by, you'll get your wings. But in real life they act like death is a big tragedy. They don't *really* believe they're going to float around on clouds or anything.

I think the only Westerners who think of death in a positive way are people in a lot of pain, ones with fatal diseases who feel the suffering every day and they're thinking, "Well yeah, if I was to, you know, go away, at least I'd be done with the suffering and I would free my soul. . . ."

A lot of people are afraid to cry when a loved one dies, or to even talk about it. In some other countries they're more loose and when you're more loose you can talk about what your fears are, openly, with your mother, with your brother, with your dog even. Here we require trained professionals to talk to, and it's amazing how that clogs up our life. Here it seems very closed and people can't talk about it.

There was this one episode of *Murphy Brown* where she had some spare time and she was reading this baby book and she read this section on how to talk to your kids about death and all of a sudden she realized that she didn't really know much about death and she had to go around and ask people.

She's not your average American and she wanted to talk about it, like asking people, "What's your opinion?" And everybody was afraid of her. They were saying, "Do we have to talk about this now?" And, "You're not going to give me the death talk now are you?" you know, all her friends. One of them was a very uptight person who goes to church but is still mixed up, and he was saying, "Do we really have to talk about this?"

I'm not sure exactly how it came out. I think she saw that nobody really knew about death . . . it was more undiscovered than thinkable.

I've been to India and I've seen the burning ghats and for Indians death is like a freeing of the spirit from the body, and then they burn the body and put it in the river in Benares and that gives them good karma for the next life. But here in the West, you know, they make death out to be a lot heavier and a lot worse than the Indians do.

It's funny how the lack of knowledge and lack of openness really sticks out, especially in America and Europe, more in the first-world countries than the third. Because I think the third-world countries, a lot of it is poverty and they don't have the good life that the West-erners do and they're thinking, "Wait till we get out and go up."

There's more science in the West. They can keep your heart going. But scientifically hearts aren't what they seem to be, mentally. Mentally hearts are something that give and take the love and every-thing. That's the way they see it in India, you know. Hanuman [a Hindu deity] is tearing open his heart and inside there's a picture of the two people he loves the most.

The heart is an emotion-keeper, and a lot of the time death opens up more emotions. But scientifically it's like, the blood goes in, the blood goes out, a heart is just a heart, as long as it pumps it's always going to be a heart. Only in your mind is your heart going to be something deeper than what it is in your body. I mean, when a heart gets broken, it's like a metaphor, you know. That's what the Indian style of heart is, it's a metaphor to the Western style of heart.

In America I think they keep all their emotions boggled up with this funeral thing. It's not a very free event. It's more like a tragedy than anything like what happens in India with a freeing of their soul. I think if people in the West looked at death in a more positive way it would be more of a releasing than a loss. It would definitely be more open.

KORBY SIAMIS
Age: 38
Television Writer and Producer, *Murphy Brown*

༄

I have a son who is three and a daughter ten months old. One rare night I came home from work early and I thought, "Okay, I've got a little time this evening; I'm going to catch up on the baby book literature." We're reading *Your Baby and Child: From Birth to Age Five,* by Penelope Leach.

I'm reading along and it's about language development and their independence and all these fun things and I turn the page and there's the heading: "Talking About Death." It completely stopped me in my tracks. I had to reread the sentence three times to believe I was really facing this. I mean, I knew that it was in the future, I just didn't expect to be facing it so soon.

I had thought of it from time to time, aware that the question would come up. When you have a child you know there's going to be that moment when you sit down with them and say, "Yes, I brought you into this world, but guess what, there's a catch." Still, I was not ready to picture that conversation, not anywhere near. So I'm reading "Talking About Death" over and over and nothing is registering and I think, probably as a deflection of the anxiety I was feeling: "Hey, this would be a good story for Murphy. Let *her* deal with this, I don't want it right now."

And it was one of those times where it just comes to you very clearly. I saw it as a series of scenes that were basically two-people conversations in which Murphy went to each of her friends and said, "What do you think happens when you die?" challenging people to talk about the one thing that nobody talks about. This was so right for her character in so many ways, as the reporter and the skeptic that she is.

The other two executive producers were very receptive to the idea. We decided we'd better pitch it to Candice [Bergen] early on because, well, death is a very personal thing. She was in love with the idea. Barely had the sentence come out of my mouth when she said, "I'm always driving people out of the room by going up to them and saying, 'So what do you think happens when you die?' " Sometimes Candice is Murphy.

The next step was to sit down with all the writers, there are ten of us, and talk it out a little bit. Of course, the first question that comes up is, can we make this funny? After all, we're doing a half-hour comedy show here and there *is* a certain obligation to entertain the audience. I mean, just how funny could we make death?

We all knew that certain points were clear choices—Murphy would go to Frank★ first as he's her best friend; Frank would have been influenced by his Catholic upbringing; the same with Miles and his Jewish beliefs. But they would also have their own neuroses in dealing with the subject, their characters would impact on their beliefs.

We knew that Corky would be the voice of total faith in a hereafter. She would be completely trusting in a way that Murphy would both question and envy somewhat. Jim was a trickier beat to get. (Writer's shorthand . . . by "beat" I mean Jim's story.) We finally decided he would share a lot of Murphy's skepticism as a reporter, someone who, like her, is used to questioning things, used to looking for answers. But Jim has a real yearning to believe in something more, and that allows him to commit to religion in a way that Murphy can't.

Basically, what we were trying to do was to show a spectrum of beliefs. As you go through the various points of view, Murphy is left as the only person without a strong faith or strong belief, her skepticism still overpowering her acceptance of an answer.

If the writers had any misgivings about the subject matter, they didn't say anything. I think that probably any writer would be excited by this. Rob Bragin eagerly accepted our "invitation" to write

★ Frank, Miles, Corky, Jim, and Eldin are all characters on the *Murphy Brown* television series.

the script. He's a very bright guy, the right combination of darkness and funny; just right to take on a story like this.

So Rob went off into the abyss and came back two weeks later with a draft called "Reaper Madness," and the question of whether or not this could be funny was, with great relief, answered. Yes, this can be funny. We knew we were definitely on the right track.

Every script goes through about five layers of rewriting and then additional changes during the week of rehearsal and production. During the course of rewriting it was a matter of going even deeper, searching for more depth, looking for something that would resonate more. As long as we were going to go up to this big subject of death and choose it off, so to speak, we didn't want to end up with something that would be seen as shallow or sketchy, funny maybe, but without any real feeling.

Rob brought wonderful things to the script, like the idea that Frank's changing beliefs and search for answers were tied to the women he had dated at various times throughout his life. When he was with a Buddhist or a Christian Scientist, those were the beliefs that he would take on. Currently he wasn't sure what he believed because he wasn't seeing anyone. It was just so right for Frank's character. Also it gave the lightness that you need. The humor had a chance to come out in this. Rob came up with the near-death experience for Miles which was funny, but also significant to include since we were going for a wide spectrum of beliefs.

So the others had their coping mechanisms but Murphy stood alone until her final scene with Eldin. And then Rob had that wonderful ending where Eldin gives Murphy as much of an answer as there could be for Murphy. Eldin, who lives more in the realm of the known than the unknown, addresses the subject in the most practical way possible. He says that his belief about life after death is that you live on in what you create, which for him is his art, and for Murphy . . . well, maybe she's got something like that. And they're standing over the crib and she looks down at her son Avery and, as much as somebody can get a satisfying answer to death in twenty-two minutes in a comedy, that was her answer.

We work in front of a live audience, so there's always that one moment where you wonder, are they going to like this episode? Is it going to mean anything to them? And with this episode that moment comes the first time Murphy says to Frank, "What do you think happens when you die?" And I'm wondering, are we going to turn around and see 120 people rapidly leaving the studio saying thanks a lot but no thanks?

Before the show, there's a warm-up session where a stand-up comic talks to the audience a little bit and . . . well, you know, warms them up. And you always watch them and judge what kind of audience this will be. Does it seem like a hot audience or a cold audience; are they smart, hip, too old, too young, too anything? This time I remember looking out at them and thinking "I hope they don't hate us, I hope it'll be okay."

As it was, it went over great. We definitely got a few of those laughs that were out of relief, where people were anxious to laugh, but the audience was with us all the way. We got a terrific response from them.

All in all we ended up being pleased that we took this subject on. It was not an easy show to do. I don't know that any of us were totally satisfied. Ultimately you don't end up with an answer that gives peace of mind to the entire world. There's no way that ten comedy writers are going to do something that writers and teachers throughout history haven't been able to do . . . but I'm really glad we did the episode.

[*"Reaper Madness" went on to win the Humanitas Prize given for exceptional film and television writing.*]

The fact is, everyone's going to die someday. To me the most interesting thing is, how come people go about their life so calmly? I grew up wondering, what *is* this? Everybody seems so calm, aren't they getting it? Why isn't everyone running around saying, "Jeez! We're all going to die?" But they don't. And since no one else is doing that, I don't do that.

And even after doing this show, I'm still not comfortable initiating conversations on the subject. I'm not Murphy Brown going up to people and saying "What do you think happens?" My husband and I never really had the conversation, "Uh, what do you think happens?" until it came up around the children and this episode. I said to one of the other writers, "What does your wife think?" and he said, "We've never talked about it." So you can know people very well and not have a clue what they think about this.

At one point at work, when we were well into it, we stopped and took a poll in the Writers' Room because we realized we didn't know what we believed ourselves. We went around the room, "Okay, life after death—yes or no?"

We came up with six votes for a hereafter of some sort, three who think this is it, and one abstention who basically said, "I don't know," and wasn't willing to come into one camp or the other. Going into it, none of us knew what the others believed. In a few cases we might have been able to guess but we didn't really know until we voted. Again, we had never talked about it. And in the Writers' Room, few subjects go untouched.

For me personally, my coping mechanism is not really that different from Murphy's when she says, "I guess I figured that if you didn't think you were going to die, you wouldn't. Hey! It's worked so far." This is a line that came from the Writers' Room but it sounds good to me!

I'm sure it would be wonderful to have no anxiety about it, to have complete calm and peace with it. That's what we wanted to show with Corky. She is not really bothered by the conversation at all, she has a very deep faith and Murphy definitely has some envy about that. But for me there are too many things about a hereafter that don't make sense. So I've chosen to focus on the here and now, and the control freak in me recognizes those things I can't control and gives up on them. You move away from the battles you can't win if you're going to be a successful control freak.

And that works fine—until you have children. That changes things. You are forced to have the conversation. It can no longer just recede into the depths of your mind. On the show, the question of what Murphy should tell her son was a natural trigger to get into the topic of death, but early in the episode you see that it's really about

Murphy's search for answers for herself. She is looking for her own answers as much as for her son's.

For me, I'm still wondering, "What do I say to my kids?" I suppose what I will do is be as open as possible and try not to let any anxiety I have get passed on. . . . Well, I guess you do let some of the anxiety come through, if you're honest, and you want to be as honest as possible with your kids. But the things I've read say that it's a big concept for them and you can easily overtalk it. You have to take your cues from them.

My son has this little train named Percy, and yesterday he put it down the heating vent and there was no retrieving it. I took the vent off and put my hand down all the way up to my shoulder in this sooty hole and the train was definitely gone. And we're telling him, "It's gone, gone for good, that's it." There was something about explaining to him that it was gone forever that foreshadowed the much bigger conversation in a way that made me very uncomfortable. But he handled the train pretty well so maybe we could work up from there. Sometimes things don't come back, sometimes they are gone forever.

I'm going to be honest with them about what I believe. I'm an agnostic, but there is a big difference between atheist and agnostic and I want my children to understand the difference. Most of all, I want them to see the other choices that are out there. With my own parents I was basically raised agnostic, but they made a point of sending us to church with friends of ours so that we would be exposed to religion if we so chose. I really appreciated my parents doing that, putting the choices out there. I think that's the most important thing you can do as a parent.

So far my kids seem very bright—no bias here—and I want them to find whatever works for them. They can become born-again Christians and if that's what works for them, then great. It'll make for interesting Thanksgiving dinners.

MARILEE LONGACRE
Age: 37
Waitress

∽

A friend of mine had died and several of the people who knew him were sitting around together, in my kitchen. This was when I was still married and we had the house. The kids were playing in the other room and we were talking and my brother-in-law described how this guy he knew had died. He had spent the day fishing, which he loved, and had a great dinner and, you know, a romantic night with his wife. Then he just quietly died in his sleep.

My daughter, who was around six or seven, walked in just in time to hear someone say, "Wow, I wish I could die like that." And she said, very matter-of-factly, "Everyone gets their own." I said, "Their own what, honey?" thinking she was talking about the sandwiches we'd made for the kids or the cake we were going to have later. And she said, "Everyone gets their own death. You don't have to share."

Then she got her glass of apple juice off the counter and walked out of the room and we all just looked at each other with our mouths hanging open. It was one of those moments, you know? Where everyone's going, "Uhh . . . yeah."

I'll never forget that. Never.

ROBIN WHITE OWEN
Age: 43
Television Producer and Media Curator

❧

As a child, I don't remember thinking about death per se. But I have to admit I'm surprised that I don't remember my own curiosity because it's on Taylor's mind a lot. Taylor is my four-year-old son. He asks about death all the time. He really wants to understand what happens when you die.

He's been talking about it seriously for about the last six months or so. I think he came to be aware of it because he sees insects die; we kill ants in the garden, if they're crawling on our food or whatever, and he sees flowers die and the grass dies and he asks about it.

"What does it mean?"

"It means they don't have a life anymore."

"What does that mean?"

"Well when something dies its life is over. It's gone. It's not around anymore."

We try to explain and then it sort of escalates from there.

"Do people die?"

"Yes, people die."

"Am I going to die?"

"Well, when you're really old, someday far away."

Right away he knew he didn't want to die. He didn't want me to die. He didn't want Daddy to die. He would say, "Don't die," and "I don't want to die." And you find yourself saying, "We're not going to die. You're not going to die." Which of course is not true, technically speaking.

I really don't want to lie to him, that is very important to me. I said, "You see, if people lived forever there wouldn't be any room for any more people. People die so that new people can come and live, so there can be new life. It's just a natural process." Which

might help adults who can look at the larger context, but his understanding of the larger context, conceptually, is not that solid yet.

Then I tried saying that death was just a part of life, just another
part of life. That's all it is. It's not a big deal. But that didn't help.
And it didn't help to say, "It's not going to happen until you're old.
You have a long life to live before you're going to die." That didn't
help at all. He was inconsolable about this. So it was really difficult to
try and explain the truth, that people do die and everybody's going
to die. He would get upset and start to cry and feel terribly sad.

The problem is, I can't give him a simple answer about what
happens after you die because I don't definitely believe one thing or
another myself. Taylor's cousins have been brought up in a very,
very, deeply religious Roman Catholic household, and they can
answer the question easily. "Oh, yeah, you die, you go to heaven,
you see the baby Jesus." That's it for them. Even the three-
and-a-half-year-old can answer that. I wish I could give Taylor such
a simple, straightforward, and comforting answer that would solve
his problems.

People who subscribe to a particular religion can just say whatever that religion teaches about death. If you're Jewish, you just say
what the Jewish religion says about death. If you're Christian, it's
clear, you go to heaven or you go to hell. I was raised in the Episcopalian religion, which preaches that when you die you go to heaven.
I guess. To tell you the truth, I didn't pay much attention to it when
I was growing up. I really didn't. I don't think I've ever actually
believed that there's a heaven with a God. I think it's pretty hard to
believe in a heaven in the way that they used to paint pictures of it,
or the illustrations in the King James Bible when I was a little kid.

Although surprisingly, to listen to people who've had near-death
experiences describe what they saw, this tunnel with light at the end
of it and then all their friends were there, it sounds like those pictures. Say, hey! Maybe that's what it is, I don't know.

Or maybe David Byrne has it right—*"Heaven is a place where
nothing ever happens."* I don't know that that would be my definition
of heaven. My definition would probably be more like, heaven is a

place where you worry just like you do when you're alive. That's probably more like it.

It's hard, because I think if I went to the doctor and he said to me, "You've got terminal cancer and you're going to die," I would be pretty upset. I would not want to leave. I would not go gentle into that good night. I would kick and scream. I would want more time to share, to see Taylor grow up, to be with my family. But I wouldn't be afraid of what happened after death. It's either nothing at all or it's going to be fine. Basically that's what I think.

The one thing in my experience that I know happens is that you *do* live on in the hearts and minds of the people who loved you. To that extent your spirit remains a presence on the earth. That I can say with certainty. But it's very hard to make a four-year-old child understand something so immaterial and conceptual. They're concerned with concrete things.

Safety is a big concern for a four-year-old. It's the fear of monsters and ghosts and bad people, the bad guys. I don't mean children run around all the time being scared. They certainly don't. But at inconvenient moments, like when you want them to go to sleep, they're scared, "Oh, but there's monsters down there, Mom." Or, "I'm afraid of the bad guys." So, of course, you say, "There aren't any monsters. Ghosts are not real. No skeletons are going to come after you."

Curiosity as well, curiosity is a huge thing with kids. "Where do you go?" "What happens to you?" They're so curious about absolutely every, every, everything. And God knows, existence is a big thing. "If you're not here, where are you?" Anything reassuring would be good to say. But I want to be honest.

You want to be honest with your children because you want them to be able to trust you no matter what. If they can't trust you, they won't turn to you when they need real advice because you'll have given them foolish lies before, along the way. It's very important to be as honest as you can, and to give them as much information as you think they can absorb at the time. So that's why I can't say, "You'll go to heaven and be with baby Jesus," because first of all

I don't believe it, and second, I don't really understand what it means. I could never say that to him.

Then one day we were reading from a children's book about Tibet, where death is presented as the beginning of a journey to another life, in which you get to choose what kind of life you want. As we were talking it seemed okay that this coming back in another life might be possible. And it was an idea that made him feel better about it.

Although I've never had any firsthand experience that would lead me to believe that reincarnation exists, I would say that if you tend to believe there's only so much matter and energy in the universe, then obviously it has to be recycled. Everything else is. So it seems quite possible that life does come back, in some way. The energy that is life reappears in some other life form, whether you end up being a person or some other living entity. I feel this is probably true. And even though I can only say it with an offhand conviction, not really with an in-my-heart conviction, still I felt okay with it for his level of understanding.

Then I heard him explaining this to his longtime baby-sitter, Gwen, and he said, "Well after you die, you just come right back to life." And Gwen is going, "Who told you *that*?" So I saw this needed some fine-tuning. In Taylor's mind it had seemed like you immediately come back to the same life.

So we've been trying to explain to him that it can be that you come back in another life but it's different from the one that you have now, or it could be that you just live on in the hearts and minds of the people who love you, or it could be that you go to heaven and you have a life in heaven. I wish they would do a unit on death at the Montessori preschool.

While I can live with the idea that possibly you have another life after this, it's very important to make it clear to Taylor that this life is unique. I mean, we live in a culture where people are shooting each other to death all the time. And little boys play with guns. Even if they don't have guns, they use their fingers, they use sticks, anything. So I think it's really important to make it clear to him that if you kill somebody it's a terribly serious business. They lose their life. It means they don't come back, finished, kaput, gone.

It's fine to say, "Well, yes there is a kind of life after," but you have to be really clear about teaching the importance of *this* life, the value of each individual life. You can't take life just because there's going to be another one. You have to be really clear about describing those differences. "You don't kill bugs or plants or things just for the sake of it. Yes, it's still a life and it counts for something. If the ant is crawling over your cereal, squish it, right, but you don't have to kill them on the ground. It's okay for them to live on the ground. You should let them live." It's important for him to know that once life is gone, it is gone.

I think it's possible to teach children to be ethical and to have humanistic moral values, without having to teach them in the context of a religion, a certifiable, I'm-a-Christian, I'm-a-Jew religion. But I'm not sure about how to help them understand about death without religion. The problem is, religious ideas about death are so tied up with reward and punishment. I find it hard to subscribe to the idea that certain things will happen to you depending on how you've lived your life. If you live a good life then you'll have a good afterlife. It's like, if you're a good boy now then you can have an ice cream later. That kind of relationship seems more punitive than anything else. It's the stick. I think it's important to live a good life, to do the right thing, because that's how you're going to live with yourself. Not because you're going to get something for it after you die.

So we're working on all this. Then, recently, I was talking to a friend who had been to a conference and heard Ram Dass talking about death. Ram Dass said he had this spiritual advisor and he asked this advisor what he should tell people who are dying, what he should tell people about death. And the advisor said, "Tell them it's absolutely safe."

When I heard that, it made perfect sense to me, and I realized that that kind of reassurance was what a child would need. I thought it might really work for him as an answer. The next time he asked about it I said, "Taylor, I'm not really sure what happens, but I know that whatever happens, you'll be safe."

And that was the answer he needed to hear. I could see a huge sense of relief come over his face, literally like a wave washing over the shore. And he didn't ask about it again for maybe a week. The next time it came up, I gave him the same answer and it really satisfied him.

And it satisfies me as well. I think it probably is safe. I think that answer is quite profound. There's no proof that it's accurate, but it's such a simple answer and it's not hard to believe really, intuitively. It doesn't posit a heaven, a hell, a this, a that, it's not a value judgment, it's just—there. It's elegant in its simplicity. It speaks to a profound need that people have, the need to know that they're going to be okay. I think that's what all of us really want, in the end.

Now that he feels more secure in that area the questions aren't so much about what happens when you die, but more about religion. "What is God? What is the devil?" Often that ends up being a discussion that involves death because Christianity suggests that when you die you get to go and be with God, and in that way, death becomes a part of the definition of God. Now I'm trying to define God differently, but that's another story. . . .

CHARLIE LORD
Age: 60
Bureau Director, Children's Express
Past Headmaster, St. Timothy's School

❦

Through my school headmastering days I've been constantly struck by kids facing their first death. They aren't prepared. And we aren't prepared, as educators, to deal with it either. In the educational system we mirror the society as a whole in that we pretty much ignore it. If we deal with death it's because we're reading about "Death in Literature," which is really about literature, not about death. Ethics and values courses of various types may touch on it slightly, but none of this prepares you for a real death.

One of the toughest moments of my professional life was when I was at St. Timothy's, a boarding school outside of Baltimore. A young girl there had been constantly misbehaving and was obviously crying out that she didn't want to be where she was. In the fall of the year I had been forced to send her home. She was from Washington and her half sister was still at St. Tim's. On a Saturday night in the spring, she was riding on the back of a motorcycle and was killed in an accident in Washington. Her half sister got the word and her family came and picked her up. Then, on Sunday afternoon in the school chapel, I had to tell the students, all of whom knew her, that she'd been killed.

Suddenly, this group of over a hundred young women was dealing with a death that came pretty close to them because it was someone they'd known, lived with, roomed with and so forth. And it was the death of someone their own age, which is scary. I felt very inadequate, even at giving any context to death. Counselors and others in the adult community helped out and we talked about it, but the standard "Well, she's now happily in heaven" approach to death was certainly not going to go across with these kids. And I didn't believe it either, not in any way that helped to deal with the really hard part, this being a life that had been snuffed out much too soon.

Since I've been at Children's Express [a nonprofit program designed to empower young people from differing socioeconomic, racial, and cultural backgrounds] I've been working with a number of children and teens who live surrounded by death. There's a young man here right now who puts the friends he grew up with into three categories: (1) dead; (2) in prison for drug dealing; or (3) dealing and out of prison.

This program helps to show kids that there's an alternative, although you don't make any money working at Children's Express, and you can make a heck of a lot of money on the streets of Washington if you want to take some huge risks. Fighting off the attraction of drug dealing is very, very tough. You can understand why easily enough.

I've seen the teens who say, "I probably won't make it to twenty-one," and I've read about kids planning their funerals or whatever. That very depressing feeling of: "I'm licked. There's no way out of here." I do know those children exist and I know our own young people here who talk about some of those kids. But our young people don't feel that way. I think they see an alternative.

If you put a bunch of kids together in a room you're going to get some wonderful things happening. A lot of adults are scared of doing that, but it works. The youngsters deal with each other, they support each other.

The thrust has been to try to bring in inner-city kids from the Washington area, because that's where the need is greatest, where budgets and programs have all been cut. So they get to know each other where they probably wouldn't otherwise. It shows the better-off, middle-class youth that they are indeed fortunate, and shows the kids who are in a tough situation that there's hope.

Hope is the important thing. And I do see hope in these kids, most definitely. There are a couple that I really worry about but I think most of those here, if they can make it safely into college age, into their young adulthood, they'll be fine. They're going to be fine if they don't get . . .

There's a young man in the program here who was standing on a street corner and someone mistook him for someone else. It was a drug thing. They drove by in a car, mistook him for someone else and shot him. He lived. He wasn't expected to live but he did. Now that was completely random. It was a complete mistaken-identity situation and it makes you realize how vulnerable these kids are.

For your mainstream, middle-class teen in a normal situation, usually the first death they deal with is the grandparent death, which tends to strike when they're fourteen, fifteen, sixteen, or seventeen years old. That death is usually muted by the fact that the child often didn't really know the grandparent that well, or didn't spend much time with them as they got older; and they don't see the person dying. Which speaks to how, as a culture, we not only avoid death, we avoid old age. I don't think there's anyplace in the world that deals with old age worse than the United States. And this affects our attitude about death.

When I was teaching a course on the Middle East at Maumee Valley Country Day School, in Toledo, Ohio, I remember showing a film describing a particular nomadic group from that region. The nomadic trail crossed a river at a point where they would go, with all their animals, from the higher land to the lower land. In all the different seasons they would always have to cross this river. The older people, the grandparent-age people, when they could no longer make it across the river on their own, sat down on the riverbank and said "All right, that's it. We're not crossing the river." And that was their statement that they were going to die. The point was that the tribe had to get the cattle across the river and the grandparents knew if they could no longer help to do that, their contribution to the society was done and it was time for them to bow out.

Well, I'll never forget the reaction of the seniors in the class who said, "How can you do that? How can you just leave them to die, instead of helping them across the river?" They were shocked. So then I asked them, "How do we deal with it?" I asked them to consider the difference between putting people in a nursing home and leaving people sitting on the edge of the river. Which one was more humane? We had some very interesting conversations about it.

Old age and death are connected that way, in that shuffle-it-out-of-sight way. My mother died at home, as did my father, and under circumstances which did seem to be an extension of life, if you will, with dignity and with love, care, and concern. Too few people have that opportunity. We usually end up in a hospital with all kinds of tubes in us and it's horrible.

It's so much a matter of circumstances and luck. Let's face it, my father would not have died at home if he hadn't remarried after my mother died. He was lucky in that way or he might well have wound up in a hospital. I was living in Scotland and my brother was ambassador to China and our father was living in Florida when he became ill. It's your circumstances that dictate how and where you die. And the kid on the street corner has no choice.

I go back to the old people sitting on the bank of the river and now that I've hit sixty I think about it a lot. I don't mean I sit around all day wondering what it's like to die, but I do think about it more than I used to. I think that for me, having seen the compassionate and dignified way in which my parents and my wife's parents died, with the support of their children and the support of the hospice approach, it makes me feel better about when my turn comes.

It's too bad we can't have better models for dying; to somehow die in a way that is okay, that allows the next generation coming along to see it doesn't have to be as it's depicted on TV or the way these poor kids are exposed to it in downtown Washington or east Los Angeles.

CARL
Age: 19

⁓

The people that die around me, it's like I know it's going to happen. It's coming to them 'cause they're out there selling drugs. My cousin died last year. His come 'cause he was trying to rob a store. Everybody knew it was coming to him. You just get caught up in it. You hang out with the wrong friends, the gangs, the next thing, you go to drugs.

This boy I went to school with died. He was shot. I came home one day and there's the yellow police tape, you know, "Don't Cross," and I said, "What happened?" They said, "Go upstairs." My mother told me, "Duval died." I was in second grade with the guy.

Lately I feel it's like the wild West, everybody shooting everybody up. I'm afraid I'm going to get shot in the street. You look at these kids, people dying over one boy looking wrong at another boy. That's ridiculous. That's a whole life wasted right there.

You got to be prepared for what's going to happen. For me, I live in New York and I hate to say it, but I carry something on me where ever I go. If somebody tries to kill me I'm going to kill them before they kill me. If this person's trying to take me out, I'm not going to let that happen.

But sometimes things just happen to you and you can't be prepared. You can't see death coming along. He got a black cape. When I try to think about what death is, it's like trying to think about before I was born, trying to remember where I came from before. I can't do that. It's like you just wake up and you're here, you understand what I'm saying? Like one day you just wake up and you're here.

And another thing. I heard that people said they died and then came back, and it's always the same story. I've heard this several times. They say they see a light and they go to this light, and then they have a choice either to go through the light or come back. And some people stay there for a while and then they come back.

Recently I've seen this lady on TV, I think her name is Betty Eadie. I'm gonna get her book because she died and came back, and other people who died and came back told a similar story to the one she's telling. She said there is a heaven and angels and everything. She went out of her body and then she went somewhere into space. I know a lot of people believe in it but . . . I'm wondering, is she doing this for real or is this a gig? It's a question running through my mind. I think if you really *really* believe, it could happen . . . maybe.

But it's a big question and it can slow you down. If you think about death it kind of slows you down in life. Besides, it's just a question game. I could get to be thirty-five years old and I'd still be asking questions about death because who understands it?

CHRIS
Age: 19
Student

❧

When I was young I always wanted someone to tell me what it was like to die. I kept on asking, "What happens when you die? What happens when you die?" You get older and you realize—no one knows. You can only come to what you yourself *think* it is and what you *believe* it is. That's about it. No one can prove it one way or the other. No one can say, "We have papers, we have this and that to prove it." I'm not saying, "Seeing is believing," I'm just saying everyone has to figure it out on their own. It's your own choice and it's hard to choose.

I feel like I'm choosing not to believe. I just feel when it ends it ends. Life is something that ends. It's like the end of a song. You can play it back and remember, like you remember someone who died, but I don't think there's any existence afterwards.

Still, I think it's important to think about it. Absolutely. Because you don't know how you're going to deal with it if you don't think about it. I think about my friends dying. I think about my parents dying. It's something I feel I should prepare for. Of course, you can never prepare yourself emotionally, can you? Even if you know it's going to happen, you're still going to have that loss inside. I mean, emotionally. That's the hardest part of it.

I guess we're lucky to have a consciousness for these questions, but I don't think it was given to us by something else. I think we've grown into it, we've progressed, we've adapted. I think anything's possible over time, even for animals to grow a consciousness. Look how we have grown this brain we have. We've just grown into our understanding and death has helped us do that in a way. Death keeps us wondering and keeps us going. In all honesty, I think it's the thing that keeps us developing. It's the biggest, most curious question we have.

WESTERN IDEAS ABOUT DEATH
CHRONOLOGY PART 3

❧

Throughout the Middle Ages, no one questions what happens when you die. The religious explanation is accepted the way we accept the value of money; and Christianity is like our monetary system—all deaths are "backed by the full faith and credit" of the Holy Roman Church.

1200s	In Western Europe, the language, symbols, and customs of medieval society are dominated by Christianity. It is considered extremely wicked to disregard your own mortality, for to do so is to place yourself outside the strictures of the church and thus, of society. If there are any atheists, they keep their mouths shut.
	Death is perceived as a collective experience. While the loss of an individual is mourned, the sense of death in general is like a seasonal event, anticipated, unquestioned, and prepared for.
	The afterlife is portrayed as a kind of suspended sleep until the day of the Apocalypse or the Second Advent (Second Coming of Christ). On this day, which is widely believed to be imminent, the dead will

awaken and their bodies will be lifted up into heaven
or thrown into hell.

1300s   Beginning in 1347, bubonic and pneumonic plagues
sweep through Europe for the next several centuries.
The death toll is extensive, reaching as high as 70
percent of the population in some areas. Between
the years 1348 and 1377, 40 percent of the global
population dies. A chronicler in Siena writes: *"No
one wept for the dead because everyone expected death himself."*

1400s   The world does not end and religious doctrine
changes to accommodate that fact. The verdict on
each soul is no longer delayed until the Apocalypse
but is now made at the time of death.

The deathbed scene, which heretofore has been a
comforting ritual, becomes a test wherein devils and
angels fight for the dying man's immortal soul. Un-
faltering faith at the moment of death is key to salvation.

In 1466, the *Ars Moriendi* (*The Art of Dying*) is published using a new type of printing which combines
pictures with text, making contents accessible to the
vast majority of the population who cannot read.
This very popular work serves as a kind of instruction manual to prepare you for the test of death.

The practice since antiquity of strictly separating
burial places from towns has been completely re-
versed. The coexistence of the living and the dead
has become so common that cemeteries serve as a
kind of village green.

The Council of Rouen is compelled to forbid dancing and gambling, jugglers, theatrical troops, musi-

cians, and others from carrying on "their doubtful trades" in the cemeteries. This declaration is, for the most part, ignored.

The individual tomb, inscribed and set apart, becomes more common. What had been reserved for the commemoration of the great and powerful is now sought by ordinary people, who before this were buried in common or unmarked graves.

In some parts of Europe, funerary art becomes grotesque, depicting morbid details of decomposition. Often attributed to the horrors of raging pandemics throughout the Middle Ages, these creepy images also hint at the beginning of a significant change in the concept of mortality, from a collective acceptance to a more personalized notion of individual loss.

We begin to see the first flicker of the concept of death as a failure inherent in human nature.

&

I remember when I was young, when I was twelve, thirteen, fourteen, those years, death was not real hard to deal with because it was kind of natural. You go, "Okay, another homeboy died, this is what you do, let's have the car wash to get the money together and then we'll go to his wake and then we'll go to his funeral." It was very routine, very normal.

As I got older I started to see more, to understand life a little better, and death got harder. More and more homeboys were dying because things were becoming increasingly more violent. I couldn't deal with the death because it was so hard, the senselessness of it. "How could they just come over and kill him?" "They didn't even have a beef with him, they were just trying to kill a Dog Patcher." It hurt more and I'd agonize over it more as I got older.

Then, while working at Whittier, where I did the gang risk-intervention pilot program, I began to realize that the kids out there *wanted* to die. You'd be talking to them and you'd realize that they aspired to go down in glory, that their plans were to die for the barrio name. Now that was really hard to deal with. That was a big shift from when I was in a gang.

I grew up in Dogpatch, in Paramount in L.A. Joining a gang is what you do when you're a young person in that area. That's just what happens. You go through this process of hanging around with everybody, then you get jumped in and then you're from the neighborhood and that's the way it goes. That's the life.

Getting "jumped in" is an initiation. You have five, six girls around you and they're going to see what you've got, they're going to see what you're made of. Are you going to fight back? Are you really down for your neighborhood? You get jumped in. You're supposed to fight back.

I came in when I was twelve years old. That's the average age. That's the thing about our kids, our communities, you grow up fast. You see a lot of things that maybe other kids don't see. You might say—things that "normal" kids don't see, but these *are* normal kids because that's life in the barrio. It's normal to grow up fast there. You see a lot of things.

You have to understand, there's a tremendous amount of pride and tradition in the barrio. A lot of the culture comes from there. That's where you listened to the music and where you learned about your own heritage and customs versus mainstream society. It's been called a subculture and it definitely is, in that this is where you learn about being Chicano, this is where you learn about family values, tradition, loyalty, and all these things.

Through the gang and through the neighborhood I try to find pieces of my culture. What is my culture? My parents are from Mexico but I was born and raised in the U.S. I'm not Mexican, I'm not really American, so what am I? I'm Chicana. The Chicano culture was in the neighborhood. The stability was in the neighborhood.

Gangs were very much about community. Everybody knows each other and you know everybody. "Okay, they're on this street, and their grandmother is so and so." You learn the family ties and all that makes a community. So gangs don't have to be a bad thing, but they became increasingly violent and increasingly lost the tradition that kept them together as community and they turned into what we now know as gangs. I think I caught the tail end of the traditional way. There was always violence, but there was more integrity and, well really, honesty.

Death was there of course. Homeboys died all the time. And sure, we've always had the rival. There's a neighborhood that we just do not get along with and never have and they'd always come over, and they have killed us, and my homeboys have gone over there and they've killed over there. But it was different when I was young.

There were unwritten rules of conduct, unwritten codes. Everybody knew those rules and there was a certain respect, a mutual respect. You adhered to those codes and there were certain things you didn't do. If you saw somebody with their parents you didn't go up there and act crazy. You took care of it on your own time, your own way. And none of this going through the back door trying to make sure nobody sees you. If you had something to take care of with someone, you confronted them, you took care of it, and you parted having respect for each other.

Now all these drive-bys; there isn't a real target, you just go out and shoot. They even shoot up a wake. That was not the way it was done when I was growing up. It's really changed. Now you can't even get through the car wash.

The car wash is a fund raiser. When somebody dies, we hold a car wash to raise money to help the parents pay for the funeral and everything. Everything is donated, rags, soap, etc., and everyone brings their cars; parents, passersby, people in the community all bring their cars, to help raise money for the parents. Because we're poor people and there's just not enough money, these car washes are very important.

I remember a couple of years ago, I went to a car wash for one of the guys in my neighborhood who had been killed. We had it for several days, over a weekend. I went and the next morning when we came back, the rival neighborhood, who had killed him, had written something on the wall that hurt a lot, because they were just mocking the death. When I got there that morning and saw that, it was such a painful thing. How could they mock our grief? And several times during that car wash, they passed by. Again, just to mock and flash out with their hand signs. They didn't use guns, they didn't shoot, they were passing by and going through the hand signs. That would never have happened when I was growing up. There was respect for a funeral.

Now there's a lot of immigrant kids who come from places where they have a different view of death. Kids from El Salvador, for instance. There's no respect for life and not a lot of respect for themselves or for things around them because they feel no connection to anything. They don't have that sense of looking for something. They see it all differently. I hear Chicano gang members say, "Don't mess with Mara Salvaduca, they're crazy."

That's just one factor and there are a lot of other factors involved; it's not a simple thing. There used to be intervention programs that helped kids find alternatives. Then they got cut out in funding cutbacks. That's been a big change over the last ten years or so. Now the kids don't see any options. They cannot visualize themselves at eighteen years old, at twenty-five years old. They're not goal-oriented because there are no goals they feel they can reach. What is there? There's prison or there's death. Well, you know, prison's not so great, maybe dying is better.

Many of them are very self-destructive. Their thoughts about death are actually suicidal. They've grown up in the Catholic tradition so there's that prohibition, but they're working on a kind of indirect suicide. What they've picked up is maybe a general feeling of God and the idea that death means maybe you'll sleep, maybe there's souls and spirits. But I don't think these kids really think about what might be afterwards or ask themselves if there is anything. It's more abstract.

Mostly from the Church you use the rituals and the ceremonies. You have the baptisms, you have the *quinceaños,* and when you die, we have our community priest there doing the last rites if they make it in time or doing the ceremonies at the funerals. So it's very much ritual. Not so much the concept of the religion, but the ritual is very important.

The wake, the funeral is very much about ceremony. Going down in a blaze of glory includes the idea of a big funeral, all the cars and everything. A friend of mine passed away this past year and he had a tremendous funeral. There were so many people there and so many cars. The procession went through the neighborhood before they took him to the cemetery. The whole thing was videotaped. It was very much staged, his family planned it like that because of who he was. This particular guy, he had that big name in the neighborhood. He was raised to be bad in the barrio. And he was. And that's the way he went out. So his ceremony at the end had to be this big huge thing, and it was.

I keep seeing this image from when I worked at the Whittier program. There was this one young guy, and a counselor asked him, "What do you see for yourself in the next five years?" With complete calm, like he was talking about which school he wanted to attend, he said, "Well, I'm going to make a name for myself in the neighborhood, then I'll get killed for it." He wasn't joking. He meant it. He had visualized his death. He'd seen death happen, he had seen other homeboys get shot. He had seen his brother killed as well. This was his goal, his role in life . . . to die.

MELISSA   CYNTHIA   TERRY
Age: 14   Age: 13   Age: 13
Students/Junior High School

❧

CYNTHIA: If you're not scared of dying then you have nothing to worry about. If you're scared of dying you shouldn't even be in a gang or in a crew. If you're scared of dying then you got a load on your shoulders.

MELISSA: Being in a gang is good in one way but in another way it's bad. If you ever get in trouble they'll take up for you, back you up, or if somebody messes with you, they'll take care of them.

TERRY: But the negative side is like, let's say you have to go out with them and do a drive-by or something like that. And if you get shot maybe they'll leave you behind. I don't think I'd do it but I would go along in the car maybe, or something like that.

CYNTHIA: I wouldn't go out and kill anybody because you'd be taking away their life just like they'd be taking away your life if they kill you.

TERRY: I would. I would kill somebody. If I really hated them or they did something to my family, I would kill them.

MELISSA: Well, yeah, of course, if they did it to your family. I'm waiting for my stepdad to get out of jail. I don't want him to get out. He tried to kill my mom. I'd kill him if I had to. I don't like him at all. Nobody likes him.

CYNTHIA: Oh well, yeah, that's different. I'd kill somebody if they were gonna mess with my family. That's different.

TERRY: But it really takes guts to do that. You can say it right now but to tell you the truth, I don't think many people can really do it.

CYNTHIA: My brother was shot. Somebody came by in a car and shot him three times and he ran all the way to the house and it was ugly 'cause he was shot in the stomach and through his arm and his leg. He wasn't crying or anything, he was stumbling around and holding his stomach, but when he got out of the hospital he told me that I'd better be careful 'cause our house is marked and they don't know if there's gonna be other drive-bys and stuff. So we're real careful by my house.

TERRY: Sometimes you get in trouble because of your brothers and sisters, that's one thing. My sister belonged to a gang and they didn't get along with the gang that was fighting with them. There'd be drive-bys and the first thing was we'd have to get my brothers down on the floor, that whole thing. Even if it wasn't meant for us, still, you'd be scared; you'd be traumatized, you know? It was the thought that we had in our head that got to us.

CYNTHIA: A lot of kids are in gangs. There's QBL and KBL, "Queens Becoming Legend" for the girls and "Kings Becoming Legend" for the guys.

TERRY: I was thinking about joining but I didn't yet. It's not easy. They test you. They jump you and practically kill you or they have gang fights and stuff. That's why you have to really think about it. And besides, my mom is really strict. I probably wouldn't be able to be in a gang.

But if you see a guy with tattoos all over and he says, "Hey, no problem, so I'm going to die, big deal," me, I kind of have respect for that person because they're saying what they'd die for. If you mess with them, boom. So you have to have respect for them. That's kind of the whole point of gangs too—respect. Respect between people.

CYNTHIA: Once when this kid died, he was fourteen, we went to his funeral. You go up to the altar to see the person who's lying there and you think, if it was you they'd come up to the altar to see you. He was in this group that used to do karate, and while we're up there looking at the dead person, they did this karate thing. It was great. And at the wake, we got shirts that said, "In memory of . . ." with his nickname, you know? And they took pictures; his girlfriend took pictures kissing him and she was crying and it was sad. It hurts you know, 'cause his mom was crying.

TERRY: The guys can hold it in, but when they get back to their room or somewhere they'll cry.

CYNTHIA: They have big wakes and they have car washes, anything to earn lots and lots of money for their homeboy. It's a big deal.

TERRY: You have to be careful too, 'cause it gives the other gang a chance at you.

CYNTHIA: You're having a funeral for that person and they come by and shoot whoever they can, even little kids and everything. Right now there's supposed to be a truce between the gangs, right? But still they say Mexicans are killing Mexicans and black people are killing black people; they're killing their own races and pretty soon, they say, they're going to be killing off everybody.

It wasn't always like that. A long time ago, my brother, he's twenty-four right now, he used to be from a dancing crew when he was younger and there used to be other dancing crews, like break dancing and stuff? And his crew would dance against other people. When they were gonna fight fist to fist, they wouldn't fight, they'd break-dance to see who would win and whoever had the best moves would win, and the other crew just left in shame. But like I said, that was a long time ago.

TERRY: I wish it was like that now.

MARTA ARQÜELLO
Age: 35
Project Director
University of California Center for the Study
of Latino Health

✑

In these communities the parents live with the fear that they will lose their kids to violence. It's a constant fear, kids dying suddenly, with randomness. It's not the same as when you grow up in Latin America where you feel your kids are going to be safe. You're not scared whenever they're not home, you're not scared if they're out and about for a little while. But here there is a real sense that there isn't anything they can do. They're hanging on to whatever will make them feel that somehow it'll be okay for their kids . . . if nobody shoots them, if they don't get killed by drugs, by a nut, whatever. They live all the time with that bigger anxiety. I'm working with some parents who have had two kids killed. There's a sense of desperation, real desperation.

To have hope under such conditions you have to be very, very strong and the hope has to be reinforced, and there is nothing reinforcing it. I've seen that get much worse in the last ten, twelve years. Everybody's depressed. Frankly, I'm less worried about physical death than I am about psychic death, this depression, this hopelessness that's happening.

To me *that* is what requires our attention; that's what needs the technical application of everything we're supposed to be so good at, instead of applying our expertise to having more children and keeping dying people alive longer. I mean, think about this business of cloning and genetic engineering and all of that. It seems like white people are really obsessed with not dying; with finding a way to keep on living, applying all that technology in this insane effort. But we're all going to die anyway. Ultimately you have to accept it.

It scares me to think that we now have the power to engineer people, to make birth technological, all of these developments. The white society is doing this at a time when their population is decreasing and, at the same time, allowing things to deteriorate so much in certain communities. I hate to be paranoid, and I really don't want this to sound like I'm nuts, but think about it; is it continuing racism that's spurring on this whole technological drive? We can't see fit to provide creative education, to provide hope, but we can somehow manage to maintain old people on all these machines, or to provide in vitro fertilization to rich people. Children are left alone everywhere while we apply our technology to helping a few infertile couples have their own.

In the meantime some of these kids are living in a war zone. It's not much different from when I lived in Nicaragua where you always heard bullets and you never knew what they meant. And you woke up the next morning and there were no bodies. Yet, in the capital, all night you heard the helicopters, the shooting. It's the same here in some neighborhoods.

It's no surprise that these kids universalize their own experience with death. And when you confront them with the need to take care of themselves in regard to risks like AIDS, or smoking cigarettes, they say, "Hey, I'm going to die anyway." The reality is—there is so much potential for their destruction. It's a miracle if they *aren't* dead inside.

REBECCA WALKER
Age: 26
Writer and Activist

❧

When I think of death, when I think of the people I've known who have died, I feel that they've accessed a kind of bliss. I think we go back into the collective unconscious and it's joyful in some way. That's my vision of it.

Now I'm describing a very intuitive, instinctive feeling I have, but you have to be careful talking about the idea of bliss in death because it's been used by established religious institutions in a political way, where the bliss of the afterlife is used to justify the misery of the present.

When I was thinking about talking to you, I thought about these kids, the kids with guns, the kids in gangs. Many of them, and a lot of older people for that matter, are dead already. Dead in the sense of shut off emotionally, finished, gone to nowhere. And it's really because, in the lives they are given, there is no joy, no space for understanding the preciousness of life, no spiritual experience, certainly no bliss.

I think that *that* is death. Maybe we should change our whole vocabulary around the subject because, if there is a continuum, death seems to be a misnomer. It shouldn't be "life" and "death," it should be something else. If you transcend, if you do go on, if there is this sort of eternal consciousness—and of course those are big ifs, but let's say there is—then we're really talking about different *kinds* of life. It should be "earth-life" or "flower-life" or "later-life" or something.

And with the kids and people who have died while they're still living, maybe they're trying to get out of this earth-life. Maybe it would be a relief for them to get out of earth-life and into a different life.

My work is focused on looking at how we construct identities.

Trying to figure out what happens when you break down "us" and "them," "male" and "female," "black" and "white," all those binaries, the opposing identities that we've constructed for ourselves. How do we move beyond identity politics? How do we make room for a third thing, a third power, a third wave. Not the "either/or" but the "and." A new vision of multiplicity and diversity that's not hierarchical.

I think the measure can no longer be about how much money you have or what your race is. The measure is really more about how much love did you get. How much self-love have you internalized? How engaged can you become? How many empowering models of yourself are out there for you? It's not really about black or white or rich or poor, at this point. It's about everything we always said was basic. Love. Self-worth. Safety. For everybody. A sense of inherent worth and value. I think that's the new measure.

If we could dissolve some of the old identities that keep us locked into such a rigid state of being; if we could somehow disrobe, take that armor off, take off all the armors of identity that are put onto us by this world, then we would get closer to that state of bliss that I was talking of. We could find more joy if what we are inside could be released, like a flower blooms, without agonizing, without education, without trying to make you into something; you just happen of your own volition.

Maybe life-and-death is another set of binaries, or polarized identities that need to fall away to reveal some kind of continuum. And death is a turning point where you're allowed to have that, where you don't have to try to be free anymore, you really *are* free. The challenge is finding the political reality in that.

And then there's this media idea of a generation of nihilists, a whole group of people who are looking for meaning and aren't finding it, becoming alienated and suicidal. That's the media, but the reality I see is more a parallel with the civil rights community, a kind of twenty-something service movement, which is growing at an incredible rate. The young people I know are, in some way, descendants of the civil rights movement. They have seen the ways that people can make change and transform their communities, and are now coming together to try to continue that kind of work, taking up that torch. These are people who really *do* have hope for the future, and some sense, in whatever form, of some kind of interconnectedness.

I had a dear friend who threatened to commit suicide when we were at Yale. She just felt that the racism at school was so overwhelming, and that there was no space for her lovely black female self to emerge. I remember telling her, "Honey, it's just not worth it to kill yourself. Don't take you from us. We need you." She was a poet. I remember saying, "Write about it."

When you start to understand that you only change it by bringing yourself and your full experience to the table, that's a significant way of engaging the nihilism, the hopelessness, of countering that walking deadness. Engagement, in turn, gives you more meaning, because you begin to feel that your expression will help change things. So it's engagement rather than disengagement that's always been my trip. Personally, I think that's the *real* difference between life and death.

WESTERN IDEAS ABOUT DEATH CHRONOLOGY PART 4

❦

The *Danse Macabre* shows a group of people, hands linked together as they skip off toward the horizon in a "Dance of Death." It is a pervasive image representing the triumph of death over all people, regardless of age or class, and it is used as a common reminder of mortality in much the same way that Smokey the Bear will remind us to prevent forest fires almost five hundred years later.

1500s   Memento mori—cups, utensils, brooches, rings, and other jewelry decorated with a skeleton, death's-head, or inscriptions—are given as mourning gifts from the deceased's family to friends and acquaintances.

                Until now, mourners have often worn brightly colored clothing in honor of the deceased, but when Philip II of Spain wears all black following the death of his second wife, his court "follows suit," setting an international fashion trend. Black becomes the official color of mourning, sometimes worn with a white scarf or cap.

                As the influence of the Roman Church begins to decrease, images of death become eroticized. Surrender to the overwhelming compulsion of passion

becomes a metaphor for surrender to the overwhelming compulsion of death. Where death had
been treated with familiarity, it now begins to be
seen as a separation from the familiar, and a plunge
into the irrational.

Laws against suicide make it a triple crime of murder, high treason, and heresy. Because you (and your
body) belong to God and king, the attempt to kill
yourself is considered an act of defiance toward these
authorities.

The Roman Catholic orthodoxy teaches that even a
bad life can be redeemed by a deathbed conversion
or a condemned soul helped through purgatory if
prayers and offerings are made by the living. Money
and bequests given to priests to provide these prayers
essentially become payments for the promise of a
good afterlife.

The Protestant Reformation challenges Catholic
doctrine, teaching that a good death and the soul's
salvation is dependent on your behavior in life rather
than the indulgence of the church.

Protestants maintain that at the time of death there
isn't much anyone can do for you, you're in the
hands of God. Therefore, the actual moment of
death as the focal point for religious ritual becomes
less important.

1600s   Prior to this time, most deathbed and funerary ritual
has been designed to help the dying person journey
to his or her proper place and condition after death.
Now we begin to see a change that will lead to ritual
focused toward the living, leaving the dead on their

own and paving the way for the modern attitude toward more private or solitary death.

Because the new Protestant sects are as intolerant of divergent views as is the old Roman Church, everyone continues to fight over how to live and how to die. Many groups seek a "New Jerusalem" and head out for the recently discovered world across the ocean.

FATHER GARY GELFENBIEN
Age: 51
Roman Catholic Priest

ℭ

One of the biggest dilemmas in the church today is how to maintain the power of ritual and the comfort it provides, but do it in the context of the modern world. The old ritual has power. Something familiar has power. If someone quotes Shakespeare, people respond to it. We may mock these things when we're high school kids, but when we get older and someone does it in the right way at the right moment, it's powerful. You're struck by it and you stop. You've heard these phrases, they have meaning to you.

Now the church is more colloquial than ever. It speaks a contemporary language, you can understand it, it's not angry. Many priests are struggling to make meaningful gestures within the ritual, beautiful gestures, they're not just cranking it out, you know? But people reached a stage where they backed away. Only thirty percent of Catholics practice in this country, less than five percent in France, seven percent or so in Italy. It's a crying shame because you can see the comfort in the ritual of the church, especially when it comes to death and grief. I see the comfort in the visitors who come. But I also see the pale things. By that I mean I see where I'm not permitted to do all that the church can do, because people don't want it.

Often the family is not "churched." They have pulled away from going to mass. They may still want to have their babies baptized, or be married in church, but they are not active Eucharistic Catholics. Because of this, at death, they may hesitate to bring the body to the church and only want to have something in the funeral home. I always tell them, if we could at least pour water over the coffin or do something of ritual significance, it would help.

I'm always reminded of the Pietà—the image of the Virgin Mary holding her Son, Jesus, and the lamentation and weeping for that which was, but is no longer. The vessel of the spirit—the body—the loss of that person's body, this matters. It's a great loss and it's hard to deal with and the rites help you to do that. They bring in the coffin holding the body, and you pour water over it. Some priests sprinkle the water, but I pour it over so it literally splashes over the pallbearers' shoes (they always try to discreetly move their feet away as it cascades down). In doing that I'm saying, "You were baptized into Christ, you were baptized into his death as well as his Resurrection," and splash! all this water goes cascading down.

Then you place the pall over the coffin. I have the family help me do that. Together we put this great cloth over the coffin. You blanket the person with love, they're clothed in a new life in Christ. Incense may be used at different times, but I prefer to incense after the pall has been placed on the coffin. The scented smoke surrounds the draped coffin. All of this is really saying, "Thank you, thank you for this cherished human life and the sweetness of existence."

Throughout history the ritual gesture has been fundamental when dealing with death. One example is the altar stone. In early Roman churches the altar site was actually built over the place where a martyr or a saint was buried. It was hallowed ground. Now there is an altar stone or what is called a Greek corporal, a cloth placed on top of the altar itself, underneath the altar cloth. It has a little container sewn into the cloth for a saint's bone or relic. The old ritual reminders have been retained in this way. It does not have the same emphasis now, but it is still traditionally present.

The household gods of the Romans were part of a whole system for remembering the dead, and the Roman Catholic Church continues the practice of praying for the dead. Scripture and tradition hold that it is important to pray for the dead during their time of refinement, the purgatory experience.

Historically it was believed that you could not be in the presence of the perfect God who made all things, until you had been refined, until you were purified and prepared for what is called the "beatific vision." Until you had, in a way, "owned" who you were and what you had done. The purgation idea is that the mercy of God has brought you to this point and you need to take responsibility for your past.

This can be related to the Egyptian Book of the Dead, where the pharaoh's heart was placed on one side of the scale against a feather on the other, the feather being the hieroglyph for "truth." You find traces of this same imagery in the stone sculpture of the Cathedral of Notre Dame in Paris, or at Chartres, where the scales of truth are held by Saint Michael the Archangel, but instead of the heart on the scales there's a little person. This little miniature person, looking like a little doll, represents the soul. On the other side, a group of devils tries to weigh down the scale in their favor. They attempt to bring the soul into their state of alienation, which will throw it into the maw of hell, literally into the jaws of the dragon or into a blazing furnace.

The idea of Christ as the eternal judge developed and became a real emphasis in the medieval period when artisans portrayed these frightening horrors. Michelangelo used this same approach in the 1500s. In his Sistine Chapel frescoes, the figure of Christ in "The Last Judgment" raises his right hand and arm in a gesture of rejection—casting sinners down to their dismal fate in hell. In this judgment scene there is a lost soul who has his hand over one eye; his other eye looks out in horror as demons drag him down into the infernal area where boats of death bring the souls to their destiny.

Purgatory was never portrayed as such a grizzly scene but as the place where the person was refined, like gold in the fire. Maybe there's an insight from these historic images. Perhaps this is the reality of the moment of death, where we see ourselves as we really are, before the incredible love of God. When we face God and we see the One who is love upon love, grace upon grace.

Has the idea of purgatory been packed away in the historic annals of Catholic theology? I don't think so, it's just that we do not talk about it in those terms very often. Today we would talk about our lives before God, as we pass through the veil of death, when time and space as we know it is changed. We enter into the light of God and that light displays the reality of who we are.

During the Second Vatican Council, the Sacrament of the Sick was restored. What had come to be known as "last rites" had historically been a sacrament intended for the sick. In the Letter of James we hear,

> Are there any among you who are ill? Let them send for the priests of the church, let the priests pray over them, anointing them with oil . . .

This anointing was intended to be a help so people could go on, rather than a ritual for the end of life. Unfortunately the sacrament became distorted into a send-off; it became the last anointing (extreme unction). When someone sent for the priest this was an indication of impending death. Because of that history, today people can become quite frightened when the priest comes into the sickroom. He will often find it necessary to reassure them that he is not performing the last rites but the Sacrament of the Sick.

Of course, it is possible that the priest may be called when one is dying. But again, the idea is to bring comfort, not necessarily to perform a rite over a dead body. We want to anoint someone when they are aware, before they're on the morphine drip and have lost consciousness. The idea is that the ritual is a comfort to people who are ill as well as a comfort for those around them.

In the rite itself, the priest is directed to bring Communion for the individual. First there is the blessing with water: "Like a stream in a parched land, may the grace of the Lord refresh our lives."

The ritual directs the priest to "lay on hands." This is an old Judeo-Christian tradition, placing hands on the person to pray for God's spirit to enter them. Then there is a penitential rite which includes confession of sins, and the *Confiteor,* the prayer seeking forgiveness:

> "I confess to Almighty God, I may have sinned in my thoughts, in my words and what I have done and what I have failed to do."

Basically this is an acknowledgment of failure and the willingness to change.

After the confessional rite, the priest anoints the person on the forehead and on the hands, in the name of the Lord. The oil used for the anointing is blessed by the bishop each year at chrism mass at the beginning of Holy Week.

The whole idea of anointing is quite fascinating. In the old rite all the senses were anointed: the forehead, the lips, the nostrils, the eyes, the hands, and the feet. Again, if you go back to the Egyptians you find the early history for all this. They lived in an extremely dry desert climate where oil was both soothing and precious. It was a luxurious commodity, a negotiable bond. Grave robbers who ransacked the pharaohs' tombs were in search of perfumed oil as well as gold and jewels. Even today, in any hospital situation, patients are massaged with lotion. It's medicinal and comforting. Anointing isn't simply a ritual gesture, it's a practical gesture.

The prayer for this anointing is quite positive:

"Father in heaven, through this holy anointing, grant this person comfort in their suffering; when he or she is afraid, give them courage; when afflicted, give them patience; when dejected, afford them hope. When alone, assure them of the support of your holy people."

That's really the point, to surround the person with a loving bedside, to be right there with them, to support them at this crucial time.

During the Reformation, while reformers were smashing church windows throughout England, the Roman Catholic Church began to address issues in a Counter-Reformation, clarifying and restating doctrine. Their position was, "We're still right whether you broke away or not;" and in their architecture, in the use of marble, mosaic, fresco, and paintings, they were presenting their view of paradise. What the reformers were expressing simply—plain churches with no decoration—was in direct contrast to the elaborate interiors of the Baroque churches in Rome. These spectacular interiors have breathtaking figures in the heavens with Mary, the Mother of Christ, and the saints. Paradise is bursting with light above your head. It is as if the church were saying, "We offer you the saints and glory, the very Light of God. We offer you the Mother of Jesus, we offer you paradise with Christ the Lord."

That paradise is echoed on earth in the church and her sacraments. St. Peter's in Rome with the bronze glories of Bernini, with the saints and sunbursts of cascading angels, all these were a promise, as were the earlier mosaic interiors of the Byzantine churchs and the dazzling stained glass of the medieval cathedrals. It's so beautiful really, so powerful, expressing a real wonder—the wonder of the vessel of the body, destined for glory in paradise. With the old anointing, you anointed all the senses, the nostrils and the lips and the eyes—a luxurious fullness.

We're in an age of complete obsession with sexual and physical expression. It doesn't take watching the movie *Bull Durham* to know that people want a full experience, they want it to be real. There is something in this sensuality that is embraced in the sacraments and imagery of the church. People long for it. It touches the deepest part of being human, and it is expressed in ritual. The believing community in every expression is saying that there is something real here, something full, and we still have the need for it.

REVEREND BARBARA ST. ANDREWS
Age: 49
Episcopal Priest

~~~

I was at a conference once on traditional religions and "New Age" ideas, the kind of thing I think is very important, bringing together the old and the new, and someone there spoke about the power of language, the ancient power of certain words. It was some time ago and I can't remember his name but I do remember what he said because it struck me as a great example of the way old beliefs and new scientific ideas could be seen as similar.

He talked about Sanskrit, describing it as a language where the sound of the word was closely related to the thing the word was describing; and he talked about mantras, words or sounds used in Eastern religions to produce certain effects; and he talked about spells and hexes, incantations, all that sort of thing. It was fascinating.

He said that the sound of certain words held certain kinds of power. That there were ancient secrets in the *sounds* of the words, sounds that could help people in different ways, including when they were dying. He mentioned the last rites in the Catholic Church and the Buddhist practice of reciting certain prayers and chants as someone dies. The idea was that these "magic" words would help you to go to heaven or move through the Bardos, which is the Buddhist name for the afterdeath state.

I know that the Tibetan Book of the Dead is based on the idea that the dead person can still hear and so you read it to them to help guide them along. This man's idea was that there could be ancient words that were the "keys to the kingdom." That's how he put it. If you could get the right words and they were said at the right time, you could guarantee a good passage for yourself. These words, these prayers, were *pass*words. Literally.

Now this may sound very extreme or even slightly lunatic but personally, I think it's fascinating. Being a priest, when I think of liturgy, of prayer, that's the way I think about it. These words, said so many times over and over and over throughout history, definitely do have a power inherent within them. It's almost as if the words themselves can make something happen. But to me the important point would have to be that it's not a blind faith in the words alone. Our intelligence can show us exactly how these things can happen if you think of the words in terms of soundwaves and the kinds of healing effects we know that sound can have. It made me think of the studies that have been done showing how you can actually depress someone's immune system if they are bombarded with noise pollution and how the opposite is also true. If people hear pleasant sounds they feel better. I think it's in that same category of phenomena. Sounds can actually affect how you feel, they can affect physical things, so why shouldn't they be able to affect the consciousness during that passage at death? This isn't that fanciful an idea, it's really very reasonable.

To me, human reason is one of the key elements of religious practice. This is one of the things that's distinctive about the Episcopal Church. We put a great deal of emphasis on the reason that God gave us, on our intellect, on the assumption that we can figure things out for ourselves.

Episcopalians base their faith on what's called the Lambeth Quadrilateral, the fourfold foundation of Episcopal belief. There is tradition, there is Scripture, there are the bishops, and there is reason, our own ability as human beings to reason things out for ourselves.

To me, as a twentieth-century Christian with an appreciation for science, a lot of the discoveries being made in the new physics make sense in terms of my religious beliefs. For instance, one of the great comforts of Christianity is that we can trust that there is something, some form of life that continues beyond the grave. Although death is, in one sense, horribly tragic, and life can be viewed as an extended grief process because we're always losing something, even if it's just our youth, still, I take comfort in the idea that the continuity of things is quite likely. If matter and energy are interchangeable, as Einstein says and the new physics teaches, all the intimations that life continues after death become more explainable in scientific terms

and therefore more believable. What was a comforting "belief" becomes a reality. That is the excitement of working in the ministry. I
can offer that comfort when it is needed.

I've spent a lot of time in hospitals and nursing homes and minis-
tering to the ill and elderly. As a priest, I am one of the privileged
people who can walk by the nurse in ICU and be right there in the
middle of the situation. So I see how people die and I see it from the
point of view of someone who is focusing on that.

I pay a lot of attention when someone's getting close to death;
it's my job to pay attention to what they say and what they do.
People want comfort and often they want to let go. Unfortunately,
the medical professionals are often totally focused on the material
world and all their energies are heroically directed toward maintaining the physical life. This makes sense. If you only believe in the
material world then it's an enormous tragedy if you lose a person to
death. But from a priest's perspective sometimes it's a great healing
when a person lets go of this life and goes on.

At the time of death we can provide absolution, forgiveness of
sins, and holy unction. All are ministries of the church, although we
don't believe that your chance of being received by a loving God is
mitigated by whether you did or didn't get the priest there in time.

I work with many, many Catholics and more and more, I think,
we are softening our theological views to reciprocate and understand
one another's point of view. Although it wasn't always the case
throughout history, the little differences in how we do things usually
don't have too much to do with the reality of what we believe. We
basically respect one another and work together. At times when
there hasn't been a Catholic priest available, I've gone in and helped
out. One time a dying woman looked up at me and said, "Thank
you, Sister." She assumed I was a nun and that was just fine. I said,
"You're welcome." If that was a healing ministry, so be it. When
you get caught up in semantics you just miss the point.

And when someone is dying, the point is that Jesus Christ somehow, in some way, transcended the barrier of death. As a Christian I
believe that everything begins and ends with a conviction that Jesus
somehow transcends death in a way that makes him contemporane-

ous with man in a spiritual sense, contemporaneous with me. So when I am in need or trouble or loss, I can reach out and there is this personal God who meets me. Not a vague impersonal force or idea, but a personal God who understands loss and suffering and death, who experienced loss and suffering and death.

I think it's so helpful to know that Jesus felt the same sorts of things I feel sometimes. Even he who had the keys to the kingdom said to his disciple Peter, "Do you love me?" And he repeated it three times. I think that's the final question that is always left to be answered in every circumstance or relationship, "Do you love me?" I've seen this many times as people face death. What they really want is to know they are loved. Maybe they haven't even been aware of that need before. Up to then, other things have seemed more important or they haven't had the time to think about it. But that's what it comes down to—"Do you love me?" Sometimes we have to get to where we really understand that life is finite before we have the courage to ask or to answer that question.

[*The Reverend Barbara St. Andrews was killed in an automobile accident several weeks after this interview was completed.*]

MARGARET FIELDING
Age: 48
Wife and Mother

❧

Basically I'm a quiet person. I don't like to make a fuss about anything. I was raised in that way, not to upset anybody, not to make a
fuss. "Be seen and not heard," that kind of thing. I remember once
there was a news story on television where people were crying and
screaming at a funeral, gathered all around a grave, one of the men
actually jumping into the grave, the women wailing and fainting and
the men crying too. It was in the Middle East somewhere. It looked
completely foreign to me and I don't want to sound prejudiced or
anything because I know there are many different ways to be in this
world, but it bothered me. It made me very uncomfortable. I
thought to myself, "How can they behave like that? How can they
be so undignified?"

Last year my aunt died. She lived on the West Coast and she had
her own life. Her husband had been dead for some time and she had
her physical problems, but we assumed that for the most part she was
okay. Then all of a sudden one day she collapsed and they took her
to the hospital and found out she had cancer everywhere and that
was that.

She had a living will and a medical proxy and everything was all
set up so that she wouldn't have to be kept alive or treated if she
didn't want it. She asked to be put in the palliative care unit and they
gave her morphine and she died ten days later. Just like that.

By the time we were notified and managed to get out there she
was unconscious and I didn't get a chance to talk to her or anything.
I felt terrible about that. I had really wanted to talk to her one last
time, to let her know how much she meant to me.

When I was a little girl she was such an exotic figure in my life.
Her name was Lillian but she was called Lily. She was my wild aunt
Lily, my mother's sister and sort of the black sheep, well, more like

the gray sheep in my very white-sheep family, if you know what I mean. She didn't marry until very late in life. She had "affairs." You must realize this was the fifties and that sort of thing just wasn't done. I knew my mother and father didn't approve of her but I liked her a lot. She was smart and funny and she wore the greatest clothes. At least I thought they were great, my mother thought they were "inappropriate."

We lost touch when she moved to Europe. Then I went to college and married shortly after graduation. I didn't hear much of her for a long time and then, about ten years ago, after my mother died, we got to know each other a bit better. We were very different from one another but still, I liked her. We would talk on the phone every once in a while and we wrote to each other occasionally. If I had known she was ill I would have . . . well, I would have been in touch more, I would have . . .

Well, anyway, the thing I wanted to tell you was—she had made arrangements to be cremated and had left a letter of instruction asking that there be no funeral or memorial service or anything. I knew she was pretty much an atheist and these were true and heartfelt wishes on her part, so of course we respected that. She was estranged from the rest of the family. I think I was the only one she was still in touch with. There were some friends of hers out there who did have some kind of party after the cremation. They invited us to come but we didn't know them and we had to get back to our own life, so we didn't attend. It was all very quick and very . . . clinical.

I went back home and of course my life continued as usual but I found myself feeling preoccupied and sad. At first my husband said this was understandable and to be expected, but it didn't go away. Instead of easing off, my sadness became stronger and stronger. I remember one night, many months after she had died, I found myself crying and crying and my husband said, "What's the matter with you? You weren't this upset when your own mother died." He couldn't understand it, he thought it was inappropriate. It was true, when my mother died I hadn't felt anywhere near as sad. With her it had all seemed natural and had happened over time and then I'd had a lot to do with the arrangements and all the family coming in and just so much to take care of. I didn't go through anything like this. This just kept getting worse and worse, this feeling of tremendous sadness. I'd find myself crying at the most unexpected moments.

Then finally one day I realized I was really angry. I was angry because everything had happened so quickly. She had died so quickly, there was no real acknowledgment of it, no funeral, no memorial service, nothing. And the rest of the family had pretty much ignored it and there was no one to talk to about it, no one to . . . I don't know, no one to pay attention to how important it felt to me.

But most of all, I was angry because everything just kept on going, as if nothing had happened. Everybody wanted everything to be "normal." But for me it wasn't normal at all. This woman had died and it mattered. More than that, I'd never really had the chance to tell her how much she meant to me and *that* mattered very much indeed. I needed to stop and . . . I don't know what exactly, just stop and not have to go on as if it was nothing.

I had a friend whose wife was killed in a car accident. He loved her tremendously and it was terrible for him, just terrible. He told me that once the shock had worn off, the thing that bothered him the most was when he would wake up in the morning and everything was still going on, the world was still going on. He said every morning it was a surprise to him. He'd look out at people and wonder— how could they do what they were doing when death was in the world? Not just her death, but death in general. It seemed to him we were all in danger, that everyone was in danger of losing their most loved ones. Everyone was in danger of dying themselves, at any moment. How could they just ignore it? I remember him saying to me, "Maggie, it took *years* before I could go back to acting as if death wasn't real."

And on top of that, after a while people started telling him he should "get over it," and "get on with his life." It was shocking to him how quickly people did that, how much everyone seemed to want him to go back to "normal" life. He said it was as if they *needed* him to forget the whole thing.

I've thought about that a lot lately. I think he was right. I think people actually *need* to act like death isn't very important. That's what happened to me. My husband, my children, my friends, none of them showed in any way that they understood how badly I felt. They acted as if—this is no big deal, let's get back to normal.

Now I know that when Lily died, it cannot be compared to losing your spouse or your child. She was elderly and I didn't see her every day or anything. You're supposed to accept a "natural" death. But it didn't feel "natural" to me. It felt sudden and awful. I lost something really important. I'm not sure I could articulate exactly what it was, or that I would talk about it if I could, but I did lose something and we didn't acknowledge it, we didn't really stop. Nobody said, "Yeah, I know," or "I feel sad too." I felt terribly alone and I felt, finally, very angry. And I thought about that news program and the way those people had acted at that funeral and I understood it a little better. In some sort of way I wanted to cry out like that, I wanted everyone who knew her to be together and cry together and just show, in some real way, how awful it was that she was dead and we didn't get to say good-bye.

❧

In ancient Greek culture they observed a year of mourning after a person died. You dressed in black and during the year you would remember what happened the previous year on that date, when the person was alive. You would say, "May 26—oh, we were on a picnic. She was doing this and that." "June 27—it was raining and she was doing this and that." You remember, very specifically, for a year and then, when the year is over, you have a final ceremony in which you put the name of the person on the tomb, you take off the black clothes and you say, "Now life starts again, life continues." From then on, they carry the dead as part of their lives, but they don't mourn eternally. Those ceremonies, those rites are necessary to a culture and it would help people understand death better and manage it easier if we had more effective rituals here.

My daughter, Paula, who was twenty-nine years old, died on December 6, 1992. She was sick for one year exactly. On December 6, 1991, she felt the first symptoms of a porphyria attack. Porphyria is a condition that some people are born with. It's a very rare condition, very little is known about it. It's the lack of an enzyme in your metabolism. Most people who have this condition can live without any symptoms all their lives. But sometimes a series of coincidences or problems appear simultaneously and the chain of metabolism gets stuck or broken and the person falls into a coma.

In the past, they would just die in a few minutes but now, because there is intensive care, they are kept alive, in coma, for a period of time, usually two or three weeks. Then, when the other enzymes of the metabolism have time to rebalance things and make up for the one that is missing, they recover completely.

Paula had the flu, she started vomiting, her body was very stressed out. A series of things happened to provoke a porphyria attack and she went to the hospital. This was in Madrid. She told them she had porphyria and they didn't know what it was. They said, "No, it's the flu," and they sent her back home. Two days later she went back to the hospital and a few hours later she fell into a coma that would be normal in a porphyria attack but they didn't know how to treat it. She didn't receive enough oxygen, her sodium plummeted, they gave her the wrong drugs, it produced severe brain damage and she never recovered.

I was living here in California at the time but I moved to Madrid and I stayed with her in the hospital. At first we were expecting that she would recover. She had porphyria, we thought she was in that kind of a coma, she would wake up at any time, any moment.

I stayed with her in Madrid from December until May. In May she could finally breathe on her own, and that was the only thing that she managed to do, just breathe. So we took her off of the respirator and I brought her to the United States, to my house here, and I took care of her at home.

I trained myself to do all the things that you have to do for a patient in coma—to feed her, to move her, do the exercises, give the shots, all of it. I trained myself first and then I trained four women, loving women, all of them from Central America and Mexico. The requirement I had was that they be mothers because I wanted people who would understand what caring for a newborn baby is. That's what Paula became. Like a newborn child needing lots of affection and cuddling, constant supervision, you can never leave them alone, they have to be fed, you have to change diapers, you have to move them, you have to turn them around, they can't do anything for themselves. The only difference is, with an infant you know it will grow into a child. Paula will grow into death.

I'm a very active person, I'm always doing things, I'm a warrior really. But when Paula fell sick I stopped, everything stopped. It was like a long parenthesis in which I was separated from the world, separated from everything I had been doing, from writing, from the press, movies, people, family, everything. And I was quiet, still, in silence with her.

Paula gave me an opportunity to stop and ask myself the questions that I had been postponing. Stop and face death. Stop and face love. Stop and see myself in some real perspective also. As I was trying to help her I was really helping myself. It was a strange time, a very quiet, extremely painful time, that had rewards at the end. I'm seeing the rewards now. I did not see them at the beginning because I was in so much pain that I could not see anything good about it. I was angry at the beginning because I thought this could be avoided. For a long time I denied the reality of her condition. For a very long time I hoped that she would recover. I did not accept the fact that her brain was dead. I tried alternative medicine. I tried everything, you name it. Shamans, witches, homeopathy, mattresses with magnets that came from Japan, herbs, everything, even praying to gods that I did not believe in, anything that might work I tried.

Then there came a point in November, after eleven months, when I realized that I had to let go, that what I was doing was insane. Paula had been in coma for eleven months. I was hurting the rest of the family and hurting Paula too. I don't know what triggered it, or why it happened on a certain day. I think it was the fact that I stopped dreaming about her. Before that, she would always appear in my dreams. All of a sudden there was this silence, this emptiness, this body on the bed and no communication. She would not come in dreams, I could not feel her, I could not feel any contact with her except the physical, touching. And then I realized that her spirit was going and I had to give up that as well.

That week her husband came to visit and I talked with him and we cried together, and he also told me, "You have to let go, we have to let go." So we went to Paula's room and locked the door. We held her in our arms and we told her that we loved her and that enough was enough, that she could go, please go. Because there was no point for her to go on deteriorating slowly and me fighting to keep her alive when she was not really alive.

I don't think Paula heard anything or felt anything, and I don't think that her death is related at all with the fact that we told her that she could go. Some people think that it happens that way. I do not think so. I think that death is something very private and it happens independently of whatever other people do or think about it. It was her private process and she was already leaving. What happened at that point was that we realized that she was leaving, and we let go inside ourselves and it became easier for *us*. But for her, she was already on that journey and it had nothing to do with anything that we did.

In the following weeks I realized that she was slowly drifting away, although nothing had changed and the doctor who was in charge said that her lungs were clear, she had no infection, she was very strong, she could live many more years. I knew that she was leaving.

On Saturday, December 5, in the morning, Inez, one of the women that helped me take care of her, was helping me as usual. Every day, starting at seven in the morning, we would bathe her, dress her, comb her hair and change the sheets and all, clean up the room. It was a wonderful process that we did every morning like a slow ceremony. There was nothing rushed in that beginning of the day. For me it was always welcoming a new day that begins with her being alive, still alive.

Paula, as all patients in coma with severe brain damage are, was very rigid. She was stiff, totally stiff. So we had to do exercises, four hours of exercises a day to give her flexibility in order to be able to dress her and move her around. On that day she was limp, totally limp, and I knew that she was going to die.

I told Inez that I wanted to be alone with her. Inez started crying and she hugged Paula and she said, "Forgive me, forgive me, forgive me." At first I was scared because I thought that maybe Inez had given her the wrong medicine or something, and she felt guilty, and I said "Inez, what are you talking about?" She said, "I want her to take my sins to heaven so that they will be forgiven." And I realized that she was giving Paula a message to take, like the mail. I thought it was such a wonderful image of what death was about.

I convinced Inez that I wanted to be alone with Paula and she left. I started doing this ceremony of preparing her for the day, only now I was preparing her for death. I brought her best clothes and I put on her wedding ring and I arranged the room in a special way. I expected to spend the day alone because my husband was working in his office, and my son Nicolas and daughter-in-law Celia and their children never come on Saturdays because that's the day they clean their house. But Celia had a premonition that something was happening and she came over, with her babies, and found me doing these things in the room. Without a word she participated in cleaning and dressing Paula. The babies started playing in the room, very quietly, very well-behaved. Then Nicolas showed up and then they called Willy, my husband, and he came also. And we spent the day in this quiet mood, waiting.

At one point we called the doctor who came and said, "Yes, she's closing down, but this can last weeks, don't expect anything soon. I will send a nurse with oxygen so that we can help her." And I said "No, no, I don't want to keep her alive, I just want to keep her comfortable." She said, "Okay. If she starts suffering, call me." And she left.

At eight o'clock, Nicolas brought flowers and candles and we improvised a ceremony to bid her farewell and tell her all the good things she had given us. To honor the gifts, the light, the love.

Then suddenly the doctor appeared again. She was worried, she didn't know very well what was going on. She brought some morphine which we ended up not using but we had it there. Paula was in our family room where the television was, where the children play, where the cat lives. It's the largest room in the house and it was also the hospital. So the doctor came in and found all of us and Paula in this room full of candles and little lights and the babies asleep at Paula's feet on her bed. And she was trapped in the atmosphere of the room, she never left, she spent the rest of the night with us. And all night it was raining outside, and we told stories and hugged and embraced.

I got in bed with Paula, holding her, and at four o'clock in the morning she stopped breathing. There was nothing, not even a sigh, she just didn't breathe anymore.

The doctor said that she was gone, and I fell asleep, embracing her, in the bed. I do not remember for how long I slept, I don't think it was very long because Celia woke me up, saying, "She's becoming rigid, we have to prepare her."

While I was asleep I had a dream. It was the same dream I had had in Madrid when she was first in coma, at the beginning of her illness. At the time we thought that Paula would wake up. It was the very first week and everybody thought that in a couple of weeks she would come out of it. Sleeping at the hotel, I dreamt of a tower, a round tower like a silo, full of pigeons. Paula was twelve years old and she was in the silo. She had a coat on and I was with her, and I heard a voice, the voice of my grandmother saying, "Paula has died." And at that moment Paula started rising up, levitating in this silo, going up, up, and all the pigeons got very scared and started making noises and there were feathers and pigeons and then I got hold of her coat and she was going up and I was going up with her and I was saying, "Don't go, don't go." And then the voice of my grand-mother said, "She has drunk the potion of death." Then, when we reached the top of the tower, I saw some very small holes and through the holes I could see a blue sky with a perfect cloud, like those paintings of Magritte, and I realized, horrified, that Paula could go through the holes and leave and I could not because I was too heavy.

When I woke up in the hotel in Madrid, I was terrified. I rushed to the hospital and knocked on the door in intensive care so desper-ately that they allowed me to see her, even though it was the middle of the night. Nothing had changed. The nurse said, "She's okay, she's alive, nothing happened, it was just a nightmare." But of course, it was a premonition.

When I fell asleep the night Paula died, I had exactly the same dream, but without the anxiety. The same silo, the same pigeons, the same voice saying, "Paula has drunk the potion of death." And I was still floating with her and holding her coat and when she left I remained there floating in the upper part of the silo. But there was no anxiety. I did not wake up with the feeling that I had to rush to the hospital or anywhere. I woke up with the knowledge and the awareness that she was dead. And her body was there in my arms.

The doctor went to write the death certificate. Nicolas took the children out of the bed and put them on the sofa and then he went to begin calling everybody because my family is scattered all over the

world. We had to call her husband, my mother, everybody. Willy
went to prepare some coffee and Celia and I improvised the last
ceremonies of death, doing what we did every morning basically,
but for the last time. It was a very solemn thing that we did together,
arranging her clothes, her hair, the room. Then we opened all the
windows so that it would be cold in the room, and we just sat there,
with a blanket, and waited. We waited for two days because we
wanted all the family to come. When everybody was there, we called
the funeral service and they cremated her.

I had two weeks of grace in which I was numb. I went through
the motions. There was a mass because she was a Catholic. I know
that I spoke at the mass but I don't remember what I said. I do
remember that we scattered the ashes and I remember where we
scattered them because that has become a holy place for me. I go
there often. But . . . after those two weeks of numbness I woke up
one moment with a total awareness that I was *never going to see her
again*. There was no telephone where I could call her, nowhere I
could send her a letter, nowhere I could find her, and at that moment the real process of grief began.

The first thing that everybody said was that I needed a therapist.
The doctor gave me tranquilizers and sleeping pills because I had lost
a lot of weight and I was not sleeping. I imagine I was not behaving
like I usually do. That is expected of a person who is grieving, of
course, but because the whole thing had gone on for so long, the
people who love me were very worried and they thought I would
not be able to go through what was coming. But I did not take any
of the pills and I did not go to the therapist. I did something else.

When my mother came, the day after Paula died, she brought a
parcel with her, and after we had scattered the ashes and all the
ceremonies were over she came into the room where I was sitting.
She gave me a cup of hot chocolate and this parcel and said, "These
are the letters that you have written me during this year." (I write
every day to my mother.) "These are all the letters." It was a huge
stack of letters and she said, "Read them, in the same order that you
wrote them, so that you will remember every stage, every step of this

ordeal, and you will know then that the best thing that could happen to Paula was death. It will be easier to accept it."

The letters helped me a lot, not only to accept Paula's death, but, like in the ancient Greek culture, to go through all the days of the previous year and remember, every day, what was happening; through the letters, through the memories of her, slowly, patiently. And I have written every day. It was a ritual mourning that has become a book.

Being a writer is a privilege because you spend so many hours alone. And if you have already published a book, as I have, people respect your time when you say that you are writing. (Before no one did, but now they do.)

During that year of writing, I came to deal with Paula's death much better because I lost the feeling of separation. When you write about the past, when you write your memories, you can see life in a different perspective. You don't see each moment separated, you see it like a big tapestry that contains everything, like those Mexican murals where all the eras, all the races, all the events are conceived in one harmonious totality. That is how I can see my life and Paula's life and our relationship, from the perspective of the writer, the powerful vision of the writer who is creating something.

In that role, you feel that you can control it. You never can of course, because fiction is uncontrollable and memories are uncontrollable and life is uncontrollable. But, when you write, you must give some order to the words, to the sentences, to the pages, to the scenes. And in creating that artificial order you can see yourself, your child, life and the universe, the past and the present and the future all in one whole mural that contains everything.

If you think about it, the history of humankind is about death and about dying in childhood. It's only recently in industrialized nations in the last century that infant mortality has dropped. In most of the world, for ages, for millennia, children have died. People died very young and babies died. Parents who survived their children, you could count them by the millions, hundreds of millions. This is an experience that is not uncommon at all and I remind myself of this all the time. I remind myself that I am not the only one who is going through this.

When Paula died, I thought that it was impossible to conceive a greater pain. I forgot that this is the kind of pain that we are immersed in constantly. Life is pain, and it's only a handful of very privileged people, in very few places in the world, who can pretend that they can go through life without pain. America is the only place I've ever been where people believe they can avoid pain and the hard parts of life.

I think this assumption has actually crippled our capacity to be happy. We base happiness in material things, in being lovely, in being wealthy or healthy, in being "safe," in some defended way. When I was young, I thought that happiness was having three orgasms in a row, or being applauded, or having a dessert, or having something published for that matter. I mean, what is that? That is nothing, it doesn't mean anything. It's only through pain that we learn and we grow. Happiness comes after you have overcome the obstacles. It's not from avoiding them, it's from going through them. The only place where I find happiness now is at the end of the tunnel of pain.

Writing has given me time every day to think, to mourn, to cry, to get over the loss and live with the spirit. To live with what I have gained, not with what I have lost. I lost the daughter that I had but I have something else that she gave me.

If I had to summarize what I learned during the whole year of Paula's agony, the moment of her death and all the next year of grieving and writing, it would be: After you have lost everything, the only thing you have left is the love that you have given.

Paula could not give me anything back because she couldn't respond in any way. And after she died she left me with this incredible treasure of the love that I gave her without expecting anything— no expectations, no desires, no nothing, just the overwhelming feeling of giving.

I understand so many things that I did not understand before.

Now my way of loving is different. The way I love my husband, my grandchildren, my mother, my stepchildren, people in general—it's not based on expectations. It's just because I get so much from the loving. I have a whale of a time. That was Paula's legacy.

WESTERN IDEAS ABOUT DEATH
CHRONOLOGY PART 5

❦

Europeans begin to make their way to what they call the "New World," in North America where Native American populations live and thrive. Paleo-Indian peoples have developed many diverse nations with distinct languages, customs, and practices while sharing a worldview based on a vital connection to nature and to place.

Although a few Indian nations see death as a shadowy uncertain destiny and enact ritual ceremony designed to protect the living, the vast majority treat death as a passage from one status to another, emphasizing a direct link with the dead ancestor whose spirit influences daily life. In North America, attitudes evolve as:

c. 9000
B.C.E.

The Clovis Indian culture ritualizes animal kills to ensure the animal spirit will return to its origins, regenerate itself, and come back to provide food again.

c. 200
B.C.E.

Indian nations of the Ohio, Tennessee, and Cumberland river valleys build snake-shaped and conical mounds in which prominent people are buried with jewelry and other precious items.

c. 500
C.E.

A legend describes the Choctaw people searching for a homeland, carrying the bones of their deceased elders until, reaching the proper place, the ancestors' bones are piled high on the ground and covered with cypress bark to create the vast mound at Nunih Waya, which was called The Great Mother.

Plains Indians wrap their dead in cloth and place them on a funeral scaffold, safe from scavengers. Other tribes offer the dead, with ritual and ceremony, to the cycle of nature, scavengers, and the elements. This practice (also prevalent in parts of Asia and elsewhere) is sometimes called Sky Burial.

Meanwhile, back in Western Europe:

c. 1000   Inhabitants of various European countries begin ex-
C.E.   ploring farther and farther into unmapped territory,
             eventually coming to the homeland of the Native
             American.

c. 1500   Spanish, Italian, and Portuguese explorers establish
             settlements in the New World.

c. 1600   European colonization begins in earnest. North
             America is virtually invaded by people whose cus-
             toms and view of death have been formed by Judeo-
             Christian history.

             The colonizers reflect a range of Christian traditions,
             including Puritanism, Calvinism, and other strict
             Protestant sects, as well as Catholicism. Their view
             of death emphasizes judgment in an afterlife leading
             to the joys of heaven or the terrors of hell.

While both Europeans and Native Americans believe in the continuity of the human spirit in one form or another after death, in these two traditions assumptions about the role and place of the human spirit could not be more incompatible.

TERRY TAFOYA
Age: 42
Doctor of Clinical Psychology
Native American Shaman

✐

The concept of spirit, and the continuation of spirit beyond death, is fundamental to Native American belief. Different pueblos, different nations have variations in practice, but most Native people share the basic concept of the continuation of life. It may continue in a different form but it's believed there is an aspect of life that goes on, and a sense that those who die can have some contact with the living, in terms of a concern or caring, that may go on over a long period of time.

Joseph Campbell, an old friend of mine who's since passed away, used to deplore the fact that in English you cannot distinguish between what is concrete and what is abstract. So people get into holy wars about the Eucharist for instance. Is it representative of the blood of Christ or is it really the blood of Christ? A lot of native languages are structured differently so you don't get into that conflict at all.

For example, *Chee Iwa Xaiyama,* "There is an eagle," is understood as: There is a physical eagle. But if I say *Chee Iwa Xaiyamayai,* the *yai* suffix throws it into what we call legend language. You don't look for an eagle because you understand I'm talking about the abstraction of an eagle, the spirit of it.

In our language, when someone dies, we talk about *atamaniwitsha,* and it means this person is on his journey. *Tamanawit,* in noun form, literally means a path or a road. *Tamanawitsha* is a much broader term referring to the idea of how you're supposed to be journeying, how you're moving forward. When you die, you're still moving forward in that way. *Tamanawitsha* means, "He's going forward in his journey." Death doesn't end the journey, it's just another step along the way.

The word for the Creator is *Yaiyaima.* In English *Yaiyaima* liter-

ally would mean "Spirit of the Spirits." And that's how we concep-
tualize the Creator. We believe that in everything, not just human
beings, but in animal people, in plant people and in mountains, the
wind, the rock, there is a little flame of the Creator inside, a little
spark of the divine. That's the *yai,* that's the spirit aspect. When you
die, it's *ilikisha.* You're in the process of becoming light.

   Iliki is a root word for light, for shining. Adding *sha* on the end
of a word is like adding the suffix "ing," it makes it an active thing.
Ilikisha means that you are becoming light, you're becoming the
energy of light, that shining. That little spark of your divinity is
released and merges with all the other sparks of the Creator. In one
aspect the Creator is the combined flames of all the little individual
beings and entities, really a sum of who we are. When you die, your
spark gets released and merges back in the way that raindrops fall into
the ocean, so nothing's ever really lost but continues in another way.

   In traditional Native American communities the ritual that occurs at death is very important. A funeral is almost a kind of organizing principle. When a death occurs it's not unusual for people in
some of our reservations who are not, shall we say, strict followers of
tradition, to suddenly become very strict.

   In describing Native American funerals I'll speak specifically
about the Warm Springs Indian Reservation where my mother is on
the tribal council, but similar things happen with subtle variations in
many of the different communities. At Warm Springs there is a very
elaborate four-day ceremony that begins immediately after someone
dies. During those four days the word is sent out and people will
start merging together, coming to the place where the loss has been,
so that perhaps you'll come to the parent's house or the brother's
house or the dead person's home.

   Now these deaths may be first cousins or second cousins, but in
our way, in our language, literally, we do not make a distinction
between a first cousin and a sibling. For us, those of one generation
are brothers and sisters. So the idea that you wouldn't attend someone's funeral because they were "just a cousin" is foreign to us, it
isn't our concept. This has been a problem for a lot of Indian people
because when you work for standard employers they usually only

have bereavement leave for someone who is in your "immediate" family.

During the four-day period there are very specific activities for everyone to do. One of the things that was puzzling to me when I started attending non-Indian funerals—and I don't mean to be disrespectful of other ways of dealing with death and grief—but going to a non-Indian funeral was like going to the theater, in the sense that something's happening out there and you sit in your seat and you watch it happen. You can emote in the same way that you'd cry at a sad movie or something, but one doesn't really *do* anything. In Native American funerals there are all sorts of established methods by which one does something.

As a clinical psychologist, when working within a Western system, often times I feel words are not enough. Having a person talk about their situation is effective in some cases but in some cases people need to dance their sorrow. People need to break something. People need to create something. At most non-Indian funerals, people do not have a chance to do that.

The four-day event may begin differently in different communities. Again, I don't want to give the impression that all Indian people do exactly the same thing but, in my experience, there are some practices that are similiar in many different communities. At Warm Springs an outfit is made for the dead person, usually out of deerskin. Even if that person didn't wear traditional clothing a great deal in their living life, they're buried that way because it's important to us. Clothing appropriate to their gender is created. For example, if it was a man, then buckskin leggings, buckskin top would all be made. And not just the body, they would also wrap the head and the hands in buckskin as well, and moccasins on the feet. The deerskin will decay at the same rate as human flesh. It all goes back into the earth together.

We don't believe in embalming but because of state requirements we do put the body in a casket. The casket is made of pine wood so that it will decay too. There are spices that we use to preserve the body. There are songs that are done to help with the freeing of the spirit, there are cleansing songs, purification songs that are done as the clothing is placed on the body.

We don't really feel comfortable with the concept of autopsy, and of course some other religious groups have that feeling as well. We're taught that the body is a seed, and so you plant the seed back into the ground. You don't start cutting up the seed. This is such a strong belief that I remember there was one Indian elder who had to have a leg amputated and after it was done she had her leg frozen so that when she died her leg could be buried with her, so as much as possible she could still be complete.

The larger idea is: We are fed by the earth, we live off the plants and the animals from the earth. Those are gifts to us. We pay for it by feeding the earth. We're put back into the earth so that our bodies become the earth again to feed the plants and feed the animals so there's a never-ending turning of the circle.

Our belief is that during the four-day ceremony the spirit of the person will retrace the steps he or she took in life, and that's why we don't bury the body for four days. That's the time when the spirit makes its journey. You're retouching all those things that you experienced in life, to take with you.

If someone has a vision or a dream of the person who's passed away during the four days after the death, we consider that very good, or maybe I should say *appropriate*. It's a way the person says good-bye, touching base and letting you know they're moving on.

It's always interesting to me to arrive during the middle of a funeral. The women will be working on the clothing and they're joking and laughing, enjoying one another's company because sometimes these are people you don't see every day, but just on Christmas or a family reunion or something, and so they're joking and laughing. Then someone new comes in, maybe a relative or friend or somebody who has just driven in or flown in or whatever. The moment that new person opens the door the women will start keening. They'll make a high-pitched crying sound. It's like a switch is turned on and suddenly all the emotion is there. It's a way of incorporating that new person into the mourning process.

Even though people are not showing any particularly strong emotion right before that person arrives, the moment they arrive, they'll turn it on. It will start and will go on for a few minutes so that person feels as though they've entered into the sense of loss. Everyone then goes back and does the things they'd been doing before the new person arrived. We're a very practical people.

It's important that newly arrived individuals are joined into the circle. So, for example, during the religious ceremonies that take place after the dressing's done, if people have just come they will walk around and shake the hand of everybody in the ceremonial space—and that may be literally hundreds of people—so that everybody is recognized and acknowledged as being part of the process. And it's not just the immediate family. Even if you're not related to the person, this would still be done for you, to let people know that we are all of one heart, we are all of one mind in this undertaking. "Undertaking" is not a pun I wanted to make in this respect. It would also be done for other kinds of high holy days, not just for funerals.

Around a death, there are almost always ceremonies and rituals that involve social or even economic mobilization. One such example is what in English is called a giveaway, a ceremony where things are given away. In very traditional households, anything the dead person touched on a regular basis, such as pots and pans, plates, silverware, all will be collected and given away.

In many of our communities we believe that a human body has a certain kind of energy, a certain kind of power. In the Hawaiian culture this is called *mana*. It's called by different things in our communities, but the idea is that there's a kind of energy signature, a signature of the spirit power of that person if you will. Something that they used on a regular basis is infused with that energy signature. The objects that the person owned in life will be separated out. Those objects are then collected, cleansed and sung over and taken to the longhouse where the ceremonies will take place.

During the giveaway ceremony a speaker will take items and hold them up for everyone to see. For example, if the person was a rancher the speaker would hold up his saddle and say, "Look at this saddle. This is a saddle he used to use. Look at it, we'll never see him use it any longer. This is the rope that he used to use. Look at it, we'll never see him use this rope anymore."

One of my younger brothers was killed in a car crash. He was a championship fancy dancer and so they held up the bustle with the feathers he would wear when he would dance, and said, "Look, this is what he used to wear when he would win the championships."

In psychological research on issues of grief and bereavement, one of the things that you see very consistently in the literature is that if you don't have that kind of reality check, a lot of times the healing doesn't take place. For example, when people are missing in action from a war, or in a death where the body's never recovered, the survivors will often not be able to complete their grieving process. This is our way of institutionalizing the idea of forcing people to confront the reality of the loss. And while that's being done, photographs are being passed around so that you'll see the person in different stages of their life, you'll make that connection—"Yes, we acknowledge this and it's done, it's over."

And that's exactly the structure. "Look at this. You're not going to see him do this any longer. You're not going to watch her use this any longer." So you can't do denial. It's right there in front of you. Again, from the psychological research, we see the utility of this, and it's something that was automatically built into our traditional system.

Then a lot of those things are given away. I remember when my first brother died, our family not only gave away the standard things like the cups and saucers and dishes, they ripped up the carpet and gave all the carpet away. They gave all the furniture away. For us there's a saying that joy shared is doubled and sorrow shared is halved. So when you have sorrow you give away things, and people take a piece of your sorrow with them when they receive that gift.

Objects that are special heirlooms or lineage objects are put away. After a year's period of time those things are taken out and they're usually given away to family members. For example, when my grandmother died her things were put away. After a year they were brought out and given to the grandchildren. I was given a cornhusk bag, a belt bag that you wear on the side of your belt (Indian people never knew they invented pockets). It was of her own making when she was a young woman. So that was my receiving heirloom to always remind me of who she was and of my relationship with my grandmother.

Now, moving on to the third day, usually starting around sundown, they'll begin the funeral. These things are not tied to a time clock, but this is a rough approximation. They'll start up the funeral and people will, what we call *washat*. *Washat* means to dance, but it has the connotation of religious dancing or a worship dance. If you've never seen it, it's difficult to describe. It's kind of a skipping dance, a sideways skipping, very pretty to watch because it has a very strong rhythm to it. Usually it's younger people who *washat*.

Dressed in very traditional clothing, women and girls will wear their wing dresses and men and boys will wear ribbon shirts and leggings, moccasins, usually with their hair in braids, wrapped in otter fur or beaver fur. They'll dance as a group with the men and the boys on one side, and the girls and women on the other side. On a regular basis this dancing is done on Sunday, the same way that Christian people will go to Sunday church services. But during Sunday services it's usually three times seven or twenty-one dances. With funerals it is seven times seven dances, and so it's forty-nine dances. In my experience, when I dance that much, by the last four or five dances, my feet will bleed.

In thinking about it from a clinical standpoint, when you dance so much that your feet bleed, you are experiencing on a physical level what you're feeling on an emotional level. The pain inside externalizes itself. At the same time, when the healing process comes, and your feet start to heal, it's also a very concrete reminder that internally you're healing as well.

When I lost my grandmother my hair was cut. If you have long hair, usually one of the first things you do when you wake up in the morning is braid it. I would wake up and go to braid my hair and it wouldn't be there. And it would make me think about the loss of my grandmother. As the months went by and my hair grew out, again, it was like the healing of the blisters from dancing so much. It was a symbolic, external reminder that I was healing inside. And when my hair grows out to the length it was before the loss, it's a signal that my grieving is over as well—at least, that active part of the grieving is finished and we return to normal.

While they're doing these seven times seven dances, the casket is in the center of the longhouse and the drummers are singing their songs. Then at one point they'll stop the traditional activities and open the floor up to people who don't walk this way. People who are Mormons or Baptists or Catholics. They'll all be invited to come out and if they have something to offer, the floor is open to them. My favorite part of that is the Ladies Auxiliary of the Veterans of Foreign Wars. Usually these are little old Indian ladies who are dressed in their very traditional clothing and they go through, word for word from this little tiny handbook, what Ladies Auxiliaries of Veterans of Foreign Wars do. They put little flowers on the casket and say some kind of little prayer. It's very sweet. Then they're finished and the Baptists will come in and do something. They finish and the Mormons will come in, etc.

And while they're doing that there's usually a medicine person over in a different part of the longhouse doing medicine singing over the objects of that person. To purify or to clean them, if you will, of that person's energy. The energy signature is erased so there's nothing to hold the dead person back, nothing that continues to tie that person to this particular time and place.

There will usually be an internal circle within the larger circle. The smaller circle is that of the immediate family who will be closer to the casket and they'll say words of good-bye and talk of their experiences and make statements that they may have wanted to say while the person was living. It's all done openly within the community. The dances will then resume once everybody's had a chance to do what they want to do or say.

Not everybody stays up for every part of the ceremonies. Some people go back to the longhouse, or go back to where they've been staying, and they'll eat or take an opportunity to catch up on some sleep. But it's not unusual during this four-day period of time, particularly for those people who are most involved, the immediate family members and the others who are very close to the dead person, to go for twenty-four hours, forty-eight hours without sleep, because this is happening all night long. And the dancing goes on continually all night.

People are fed the traditional foods and they'll bring out a little symbolic meal for the dead person. In some of the Pueblos it's not unusual during certain times of year, the Day of the Dead, Halloween, All Saints' Day, for example, to put little miniature versions of food at the grave site. It's very similar to what is done in Mexico and some other communities as well, to feed the ancestors, to feed the people that you've lost. Of course we understand that nobody's going to eat that food, but the spirit of the food, the *yai* of the food is feeding the *yai* of the person. The spirit of the food is offered to the dead person in the same way that the physical food is offered to the living people who are attending.

All these things are done to songs. There are cleansing songs, preparation songs, table songs sung when the food is being placed on the table. Then, after the dancing is done and the feasting is done, when the dawn of the fourth day comes people will continue singing as they escort the body to the graveyard site. When they arrive there more songs are sung and then someone will hold a shovel with the dirt in it, and each person who is at the grave site will take a handful of the dirt and put it into the grave so we all bury the body collectively.

What I've described so far are all the things you would see if you were, for example, a teacher or a nurse at Warm Springs or Yakima, or the other places where this is done. It's open to everybody who wants to walk through the door. This, of course, is different in different communities, but in the communities that I'm familiar with, that's the case.

Then there is also what's called a *Palaxsiks* ceremony. A *Palaxsiks* ceremony is usually done in people's homes, so most non-Indian people have not seen this. After a period of time has gone by, a week or more after the burial, the family will gather together. In the old days they would come into the person's home, the surivivor's home. First they'll cut the hair. The hair is cut according to the intensity of the loss. If it was a spouse, for example, it would be about even to the ear. When my grandmother died, I had about six inches of my hair cut off. After the hair is cut off, they'll take the person's clothes off. In the old days, they used to do this without covering and the person would be totally exposed. This is very unusual in our culture because we don't really feel completely comfortable with nudity. We tend to be very private people. Nowadays what they'll do is hold up a Pendleton blanket to act as a screen.

As a clinical psychologist, I consider this, again, the externalization of the internal experience, the feeling of exposure, the feeling of vulnerability that death brings. The clothes are removed and those clothes are given away. Then people will come and dress, let's say the widow in this case, in dark clothing, in grays and blacks and browns, and a double set of scarves to cover up the hair.

In addition to acting out the internal sense of loss and exposure this ritual does something else. Part of it is also so that whenever you meet someone dressed like that, you know they're in bereavement. In other words, I have no way of knowing, when looking at you, whether you are mourning or not. In general, in American culture this is not signaled. In our culture, we'll know immediately by glancing at you, and it saves us embarrassment. We know to offer certain things to that person, or to interact with them in a particular way.

I used to live in San Francisco and riding the metro, for example, it wouldn't be unusual to hear someone talking with someone who would say, "How's your lover?" And there would be this terribly awkward pause and the person would say, "He died six weeks ago." That doesn't happen in our community, because the way that you dress signals to the rest of us that even if we don't know about your loss, we know that you're in the process of grieving.

Now the *Palaxsiks* ceremony is a very solemn kind of event, but a delightful aspect of it is that after it's all done, and the person is dressed in their dark clothing, there will be a trade, and this is exactly the way that they'll do it during a wedding. People go out to their cars, their pickups, and they'll bring in bundles, and the bundles might contain canned goods, or deerskin, beadwork, Indian jewelry, whatever. And you'll pick a trading partner and you'll sit down and put that bundle in front of your trading partner, and they'll put a bundle down in front of you, and then you'll open up the bundles and check it out. If they're not exactly matching, if I feel I've given you more than you've given me, you'll make a promise that at the next powwow or the next root feast or whatever event's going to be coming up, you'll make it up to me. You'll bring me a beaded dress, or moccasins, or something that will balance out the scale. Then food is served and what's been an extremely solemn, very sad event, becomes a festive one. So there's always a sense of positiveness that goes along with these things, a sense of constant renewal, if you will. And also, I suspect, from a psychological level, a sense of future projection, the idea that we continue, that we go forward. We have this anticipation.

The legends specify that you are in mourning for a year. Traditionally during this time, for this widow that we've been describing, she wouldn't do any work, she wouldn't even wash her own hair. It would all be done by her extended family, she would be taken care of. Her only responsibility is to mourn. Her only responsibility is to grieve. That's her job. That's her full-time position, for twelve months. She is not permitted to take part in social activities. This is so that she would be able to go fully into her grief.

However, there has been a real change in this practice. Because of the cash economy, many families have cut back from twelve months to three months. I think there's a price you pay for not doing it all the way, but again, because of people having to work, people having to earn a living in a different way than in the old days, the time has sometimes been reduced from the full year.

After the grieving period of time has been accomplished then another ceremony takes place that replicates the one I've just described, where people come back together and the widow will now be stripped again, all of her dark clothes will be given away, and the people who received the gifts of the first clothing will now dress her in new clothing. So again it's the circle of reciprocity. But now they'll bring colors that are bright, and it represents the butterfly. She's emerging from her cocoon and she's ready to fly again. She'll be able to take part in a ceremony, she'll be able to dance, she'll be able to live a normal life again. And again, because she's changing her clothing, people who don't know anything about the history of the death will be able to recognize that she's someone who's not in mourning, who's not in bereavement.

All of these ceremonies touch on everything that has been found, in the academic research on grief and bereavement, to be important and necessary to complete the mourning process. Again, from a psychological point of view, we have institutionalized all these things in a way that we feel is helpful to people in the healing process.

When I was on the clinical faculty at the University of Washington Medical School, it wouldn't be unusual for me to work with people who had losses or were grieving. And I found that my experiences back on our reservation and within our community were very helpful to me in this.

Sometimes I would tell people how to use some of our ceremonies or some of our approaches to help in dealing with their own loss. Not in terms of making them Indian, but in the sense of saying, "When we do this, this is the impact it has. Is there a way you can do something analogous to that, so you can act out your sorrow or make a commitment to yourself in a formal way that's ritualistic, again not at all necessarily Native American, but something that has meaning for you?"

I found this was helpful for people, from a psychological point of view, as long as I would provide them with a cognitive framework, a clear context on a structural level. If I were to tell people to do A, B, C, and D, and not explain the meaning behind it or the interpretation of it, it would seem very bizarre. But if you understand, step by step, what these things represent, then even a ritual that wasn't yours originally can become yours in a way that's important for you. There is a great need for this among many people today.

I work from this thesis: Human needs don't change, but the way in which we meet those needs, this changes. So we learn new ceremonies, we learn new rituals, and new ways of structuring, and if they don't have power, if they don't work, then forget them and keep going until you find something that does work.

A lot of traditional rituals have tremendous power, whether they're from pagan traditions or from Native American or Native Hawaiian traditions. These are rituals that have worked and that's why we pass them on from generation to generation. They've been shaped like a pebble is shaped by the waters of a river. Those things that are not really important have pretty much washed away, and the rituals are smooth like a pebble that's been washed by the water. These ceremonies are shaped by the waters of time.

Often people who are not familiar with the complexity of our culture will still be very moved by what they are seeing, even if they don't fully understand what is going on. I assume that we get more meaning out of it because we know the interpretations and associations. But even people who've never been to our ceremonies before often get very caught up in it, because they're being given permission to acknowledge death—permission, not just from one person but from a whole community. Permission to say: "This is important, this means something, this is a time to stop and pay attention to death."

WESTERN IDEAS ABOUT DEATH CHRONOLOGY PART 6

❦

Diseases brought by Europeans kill great numbers of Native Americans. Diseases suffered by colonists wipe out entire settlements. Warfare between colonizers and Indians exacts a terrible toll on both sides. Colonial America is rife with death.

1600s	Early settlers place plain headstones with simple inscriptions of names and dates over plots in graveyards not yet attached to churches. As they become more permanently established, graveyards are more often found next to church buildings, as is common in Western Europe.
1662	A book by Michael Wigglesworth entitled *The Day of Doom* becomes the first American best seller. In 1662, one out of every twenty settlers in the Bay colony owns a copy of this poem describing the hellfire and punishment awaiting sinners on Judgment Day.
1677	The first of many major smallpox epidemics breaks out in Boston. Approximately one-fifth of the city's entire population dies. Outbreaks of infectious disease periodically rage through the densely populated towns and seaports. During these epidemics legisla-

tion is passed restricting the tolling of funeral bells because they ring so often, they become a public annoyance.

The slave trade becomes firmly institutionalized in the colonies as both Africans and Native Americans are bought and sold into servitude.

Most of the African people brought to America come from a tradition that emphasizes extensive bonds of kinship continuing beyond death. In many African societies the land where the ancestors are buried is the sacred connection between self and clan, clan and cosmology. To leave this land is to be cut off from intimate communion with the power that guides both the individual and the community.

Native Americans also maintain personal and social stability through connection to ancestors and consecration of place through burial or death ritual. As Native Americans lose their land, they lose their connection to their dead and to the spiritual power that anchors their culture.

In the European settlements, graveyards are established as needed and are frequently neglected over time, or simply covered over and obliterated as the population increases and urban areas expand. There is little sense of connection between the dead, the land, and the community.

Individual ownership of land will become the economic basis of the new social order. In both the African and the Native American traditions, individual ownership of land is inconceivable as the land is, in a sense, "owned" by the dead, permeated with the spiritual source of all life, and consecrated by that presence on behalf of the tribe as a whole.

The conquest of European colonizers over Native American nations will not only destroy the Native American people and their way of life, it will remove from mainstream Western culture a view of death based on a spiritual connection to the natural world and to the dead.

BRENDA
Age: 14
Student, Indian School
Santo Domingo Pueblo

⌒

I have a friend, she's fifteen, her mother died just recently, about a month ago. She sort of got murdered. Well, actually, she *did* get murdered. I felt awful and, at the same time, depressed for her because she felt awful about it. I come from a full Native American belief. There is a story to comfort you when people die, but for her, she couldn't handle it. It was just too hard. Sometimes something really big is kind of beyond comfort, you know?

BOB GOLDEN
Age: 27
Computer Programmer

≈

There are some guys over at Carnegie Mellon who are trying to perfect a computer program that will allow you to download your consciousness into a hard drive. So when your body dies, the computer can just take over. Everything you think, everything you know, everything you think you know, will be incorporated into this machine and you will be able to live on indefinitely, without the hassle of a fragile flesh-and-blood body.

Personally I think they're nuts, but somebody's taking them seriously cause they've got some serious funding. It's spooky but it's where you wind up if you just go single-mindedly along that path of technology over nature. I don't know, maybe it's inevitable. Maybe it'll be better. If we're all machines we won't have to worry about the air or the water, all the pollution. We'll be able to exist in whatever horrible toxic mess we wind up making for ourselves.

It's like this joke a friend of mine told me. An alien being comes to earth from another galaxy where everything is different, and it is studying us and how things are here and we're explaining and we say, "So everyone is born in this way, you know, sex, and then out of the womb and then we live about, oh, on average seventy-five years or so, maybe a little longer, and then we die."

And the alien says . . . "Everyone dies?" And we say, "Yeah." And the alien says, "In seventy-five years?" And we say, "Well, yeah, you know, give or take a few years . . ." And the alien says . . . "Everyone?" And we say, "Well, yeah, actually, sooner or later we all die." And the alien shakes its head and says, "Oh, well then. That explains it."

LAURIE ANDERSON
Age: 47
Performance Artist

∽

Sometimes I think that understanding death is more about under-standing time than it is about having a belief. Although almost all organized religious thought about death has to do with judgment of some kind, karma or the Catholic Church—it's: "How much did you rack up?" "How much good did you do while you were here?"—still, I think it's also about time.

Organized religion tries to explain time, to understand time, as does science. How can we exist in time? Do we come back in time? How can there be endless time or no time or how can you be out of time or what is it to live in this little space of time between two large blank spaces of time? Time's a big mystery. Time, and how it can work.

With religion the answer to that mystery stays the same; in sci-ence the answers keep changing. The latest one I've read is the Hawking radiation theory about what happens when things implode into black holes and seemingly disappear. Do physical things disap-pear forever? Hawking says no. He says that, theoretically, out of the debris of the implosion you could reconstruct the object, the car, the tree, the person, in absolute detail; that is, if you could capture the radiation at the right moment.

This theory also proposes the existence of an infinitely long tunnel in which all of this information is forever skidding along—all of the information that made up that particular object when it disap-peared.

So I think for most people the question is: "When I implode, where do I go?" And it's a good question. At the moment, science says—"Into an infinitely long tunnel."

Personally I don't understand the concept of infinite or endless, so that answer doesn't work for me. But I do feel, as opposed to understand, I *feel* that the world is endless, that time is endless and we are endless. But it's not something I understand . . .

When I was little I was indoctrinated by a grandmother who believed very strongly in heaven, in the rewards that you'd get, the pearly crowns in heaven. She was someone who couldn't wait to die, she looked forward to it. She was going to go to heaven and be a bride. I was never quite convinced myself, because I couldn't really imagine heaven.

When she died I was maybe seventeen or so and I visited her in the hospital. Like many people who are dying she had gotten very, very light. She was incredibly excited about dying. She'd change her nightgown every few hours because she wanted to be wearing the right thing. Then she had a last-minute moment of total and utter panic when she couldn't decide whether or not to wear a hat. This was a very traumatic thing for her. She would put them on and take them off, one hat after another, and finally she died wearing one hat and holding another hat, just in case.

Since then I've gone through a lot of different ideas about what I think death is and I'm sure I'll change my mind again, but probably not as significantly as I have done. I know nothing really. I've felt some things and I believe some things but I don't *know* anything and I don't think anybody else knows anything. They might believe it but they don't know it.

Personally, I *believe* that death is a release, an interim state that's very light, full of light. And then you come back with a thud. Heavy with all the meat, you know? Bump. I think you hover about for a bit and then you give up on that when you realize you have no way of affecting things that happen and then I think it gets dark and then I think you're reborn. Perhaps into human form, perhaps into some other form of life.

I think it's important to let people go. When my friend, the artist Gordon Matta-Clark, died, he was a Buddhist and the lamas said, "Don't call him back, don't cry."

Gordon's twin had died a few months earlier and one of the axioms of being an identical twin is that they usually die within a few months of one another, six months to a year or so . . . incredibly close. Gordon's twin jumped out a window and it was shortly after that that Gordon went to the doctor and they said, "You've got cancer in every organ of your body and you have about six weeks to live." He went to Jamaica to get laetrile and did all the alternative therapies and died basically cancer free, but by that time he'd had about eight triple bypasses and his body was completely worn out.

Ultimately, for Gordon, I think it was quite an ecstatic experience and one that he decided to make very social. This was the first time I'd ever been involved in a death that was so open that way. He invited his friends to be part of it and he was writing a book about it and he would read to them from it.

I was upstate the weekend he died and I saw Gordon, sitting on the porch of the house where I was staying. As soon as I looked away he was gone. It's the only ghost I've ever seen. But ever since I saw him I'm convinced that people hang around for a bit, that they don't really know they're dead for a while. It's just too big an idea to grasp all at once. I think there are some days of confusion, so that it's especially important for the friends of that person to be as encouraging as possible to the dead person. Let them know it's okay to take off and we understand and wish them well, rather than sobbing hysterically, which will, I think, attract that person and impede them, impede their progress.

And, of course, in some cases it's a real relief when someone dies, if they've suffered terribly. That was the case with Bob Regher, a Warner Bros. record executive who was very supportive of my work. He had been a good friend to me and I spent a lot of time with him as he was dying.

He had gone to the dentist and they were drilling and they bumped into a lump in his jaw that turned out to be cancer. By the time they had carved away the offending meat there was about an eighth of his head left. He died a tremendously horrifying death. He only allowed his daughter and me to come and see him, and it was truly awful to see something with no ears, no mouth, one eye and a tiny little hole where a nose should be and know that it's your friend. He had throat cancer from years of smoking and that's how *that* can be. I would lie on his bed with him and hold his hand. Of course he wasn't able to talk so we wrote notes to each other. He was outraged about dying. I would leave and go smoke an entire pack of cigarettes in a row.

There's no doubt in my mind that there's a big fight between the life impulse and the death impulse and for many people it's a constant balancing act and struggle. I accept that struggle and I also think it's interesting and I'm not depressed by it. I think there's a lot to pay attention to in that realm, a lot of things do involve loss. This is just our life. A lot of our life is sad. A lot of it is about loss and a lot of it is about joy but I don't think it's overwhelmingly about joy, not for me anyway.

I try to pay attention to other ways of seeing the world and one of them is watching things disappear, noticing that things die all the time. Lots of things. It happens on so many levels. You can be with somebody you've known for a very long time and realize that something has fundamentally changed and you don't relate to them at all in the same way. They've become a stranger to you. That's a death as well.

On a very gross level, you can think of death as something where, after a whole lifetime of pumping up, your physical body begins to rot and three or four hours later you're a stinking mass of bone and meat. Or you can think of death as something that happens all the time, many times before the actual physical death, and then the particular instant of physical death may not be so important.

Death can be a very positive thing, and certainly with Bob it was a great relief when he finally died. But then, to see the frail piece of him that was left at the end was very moving because there was something of Bob even in this monstrosity that I was looking at. Here was this headless person who'd shrunk to a third of his size, but still there was something of him there. Actually, there were two things—there was his sense of humor and there was a tremendous anger. Those were the two warring things that were going on, and my feeling was that he was able to resolve that before he died.

I had a very positive feeling when I heard that he'd died and I trust that because I do think you get a kind of radiation from the situation. It can be a creepy feeling or a good one, and in that sense I definitely got a good one. I thought he was . . . glad.

You know, so much of our lives is about disincorporation. So many of our experiences now are mental. With your computer, even with your phone, you don't really see that person, but you feel as if you've seen them. Movies, for instance, are a way of disincorporating. I'm not saying I think heaven is virtual reality, but I do think people are getting more and more used to having mental experiences that raise the question: "Well, why *isn't* this person sort of alive?" They seem alive, they might even have the same impact on you as if they were alive. So there are ghosts everywhere. I think, theoretically, that should make it easier to be one yourself.

SHIRLEY STAPLETON
Age: 48
Secretary, Wife and Mother

༄

My experience with dying has been mostly about money. That sounds awful I know. Crass and cold. But the truth of it is, when my mother-in-law was dying, it all came down to money and trying to figure out how to pay for everything. When my parents die it will be the same. If I was going to die tomorrow, the biggest worry I'd have would be how to do it so it didn't cost too much for my family.

I know this could sound like I don't care about love and grief and all that, but I do. We do. This family loves each other very much and I care about what happens to my parents. I cared about my mother-in-law. She was always good to me. When the kids were born she helped me out a lot. It wasn't one of those things where we didn't get along or anything like that. I really liked her. I loved her. It's just that I feel so tossed around, so stretched out trying to take care of everybody, I don't have any energy left for taking care of people dying. I wish she had just dropped dead of a heart attack or something quick. For her sake as well as my own. I pray my parents will die quickly. Boom. Done and over and all you got to worry about is how to pay for the funeral. I know it sounds bad, I know it sounds awful, but if I'm honest about it, that's how I feel.

My husband, Hal, was a systems manager for a big company that laid off a lot of their middle management people about four years ago. At first we didn't realize how bad it was going to be. We thought he'd get another job doing pretty much the same thing. But there were a lot of other guys out there in the same boat and so many companies were laying people off, downsizing they called it. It was downsizing all right. It downsized us.

He was out of work for a long time. Now he's got a job as a dispatcher for a trucking company. It's hard on him. It's a real come-down. He gets depressed.

I was lucky to get a job as a secretary again, which is what I did before we got married. I mean, I'm not one of those women they talk about who wants it all. I just wanted a home and kids. That's what I wanted to do, raise my children, make a nice home. Now I work at this job because I have to. We couldn't make it without my paycheck. Thank god we didn't lose the house. We came close, but we managed to keep the house.

Hal is an only child. His dad died years and years ago. His mother hadn't been well for a long time. She had osteoporosis and bronchitis and several other ongoing problems, but she had managed to continue to live in this tiny little apartment she paid for with her dependency pension and she lived on money we sent her. Everybody called her Nanna. Her name was Hannah but the kids called her Nanna when they were little and it stuck. Everyone has called her Nanna for years. Nanna went to the doctor with pains and bleeding and she wound up in the hospital with colon cancer.

Finally the doctors said, basically, we've done all we can do, and it was up to us to figure out how to take care of her as she was dying. They wouldn't let her stay in the hospital because there wasn't any treatment to give her. That surprised me because everybody I ever knew died in a hospital but now they try to get you to take them home if they're going to take a long time to die. The insurance doesn't pay for it anymore. She wasn't being treated. She was just dying was what it was.

When we started talking to the discharge people at the hospital about taking her home, I began to realize we had a problem. It turns out that if you're at home, Medicare only pays for part-time nursing help and not for what they called "custodial care," which was fixing her food, bathing her, that kind of thing. She needed around-the-clock care. The hospital people said we should talk to the hospice people. At first I thought the hospice people would come and take care of her but it turns out you need to have somebody who does the twenty-four-hour care and then they *help* you do that. Which is nice but neither my husband nor I could leave work and stay home with her. We didn't have anybody who could do that. I found out later that in different states and different cities some hospice programs do take care of the person whether you are there or not. It's quite different from one part of the country to another. I've learned a lot about this since then, but when we were dealing with it I didn't know the score.

We started looking into nursing homes but the nice ones were all full up, they had these long waiting lists. One of them said it would be several *years* before we could even *apply* to get in. And they were very expensive and there weren't that many that were official Medicare places and even then Medicare only covered the first few weeks and then we had to pay for most of it ourselves and we're talking a lot of money here. The whole nursing home thing was such a shock for me. I didn't realize how expensive that was. And we already owed the hospital for the part of Nanna's bill that Medicare didn't cover. It was one ugly surprise after another.

The hospice social worker was really nice. She tried to help us figure things out. The hospital people were not so great. They just wanted Nanna out of there. The social worker said that the hospital couldn't discharge her if we didn't have some kind of care set up, but Hal got real upset at this point. The social worker started talking about Medicaid and Hal thought of that as welfare . . . well it *is* welfare . . . and he just freaked out. He wouldn't tell the hospital that we couldn't take care of her. He acted like it was no problem, like we had it all covered. I'm thinking to myself, "What is he talking about? How can we do this?"

I look back on it now and I realize why he did that. I mean this was his mother and he couldn't take care of her. Coming on top of his really depressing years of unsuccessful job-hunting, it just about did him in. And the way the hospital people acted, it made him feel humiliated. So he basically told them there was no problem. He put up a big front.

I let him talk me into bringing her home but it was a mistake. We put her in my son's bedroom and he slept on the convertible couch in the living room. Everybody was trying to help out but we were all really overwhelmed. It got so nuts. One person told us we needed to hire a lawyer to help Nanna "spend down" for Medicaid. That was the wrong thing in our situation. Nanna already qualifed but Hal was talking to people as if our finances were better than they were. It confused things. This whole experience made me realize how money runs everything. Everything. Including dying.

Hal couldn't take leave from his job. He'd only been there for six months. I talked my boss into a short medical leave and the hospice people came and they were really helpful. They taught me how to give her these shots for the pain and they helped with a lot of things. A nurse's aid came for an hour each day and there was a volunteer who helped with things like shopping and stuff but she could only come a couple of times a week. They were great but the whole thing was so hard.

Nanna was really out of it by this time. She was having these dreams and would cry out in the night and wake everybody up. Morphine dreams. I remember hearing something about that a long time ago, about drugs and hallucinations. Morphine dreams they call it. The hospice nurse helped me adjust the medication and we figured out a different schedule and it got better, but that experience really broke Hal down. I saw him cry one night. I'd never seen him cry before.

Thank god Nanna wasn't all that aware of what was going on. She had never really come back after the surgery. I think the anesthesia was too much for her, at her age. She didn't say much that was real clear and lucid but you could tell she was sad.

One day I came into the room and there were tears rolling down her cheeks. I went over to the bed and took her hand and I said, "Nanna, does it hurt?" And she said, real soft, she said, "It's gone." I said, "What do you mean?" And she said, "It's all broken."

She was staring off, like she was talking to someone else. I don't know what she meant. I don't know if she was talking about her body, or her life, or what—maybe she was remembering something from a long time ago. I have no idea what it was for her, but what happened to me was, it was like this floodgate opened up inside me and I just started crying. I felt this terrible terrible sadness and tiredness and loss. I remember I put my hand on her forehead and she closed her eyes and kind of moaned and then I tried to give her the shot but I was crying too much, I couldn't see. I wiped my eyes and managed to give her the shot and I stayed with her until she fell asleep but then I got out of there because I knew I was going to cry real hard and real bad and I didn't want to do it sitting next to her.

That night, lying in bed, I thought about killing her. That's the truth of it. It sounds awful when you say it out loud but I thought, if I could just give her a shot that would let her die quietly, peacefully, in her sleep, it would be the answer to everything. Putting her in a home where we didn't know if she'd be taken care of or not, you know? You hear such stories and I'm sure they're true. The way everything is set up, it just figures they'll do the least amount they can do. Maybe leave her alone for a long time, uncleaned and all that, or they tie them up to the bed . . . you hear such awful stories.

That night was a low point for me. I had gone back to work. My boss had been really great but he needed me there and if I couldn't be there he was going to have to hire someone else. The hospice people were trying to help us keep her at home but one day the volunteer didn't show up when she was supposed to and I was late to work and it just wasn't working out. Hal was tied up in knots. I was exhausted. The whole thing was really hard on the kids. I don't know for sure what Nanna felt but like I said, I think she was really sad. I lay in bed that night and I swear to God, if I'd known how to do it I think I would have just "helped" her to die right then and there. Like I said, it was a low point.

Nanna qualified for Medicaid to pay for a nursing home. Medicaid is for poor people, people on welfare. But in the end it was a matter of having to face facts. She was poor. And we couldn't afford anything else and it wasn't working out trying to do it at home.

The next horrible step was applying for Medicaid and then trying to find a nursing home that would accept her as a Medicaid patient. But finally Nanna went into this home. She died about two months later. We had a very simple funeral with a pine box and that was that. I think Hal would have borrowed the money for a fancy casket if he could have. It would have made him feel better. But we couldn't borrow any more money, and besides, I told him, it was really more dignified this way. More simple. It was . . . reality.

I think you've got to face things as they really are and not try to pretend they're different. After you die maybe you wind up somewhere nice and easy, but here, you've got to deal with difficult things and it can be real messy and hard and it can feel really, really bad. Maybe that's the difference between life and death. I wouldn't say I believe in hell. I think death brings peace. I hope it brings rest. No more worrying. I'll tell you, the idea of eternal sleep sounds pretty good to me.

We're Christians, we go to the Presbyterian church. I know it would have been a terrible sin if I had helped Nanna to die. I mean, it would have been murder. I know that. But I sure understand people who . . . well . . . people who think about it anyway.

Recently I saw something in the paper about people dying at home. The article made it sound so nice, like everybody used to live together in one big house and the babies were born there and the old people died there and they all had a great old time. I don't believe it. Not for one minute. I think the women had to take care of everybody and the only thing that made it work was if they had a lot of money. That's what I think. And I think the only thing that makes it okay now is if you have a lot of money. Then you can get help and you can have a reasonable life and you can have this wonderful experience of being able to help the dying person or whatever. But if you don't have money, it's a real serious hardship. I hope my parents just drop dead. I can't imagine what we're going to do if they get real sick and take a long time to die. I just don't know what we'll do.

JAMES BLAKE
Age: 52
Professor, Department of Student Life
Borough of Manhattan Community College

❧

My older brother died when he was thirty-four years old. He died because he did not receive proper medical care from the emergency service. He was down-and-out in a little flat in Brooklyn and he wasn't treated properly. By that time I had moved out of that community and had gone to college and gotten a degree and had a life of my own, but I always maintained a closeness with my brother.

When he died, and I discovered that he could have lived had he gotten proper medical care, it angered me so, it was another one of those things that bring you to a profound realization of the racism that exists in this country, when a person's skin color decides whether that person will or will not get what is necessary to live.

I grew up in Corona, Queens. The first time I experienced open racism head-on was when I went away to North Carolina Central University. I'd heard about it but I never really faced it like that until I went to North Carolina. I couldn't eat in the restaurant and I couldn't use a certain bathroom. There were actually store signs that said "White Only," "Colored Only." This is 1960.

I became very involved with the student movement, civil rights, integration. During that time we were all wrestling and struggling with a lot of the concepts that we'd been taught by our parents. We became estranged from our parents because we confronted the system that they had grown to accept. And of course a lot of them were concerned about our safety, wondering whether we would come back from college in a coffin or whatever.

I left the civil rights movement and became a nationalist, black power, the Pan-African Movement, etc. I wasn't a Muslim then and I didn't anticipate becoming a Muslim, but we began to echo a lot of things that I learned later were Muslim-based. "Before I'd be a slave,

I'd be buried in my grave." The idea that oppression is worse than death—this is a Muslim teaching.

I knew of Malcolm, of course. I had grown up right in the same neighborhood as Malcolm and I knew of the Black Muslims. I invited him to come and speak at the North Carolina campus and that's when I first met him personally. He was very impressive—humorous, intelligent, quick-witted. He presented an image of vitality, strong and vibrant, he gave off a powerful positive energy. The man was alive.

He gave a talk at one of the local churches and the custom was for whites to sit in the front and blacks to take whatever seats were available in the back. At that time there was complete segregation. A lot of students from Duke University were interested in hearing Malcolm and they arrived at the church and took all the seats and those of us from North Carolina Central, a black college, were standing in the back. When the Muslim brothers came in they moved all the whites and put us in the front. We were given preferential treatment. That was a profound experience.

Malcolm stood in front of the church and behind him he had the sign of the crescent and under it he had the word "Life," and next to that the sign of the cross and under it the word "Death." And he would say, "Which way do you choose? Life, the sun, moon, and stars, or this cross of death which represents the double-cross that black people have experienced from white people in this country?" This was a profoundly different perspective than any of us had at that time.

But I didn't become a Muslim then. What brought me to the Islamic faith happened later. In 1972 the New York City Police Department invaded Muhammad's Mosque #7 on 116th Street. There was a violent clash between the Muslims and the police and shots were fired. Now, police officers were beating and killing black people every day but here was a group that refused to allow police to beat them. They got the police out of the mosque and when the smoke cleared one police officer was dead and all the Muslims were alive. I said to myself, "These are some bad dudes." I wanted to know what kind of spirit, what kind of mind-set they had that would allow them to fight and to win.

I was so angry with the racism in this country and I knew that individually I was going to have a minimum impact. I wanted to be with a group, but not with people who were crying and whining and turning the other cheek. I really went to the mosque because I wanted to belong to the baddest black group in America. That's how fed up I was with racism.

I found it was truly a religion, truly a way of life. They did not preach "turn the other cheek," but they did preach balance. They ended every meeting saying: "Remember the Honorable Elijah Muhammad taught us never to be the aggressor. If we are attacked, we fight those who fight against us, but we are never to initiate it." That was what they taught. I liked that, and I joined the Nation of Islam.

For a while there I saw all whites as devils and all blacks as having the potential of being the reflection of God. It was a complete reversal of the usual racism. Where all these years we thought you were superior to us, now we realize that we're actually superior to you. It was like a medicine.

At that time, the Honorable Elijah Muhammad talked about the fact that the Christian Church's teaching about death was a false teaching. The idea that when you die you go to heaven with milk and honey and everything is rosy, this was an idea that had been used to keep black people from living on this earth, here and now, and getting what was here for them, like all other groups.

He taught that heaven and hell were really conditions of life, not places, and as long as we focused on a reward after death we would never seek the reward that God has for us here, while we live. He taught about racism and the psychology of racism in terms of the whole issue of life and death.

Now I came from a family that was very involved in the Baptist tradition. I wasn't, they were. This explanation of the afterlife as a false promise helped me understand the skepticism I'd always felt about that religion. I began to read about the slaves and how they sought heaven after slavery; how ministers were hired by the slave owners to teach the slaves about the greatness of suffering in this world and how their reward would come in the afterlife; how all through our history in this country we've been given this really convoluted notion of what death is—as if it was a reward for suffering.

But the Honorable Elijah Muhammad taught that when you're physically dead you're dead, that's it. He said the worst death is mental death and spiritual death. When you don't have knowledge of yourself and knowledge of others and knowledge of the world around you, you're not truly alive. He referred to black people as dry bones in the valley, people who are just lingering, existing on the earth but not really living. He said the black man and woman in America were living in a coffin, a mental coffin, a spiritual coffin.

He went on to say that heaven is here. You don't have to look up in the sky, the earth is already in the sky, suspended in space and better than any environment on any other planet, so what are you looking up for? You're already up and you have everything on this earth to make a heaven for yourself. He said, "Look for heaven here, now, not after death."

The Honorable Elijah Muhammad was able to masterfully present the whole notion of death as a mental and spiritual condition, and heaven and hell as conditions of this life. He showed that those young brothers who were killing each other in the hellholes of America were only falling into a trap that was laid for them by the racial supremacists of this country, that what they were doing helped the white racists to maintain their society.

He said if you self-destruct it's because you don't know who you are, you don't know where you come from. You have no knowledge of your language, your history, your religion. All that was stripped from you as slaves and for four hundred years you've been given a weak religion and a weak concept of death and a weak concept of heaven and hell. He said hell was where the black man is. What could be a greater hell than the condition that we're in, when we can't feed our babies, we have no decent schools and decent homes, our families break up and our kids die young? What greater hell can you have?

He taught that God said man can change conditions, that once you become spiritually alive and mentally alive you can change your physical condition. You can reflect God and find heaven here on this earth.

And that's the basic foundation of the teaching of Elijah Muhammad. He got black people to stop looking for something after death, and to realize that whatever they needed was right here on this planet; the hereafter was not a place but a condition here on this earth, a paradise which would thrive and be prosperous for our children after we were gone. This was the teaching on death from the Black Muslim point of view.

When somebody died under the Black Muslim faith, we would have an immediate funeral, before the sunset of the next day. No moaning, no groaning, no crying. No outward expression of emotion. There would be prayers said and then we'd pass out a mint to all of those present. At one point in the service we'd put the mint in our mouth and it would dissolve, but after it dissolved it left a sweet taste and that was symbolic of the life that we had lost. We remembered the sweetness of that person's life, we had the sweet memory of that person and that would be it.

There's no "Oh he's happy now." It was, "He's gone but his works live on, his contributions live on." According to the Honorable Elijah Muhammad, the true death is when your life is so insignificant that you made no contribution to the life of others, in this case to the liberation of your people; then your death would be like somebody who stuck their hand in a bucket of water and then took it out. It would be like it was never there. The true blessing is the positive impact you made on this earth, the works that you've done that people will remember.

In February of 1975 the Honorable Elijah Muhammad passed and with his passing came major changes. His son, Warith D. Muhammad, who was a Sunni Muslim, became the head of the Nation of Islam and he brought a more mainstream perspective to the teachings. Gradually he began to talk about Islam from the Sunni perspective. He described his father's teaching as a bridge for black people in America to cross over in order to move into mainstream

Islam. He said that if we had been introduced to Islam without the teachings of the Honorable Elijah Muhammad, we would have rejected it outright. We would have seen it as an Arab religion, and not something that was given to us as black people. He also felt it had been necessary to kind of shock people, to bring people who were stagnant and who had a deep sense of self-denial into a greater sense of who they were and a greater feeling about their potential, like a wake-up call to black people in America.

As loyal Muslims and those who loved the Honorable Elijah Muhammad and who therefore transferred that love to his son, we began to absorb these new teachings and began to look at the whole concept that Islam has no color.

Islam really has only two major principles. The reality of God, the Creator, and the idea that the sun shines on everybody equally. Islam dictates respect for every prophet of God regardless of where they come from. It's not who they are, it's who sent them. They say if Jesus, Moses, and Muhammad were to meet on the streetcorner, they would embrace one another, because, in essence, they really brought the same teachings. So this kind of universal approach began to enter into the mosque.

This seemed right to me at that point because I don't think it's natural to hate. I don't think it's our nature, and it's not a good feeling. I think we hated out of a condition, out of a circumstance. We were responding to the hatred that was perpetrated against us, in a defensive manner. What Warith D. Muhammad taught was that it's okay to respond to the hatred, but remember, you've got white devils, black devils, yellow devils, and brown devils. Satan and a satanic mind is not housed in any one particular pigmentation.

This was also appealing in that it permitted many of the believers to reconnect with our Christian brothers and sisters. Not that we're going to love everybody else and have no love for ourselves, but basically saying, if a person is good and that good is manifested, then we can reconnect to the good.

And Sunni Muslims have a different concept of death than that taught by the Honorable Elijah Muhammad. Mainstream Islam teaches that there *is* a paradise after death, a reward for goodness after death. But goodness isn't translated as suffering, goodness is translated as treating people with equity and with respect, regardless of color and regardless of their religion.

At death there is a ceremony called the *janasza*. First the physical body is cleaned with oils. If it's a male the brothers clean the body, if female, the sisters clean the body. Then it's wrapped in fine cloth and the face is turned to the east, which is Mecca. Then prayers are offered, very simple prayers, and there might be a statement or some comments made about the person. In some ways, it's the same as Christianity. The body is buried or cremated and there's a gravestone or memorial marker of some kind.

We don't believe in reincarnation. We believe that the spirit is the real essence of the person and the body is just the house that the spirit dwells in and that spirit can go on to a paradise-like existence after the physical body dies, or it can go on to a hellish condition, depending on how well you've prepared yourself on this earth.

The Holy Qur'an says, "From Allah you came, to Allah you will return." If your heart has become so hard that you refuse to believe, you return to a chastisement, it is called "a grievous chastisement." Turmoil and a troubled spirit. No peace, no real rest, no real comfort because your spirit of evil and ugliness continues after your physical body has gone, leaving you in everlasting turmoil. If you die the death of a believer, one who believes in Islam, believes in the Prophet Muhammad, believes in charity, believes in prayer, believes in fasting, believes in equity, believes in being just, then you're going to paradise. If there's any sense of pain at death, it would be because you knew a brother died an unbeliever.

But you have to remember, the most important attribute of God, of Allah, is mercy. Mainstream Islam teaches that God is all-merciful. He is forgiving, He can rehabilitate you. God does not look at just one moment of time, one moment of existence. He looks at the holistic picture—What have you done with your life? As we say in Islam, "What is your Book of Deeds?" For every good deed, you receive ten blessings, for every evil deed, you receive one equal consequence. So mathematically, good will always outweigh evil. Evil can never get ahead. In the end, everyone will return to God. *Allah-U Akbar*—Allah is the only true reality.

My Muslim name is Takbir Muhammad. It means that there is nothing greater than God. It is a reminder that God is greater than the life I experience and God is greater than the death I will experience. The Creator doesn't discriminate when it comes to death. You're going to taste death, I'm going to taste death, we are all going to taste death. No one knows the hour or the appointed time. Allah is the knower. The Holy Qur'an teaches that not a leaf falls from a tree without the permission of God. He knows why he permitted this leaf to fall from the tree at this particular time. The point is, if you're a believer, you're ready for it.

BETTY WEST
Age: 61
Mother and Homemaker

❧

You don't have to worry about the death of someone who believes. When someone is dying who does not believe, or someone like that says something to me, I just say, "Well, we've got a loving God." That's all we can say to them. We can't promise them something that's not in our power but we can hope that God will be forgiving of the ones that never made their commitment. I offer my condolences and I offer to do whatever I can to help them physically, and let it go at that.

I was raised in Hoosier country, pretty near the small town where I live now. When I was growing up, we had a farm and raised our own food. My father was a coal miner. Although most people think of the Midwest as farm country, this was a flourishing coal-mining territory around here. Through the years we've had a lot of deep mines and now we have a lot of strip mines. Of course, we have several very large farms in this area and we have a lot of cattle farms and grain farms too, but mining was the basic means of making your living. Now it's dying out. The large mines are closing and moving away.

My parents moved to this territory very young in life, when they were first married and raising their family. I was the youngest of fourteen children. My mom raised eleven, three died young. Times were tough but somehow there was always food on the table. I never dwelled on material things growing up because I didn't know all this stuff existed. I didn't know people had bathrooms inside and those kinds of things. We were not a wealthy family in material ways but we were wealthy in other ways because we had a lot of love and attention.

I grew up in a Protestant home and my family were all Protestants. We still attend the same church. I guess you follow the line of your parents. Most of the people around here have pretty much the same ideas and traditions. Our belief is that when a Christian dies they are better off than we are here. We believe we go to the Lord and later our bodies will be reclaimed, we'll have a new body, a perfect body when the Lord comes back again.

I can remember when I was young, people died at home and they kept the bodies home. The neighbors would come and they sat up all night with them and they did the kinds of things that a funeral home does now.

I had a sister who was two years older than me. She died at age four so I was only two but I remember she had a violent death. She had whooping cough then it turned into brain fever. She had such a high temperature it actually just cooked her brain. It was a hard death. It was. And it was hard on my mother.

The neighbors came and brought food and helped with everything. They cleansed the body and dressed her, they sat with the body through the night. My older brother just worshiped this little girl and he went out and bought her this pretty little white dress for them to bury her in. And they put this white dress on her and fixed her hair with a bow and she looked like a little angel.

My mother always went and helped others when there was a death, she would cook or bring food. I can remember the first time she took me with her. It wasn't a scary thing at all, it was just what you did. The tradition was different, the times were different.

And it was much less expensive. Now when they show you the clothes and casket and the vault, people tend to go overboard because they want to put them away the very best. But this is not sensible because it's all going underground and the cheaper vault and the cheaper casket would do the same thing. Especially when a family is financially strapped. To bury a person now in this territory, the very cheapest is probably around four thousand dollars. And that's not going the luxurious route, that's not first class. And the funeral home is just doing the same thing that the family and friends used to do themselves. It really went commercial.

And I'll tell you something else, I'm not so sure that the way they used to do it isn't the proper way to do it because now, when you have a family member at the funeral home and you know at four o'clock you're going to have to go in there, you dread it. This is the first time you're going to see this body dressed and prepared after death and you don't know what it's going to be like, you dread what it's going to be like in that sort of artifical setting. And if you are the wife or the mother or the closest relative, you're expected to be there for four or five hours because people are coming in. It's an awful strain for a family.

I think, probably, the old-time people had the right perspective because the friends and the family came in at the time of death or as the person was dying. It was all done together—the death, the people coming, the viewing, the helping. The body was cleaned and dressed but it didn't get fixed up in an artifical way. They lived with it in the house and it wasn't scary or anything, it just was. These things weren't separated out, do you know what I'm saying? And after the services those people were still there to comfort that family. They went all the way with them.

Now it's all separated out. There's this viewing you have to go to. You think to yourself, "Oh my, it's ten o'clock, and at one o'clock I've got to go do this." And you have this dread. And friends will come and they'll be all emotional and it makes you emotional. Me personally, I don't want to have to show my emotions. I don't want people to see me being out of control or real sad like that. I think, back then, everybody had something to do to help with the death and it made the emotional part different somehow.

You can see why it all changed but I think we've got it out of proportion. I think we are elaborating the material part of it too much. We need to get back to the basics. But it will never happen. It gets hard to change things once they get a real hold, it definitely does. We go with the tide instead of rebelling, we just go with it.

One thing I try to do about death is to be sure the children and the grandchildren understand about it. There is some that will not take their children to the funeral home or to a service, but I have always taken mine. I think it's important that they know early that death is a part of life.

Recently, when my sister-in-law died, I took my little grandson to the funeral. He had never seen a dead person in real life before. He went up to the casket, put his little hands on the side and looked in and he said, "Grandma, who is that?" And I said "That's my sister-in-law and she's asleep." And he looked again and he said, "Looks to me like somebody killed her." That's the way he said it.

I thought, I can't let him think this and I said, "No, honey, nobody killed her." And I told him how dying is a part of life and how we are Christian people and when our people die their souls are with Jesus and you don't have to worry about them. I wanted him to know that dying in real life was not television death.

I explained that we have to face death but as Christians it's easier to accept because when we die our troubles are over and we are going to be with the Lord. The Bible tells us there'll be no tears and no sorrows and we know that we'll be better off and this is a consolation.

When children die, we explain that they are going to be with God and he is going to take care of them. He's going to love them until their mommies and daddies are there with them and they'll be okay.

I have a friend whose little boy was eight years old and he was dying. When he asked if he was going to die, she looked him in the eye and she said, "Yes." She explained to him that he was going to be with God and all he said was, "Mommy, would you bury some of my little cars with me?" She was very strong in her convictions. It was very touching. And I certainly believe, as that mother did, that until a child is of an accountable age God is going to take care of him without any problem.

The truth is, you don't have to mourn the death of a Christian, and although it can be very, very hard to bear, in the end you accept death as part of life and you go on. One way or another, we are all going to die or the Lord is going to return. As Christians we know that peace lies in store.

EDITH WALLACE
Age: 87
Psychiatrist and Teacher

☙

My background was a very liberal Judaism. I always say, "My mother was an atheist, my father was a sentimentalist and I'm a Jungian who practices Sufism."

I was born in Germany and I was kicked out. Hitler didn't like me. I didn't like him either; it was mutual. Many in my family died in concentration camps. We were surrounded by the threat of death in Germany at that time. I went to Italy but Mussolini and I didn't get along either so I came to England. I was there during the Blitz, bombs were falling, people were injured and people died. Of course these are periods when you are afraid. In times like that, one is dealing with death as part of the outer life.

But I am an introvert, you see, so my life is determined by what happens inside, not by what happens outside. Let's say someone in your circle dies, sure it will affect you, but the real thing happens when you begin to think about your own death. The real thing happens when you come across the fact that life is not eternal and you can't waste it.

Now the subject of death comes up because of my age. I had a friend who lived to be ninety. She'd had a heart attack at age eighty and I asked her what influence that had on her and she said, "Until that time I thought I was indestructible." So it isn't so much about your age as it is about your inner attitude, what's going on in your inner life. When do you start to ask yourself about death and to ponder the difference it makes in your life?

I believe in synchronicity. You come to what is important to you as a result of meaningful coincidence. Life is not really linear, things don't happen in that obvious cause-and-effect way, but more as meaningful coincidence.

How I came to meet and work with Jung is a good example. As

I said, I was in England during the war and you couldn't go anywhere because the bombs were falling. Then, one Saturday, we finally got out and we went to a bookstore in Tottenham Court Road
and I picked up a book called *The Way of All Women,* by Esther
Harding. (She had been one of Jung's early students.) I already had a
Ph.D. and my medical degree but I had no idea who Jung was or
anything about him. I was simply intrigued by this book's title. I
began to work with Harding and it was very exciting. I felt I had
discovered something. I decided to become a Jungian analyst. I knew
this was the right path for me. Eventually I wound up working with
Jung himself, and with Emma Jung, his wife. I'm one of the fortunate people who is doing what she is cut out to do and it unfolded
from when I picked up that little book. All these things came about
synchronistically.

I was in my fifties when I met J. G. Bennett, another great
teacher. He had his own teaching based on Sufism and on his studies
with Gurdjieff. Gurdjieff's idea was that we're not really born with a
soul, the soul grows through the way we live, *we* develop it, *we* grow
it. That idea was interesting to me.

It's clear to me we have to learn about life, we don't know that
much to start, we have to grow into it. I see the truth of this even
more now, when I'm closer to death and want to make up for some
of the darn foolish things I've done in my life. Nothing spectacular,
just the usual human failings, being selfish and inconsiderate, that
kind of thing. I've lived a long time and I know it's important to lead
a good life, to live a life of love.

I would like to die consciously. Some people say they want to
die in their sleep, and of course they mean they don't want to suffer.
That is certainly understandable. To be in pain, to be unable to
breathe, that one wants to avoid. But to die consciously means only
that you know what's happening. You might be unconscious to the
eye of the beholder, but you're ready. You're prepared. You've settled your accounts as far as you can. Including estate planning!

Of course I'm making a little joke but it's true as well. We do
have complicated lives and one must do these practical things for the
people who survive so that they don't have any troubles. This is how

we live today. But it's a concession, it's not a substitute. As you grow nearer to death, estate planning may be necessary but it's not the only way you need to prepare, or the most important. What is important about estate planning is the love and consideration it shows for your survivors, for your loved ones.

In the Sufi tradition, we say, "Die before you die." "Be in this world but not of this world." There is another world which you need to contact now. When your ego takes the backseat, you have greater freedom and *may* contact that other world.

When Jung speaks of the Self, it could be translated into "the essence," what I like to call the original being coming to life. Then you live with that essence, not with the ego in the forefront.

Jung went to India. He saw that the Indians have the concept of Self that he was talking about, that they'd had it for a very long time. But we come from a totally different tradition. We need ego to live in our Western world. Jung put it this way, he said, "They start where we have yet to get to." I usually say, strengthen your ego first, because only a strong ego can take a backseat. Ego is a jealous power and we need the observer or we go mad, the collective unconscious takes over. That's one big difference between East and West.

In the East there is an environment that supports an egoless state, even on the outer level, materially. In India you can still go around as a *sannyasin* (a kind of monk) with a begging bowl, and you'll survive. In New York City the beggars are pushed aside, dismissed. They are certainly not admired as egoless monks. That's our culture. That's the world we live in. We can't just take some idea or another about what we should be and tack it onto what we really are. We have to be careful what we take up, we have to be careful what we swallow and what we don't swallow.

It's the same in thinking about death. In the Sufi tradition there isn't a strong emphasis on exactly what happens after death. The emphasis is on what we have done in life. I'm comfortable with that. I don't think we can speculate as to what it's going to be like, our imagination gets in the way, and our wishful thinking. Our very living may determine our vision of that world which we call "the other world." There are many things that happen in the psyche and sometimes we turn them into the belief that we are contacting the other world.

Of course we are trying to penetrate the seventh veil, as it is sometimes called, but for me the veil is still hanging there so I can't say anything. If I'm not sure about something I don't like to make a statement about it. Ask me in twenty years. If I'm not here, ask me anyway, if I can tell you anything, I will.

I think when awareness is hidden, it's hidden for a reason. Thank God we don't know what the future will bring. Think over your life. If you had known about some things beforehand, could you have stood it?

At this time it seems that we are not in a position to know many things about death, in spite of the testimony of people who have had after-death experiences and come back to tell about it. There will always be the unknowable, the mystery about death. There could be a place to which human beings can evolve where they may know more than we do now. I could perceive that for the future. We are playing with it, playing with the potential of enlightenment. There is something that is true and real, something we are moving toward, but we're not there yet.

I believe we *can* learn to grow a soul, to strive and work for understanding. But that also means don't take any crap. Don't say, "Yes that's what it is," when you don't really know it, when you haven't felt it, when you haven't experienced it for yourself. Whatever your understanding is, it has to be real.

LIN
Age: 19
Student

⌘

I won't talk to you unless you promise not to let anyone know who I am because I really really really don't want to hurt my family in any way. They are amazing people and have worked incredibly hard to make a life for us here in this country. Besides, talking to someone about things like this would be considered very, very uncool, very crass in their tradition. They don't understand the American way of talking openly about your family or how you feel about things or any of that.

My parents came from Vietnam in 1971 and at first it was very hard for them, really terrible. Although my father was an engineer in his country, here he could only find work as a laborer. My mother didn't speak English very well and couldn't get a job at all. There was discrimination and all that and they had a very hard time.

I was born here and I am an American. By the time I was born my mother had learned English and had a job. My father was doing better, making more money, and they saved every penny and did without things until they could afford a better apartment. They worked so hard and they felt very isolated I think, very alone. So they held to their religion and their traditional ways very tightly.

At home, even though they always spoke English so that we could speak well outside, still in everything else they tried to keep to the old traditions. Like the food, the holidays and all that. They are Buddhists and there are many of those traditions that are very important to them. When somebody dies you do this whole elaborate thing about it. You need to have the monk come and there's a long ritual with prayers and chants. You wear white and burn incense and it goes on for days and days.

For me, it isn't anything I can really relate to. It isn't what I feel like I am. I think the American approach to death is more realistic. You just take care of what has to be taken care of when it comes up. You don't fall back on all the superstitions of the past. The other kids I know mostly just let it take care of itself.

For me, I just want to be an American. Last year I finally left home to go to college. I won a scholarship to the school I wanted to go to but even then my family couldn't accept my moving away. I'm the oldest daughter and they really had hopes that I would stay close to home, marry, continue the traditions. But I just can't do it.

Mostly here at school it's fine, I'm accepted for what I do and it's okay. There are a few other kids dealing with some of the same things. I notice the different ways they handle it. There's this one guy here who is half Native American and he's real proud of that. He talks about his heritage and his traditions and everybody kind of admires him for his heritage and I can understand that, but they don't realize the other side of it. There's this girl here who's from Latin America. She said the same thing I feel. People don't realize that with the old traditions there's a lot of stuff they would never accept. Basically you're trapped with the family, I mean really trapped. You can't do anything on your own. In the old way, marriages are arranged, the whole thing. Everything is within the family. You have to do what they say. Before I left home sometimes it felt like I could hardly breathe in that house. And outside there is so much going on, so much I want to be a part of.

Like I said, I really love my parents and I really appreciate what they did for me. They lived through some terrible things, in Vietnam and here too. In Vietnam there were people dying, it was a war, it was horrible. And then, here, they were poor and everything and they made it so that me and my brother and sister can have a better life. They've been through a lot of bad stuff and they need those rituals and old traditions to help them feel better. But I don't need those things. It's really different for me. Most of the bad stuff I have to deal with is about being half one thing and half another. That's what I feel bad about.

When my parents die I will try to fulfill their wishes to have the rituals of their tradition. I will do this out of respect for what they've given me. But I don't want that for myself and if I ever have kids I don't want them to do all that. I want to die like an American.

WESTERN IDEAS ABOUT DEATH CHRONOLOGY PART 7

✑

As colonizers become more established in North America, their death rituals and customs become more elaborate, reflecting European traditions.

1700s   Puritans characterize death as the "King of Terrors," and encourage a strict simplicity in funeral services.

Dutch communities build houses with a *doed-kamer,* or deadroom, in which funerals are held. Cakes, marked with the initials of the deceased, a bottle of wine, and a pair of gloves are sent as an invitation to the funeral.

Settlers of German extraction open a window immediately after a death so the soul of the deceased can fly to heaven. Then a bucket of water is splashed over the doorsill and swept outward, and the door immediately closed to keep the spirit of the deceased from reentering.

The Shakers, one of a number of religious splinter groups founded during this period, develop a cradle-shaped bed for the dying. They gently rock the ill and elderly from this world into the next.

As with many other traditions, the Irish eat, drink, and often use the occasion of a death as a time for lyrical commiseration and comradeship.

Children customarily attend funerals and when the deceased is a child they often take the role of pall-bearers. One child in four dies before reaching the age of ten.

As settlers move west they find evidence of deci-mated native populations, killed by European dis-eases for which they have no immunity. Trappers and explorers describe coming upon Indian "villages of the dead."

1760   Efforts begin to discontinue public tax support of the dominant churches. The separation of church and state helps to pave the way for a more widespread acceptance of Enlightenment ideas about natural sci-ence and philosophy. A more secular view of death begins to be possible.

1776   Adult life expectancy is thirty-five years. The me-dian age of the population of the new United States is sixteen years old.

As the population increases, new Protestant sects spring up, espousing a more benign view of death than that held by the dour Puritans who had domi-nated early New England colonialism. The images of death change from the fires of hell to sweet sleep in paradise.

A harbinger of nineteenth-century Romanticism can be seen on tombstones as gloomy death's-heads are replaced by angelic cherubs.

1798   Edward Jenner develops an inoculation against smallpox. Of all the people who lived before 1800, it is
estimated that one-fifth of them had died of this disease.

The influence of the Enlightenment permeates North America,
bringing with it the idea that science can answer the mysteries of life
and death.

LARRY DOSSEY
Age: 55
Physician and Author

∽

A lot of people today seem to have a love-hate attitude toward science. They are grateful that science has made life easier, but they also blame science and technology for many of the world's problems. In addition, many feel that science is the enemy of religion and that it has stripped life of higher, spiritual meanings.

I personally believe science can be a spiritual path. Originally that was what it was. Jacob Needleman, the philosopher of religion and author, in his book *A Sense of the Cosmos,* describes how the earliest motivation of the scientist was for an unmediated confrontation with reality. This is basically the goal of the mystic—the desire for a personal encounter with what is real.

At the time science began, around the 16th century, the Church defined the workings of the universe for everybody. But the early scientists did not want to take the Church's or anyone's word for it; they wanted to see for themselves. Unfortunately, as Needleman describes the process, within a generation or two this mystical urge was lost. Science had developed a new set of rules and procedures for interpreting the world. With time, one dogma was substituted for another—the view of materialistic science for the formulas of the Church.

Today most scientists would probably deny that science was originally an attempt to come to terms with the Absolute or the transcendent; the original impulse is simply not remembered. When it is pointed out, it is usually regarded as an historical embarrassment or as a whimsical, mistaken judgment.

It is rather sad to see how we've handled some of the views of the earliest scientists. Consider Sir Isaac Newton. Working in the seventeenth century, he was convinced that his accomplishments in alchemy would be the thing for which he would be most remembered. Modern scientists are rather embarrassed that our great hero, the guy who defined the laws of motion and gravity, actually believed in alchemy and that he devoted a great deal of energy trying to decipher the hidden symbolism of the Book of Revelations. The fact is, however, that Newton was a deeply mystical, spiritual individual, who had a profound belief that the hand of God underlay the workings of the entire universe. All that has been ignored; poor Newton has been sanitized.

So, in many ways science has become distorted. In spite of this, I still think it's possible to participate in science in a very spiritual way. I agree with the view of the Jesuit paleontologist, Pierre Teilhard de Chardin: "Research is the highest form of adoration." I think many scientists would like to see a sense of sacredness restored to experimental science and to medical science as well.

Things are changing dramatically in medical science. For instance, I don't know any doctor today who would seriously argue with the contention that the mind has something important to do with the body. This recognition has been gathering strength for the past fifty years. There's a Mind/Body Clinic at Harvard Medical School. About one-fourth of the medical schools in the country have courses in alternative medicine, which emphasize mind-body interactions. Several medical schools are developing courses on the role of spirituality in healing.

To be sure, the resistance to these developments is strong. Many continue to insist that "it's all physical." There are still lots of dedicated materialists who insist on defining the mind or consciousness as equivalent to the chemistry of the brain. For them, there is no such thing as mind-body interaction, only brain-body events. Anything to preserve a completely materialistic definition of human beings! True, the materialistic view has been productive in many ways. But it is quite dismal, because it implies that when the body dies and the brain rots, that's the end of consciousness and the mind. There is no possibility of survival of death in this view.

Not only is this perspective out of tune with practically every major spiritual and religious tradition that has ever existed, I would even argue that it is bad science. Why? Because there are scores of studies which show, to put it bluntly, that there are things conscious-ness can do that the brain cannot do. This means there must be something more than brain, more than body. It's this "something more" that fascinates me.

In one of my books, *Recovering the Soul,* I developed the idea that there is some aspect of the mind that cannot be localized to specific points in space, such as a brain or body, or to specific points in time, such as the present moment. I used the term "nonlocal" to describe this phenomenon.

I chose this word after great deliberation. Nonlocality is a con-cept that has been proven in experimental quantum physics, which looks at the behavior of the smallest dimensions in nature. Physicists have shown conclusively that subatomic particles behave nonlocally, that they can't be confined to specific points in space and time. They have shown that if two particles are once in contact and are then separated, a change in one is *instantly* correlated with a change in the other, no matter how far apart they are. In some sense these distant particles behave as one, although they may be at opposite ends of the universe.

The mind behaves in the same way. Scores of studies show that people, no matter how far apart, occasionally communicate instantly with each other by sharing thoughts, emotions, and even specific information. Like the separated particles, they behave as one. No one knows *how* these phenomena occur. Whether or not the nonlo-cal events studied by physicists are responsible for the nonlocal phe-nomena experienced by humans is by no means clear, although Nobel physicist Brian Josephson of Cambridge University in En-gland has proposed this theory. Examples that have been extensively studied in scores of lab experiments involve distant or intercessory prayer; remote viewing in which detailed information is conveyed between distant persons; transpersonal imagery in which the images of one individual actually cause changes in the physiology of a per-son who is far away; and many other categories of experiments.

The spiritual implications of these experiments are quite excit-ing. They suggest strongly that some aspect of our mind can exist outside the brain and body. As I've tried to show in my writings, this quality of consciousness manifests *nonlocally* in space and time. "Nonlocal" does not mean that something is merely far-off, or that it lasts "a long time." If something is genuinely nonlocal, it is *infinite* in space and time. Regarding the mind, this implies *omnipresence, eternality, immortality.*

If our consciousness indeed possesses nonlocal qualities, it begins to sound as if we're describing something akin to the soul—something that is eternal, that does not die, that has no ending. This is why the lab experiments showing that the mind behaves nonlocally may be indirect evidence for a soul-like quality in humans.

So, something quite strange is going on. Science, which has long been the archenemy of spirituality, is shooting itself in the foot by providing indirect experimental evidence for the soul, which it has long denied.

Even though I think modern physics may hold great potential for understanding how the mind behaves, I feel very uneasy about relying on physics as the sole support for spiritual views. The problem is that physics always changes. It may be supportive of one's spiritual views today, but what happens tomorrow when it changes? And it *will* change. People talk a lot about the "new physics." To be more correct, we should be saying the "newest physics"—because today's version will surely give way to another view. In science, change is guaranteed.

But no matter how much physics changes in the future, it will not erase the ways in which the mind behaves nonlocally. These phenomena are based not on interpretation but on observation. I am particularly fascinated by the experimental evidence showing that distant, intercessory prayer has a positive effect. There are approximately 150 studies in both humans and lower organisms in this area. About two thirds of these studies show statistical significance, meaning that you cannot explain the outcomes by chance.

These studies suggest that science and spirituality might come together in harmony, after being estranged for almost two hundred years. Our world sorely needs this rapprochement, because the separation of science and religion has caused people to divide their lives schizophrenically, setting their intellect and their sense of the spiritual in opposition to each other. This split is unnatural, and has caused immense pain for great numbers of individuals who feel that their intellectual and spiritual sides are *both* valuable.

I am disturbed by the hostility I see in many "New Agers" toward science. Many actually seem to *hate* science. We ought to remember that science remains one of the best ways humans have devised to guard against certain kinds of illusions. I believe intellectual, scientific approaches can make valuable contributions in the way we order our lives, *if balanced with spiritual practice and understanding.* I often hear people advocate doing away with scientific technology in medicine, claiming it is too remote, technical, and inhumane. I think this would be silly. It's not that we need to abandon science in medicine, it's that we need to learn how to use it more wisely, more compassionately.

As we approach a new millennium, I hope we can recall the spiritual roots of science, and bear in mind that because it has profound limitations, it must be supplemented with other ways of gaining wisdom. I hope also that we can muster the courage to follow scientific evidence wherever it leads, including the evidence pointing to a soul-like quality of ourselves. If so, life on our planet may be transformed.

What choice do we really have? As André Malraux, the novelist and former minister of culture of France, said, "The twenty-first century will be spiritual, or it will not be at all."

R.I.P. HAYMAN
Age: 44
Composer, Writer and Performer

❦

I spent many years working in China on ships on the Yangtze River. There I developed heart palpitations, what's called ventricular fibrillation. The heart loses its rhythm, quivers and stops pumping blood. I blacked out two or three times but I self-revived, much to the surprise of people around me. Then one time I didn't. Fortunately I was having breakfast with a medical technician next door to a hospital in Singapore. They rushed me to the emergency room, resuscitated me and saved my life.

During the process I floated out of my body and could see the whole scene going on below me. I saw them wheeling me into the emergency room, strapping me up and getting ready to give me electroshock. I saw this frenzy of activity, but was looking at it from a completely dispassionate vantage point. I felt released—in the sense that there was an "I" at all—I felt released, particularly from my body. It was as if I were pure perception, there was no material sense and I was floating in an infinite space. A soft light kind of held me or drew me along.

I had no physicality, not even a mental separation from the profound sensation that surrounded me. And it was bright, very bright light, but I could look back and see what was going on. I could see them working on me although I was not really very interested. I felt quite joyful. It was like being reunited with something, a sensation of great beauty and transcendent love. There was a spiritual ecstasy and a feeling of finally being on the way.

Then they started calling me to come back. "Can you hear me? You're gonna be all right. Hold on!" And I'm feeling, "Oh man, why should I go back, especially to an emergency room and all this trouble?" But then, boom, they started my heart again and I was suddenly back in my body. My consciousness came back and I could feel the needles in me and everything they were doing. Typical of people who have been resuscitated, I did not enjoy this resuscitation one bit, but I was in no condition to protest.

Subsequently I was in critical care for three months because my heart kept stopping. Whenever they took me off lidocaine, my heart would stop again. It would just up and stop. They would barbecue my chest with a defibrillator, which was kept warmed up next to me all the time. Oddly enough, in between these "episodes," I felt fine except that I was in the hospital, on an IV drip, being given endless tests, the whole medical menu.

Finally the doctors did experiments on me to see which drugs might ease this condition, whatever it was. They never found the cause, what would predict it or anything to stop it. No congenital heart problems, cholesterol, hormonal problems, neurological problems, all down the line. I went through every test they had except an autopsy, which I refused to give permission for. All in due time, all in due time. I am medically referred to as an idiopath, which means my ailment has no known cause. No medicine can prevent the instability in my heart. The only treatment is resuscitation by electric shock.

As a last resort, they implanted an automatic defibrillator unit around my heart. In my belly they put a big battery pack with a computer about the size of a Walkman. It's all wired up with electrodes for shocking my heart back into rhythm. That's what keeps me alive.

The episodes recur without warning every few months, just to keep me on mortal notice. Last year it went off five times when my heart stopped. I fall down, the "box" charges up, beeps a couple times, and then boom, kicks me back to life and I get up and continue what I'm doing, without any ill effects. It feels like walking across the room on a dry day on a wool rug and you get a static shock. That's what's keeping me in this world—about 15,000 volts of mini-amperage that goes "zap."

This gives me a wry sense of things, an attitude like—"No matter what you say to me, son, you can't shock me. I have a built-in defibrillator that will bring me back every time." I'm like the Duracell rabbit, actually. I come back no matter what happens.

This is a modern miracle of technology. Guys like me—I shouldn't say guys, I should say *humans* like me, or maybe even *laboratory rats* like me—in the good old days we would have just keeled over and died. About half of fatal heart attacks are due to arrhythmia seizures similar to mine. No warning, no minor condition, nothing that can be treated. I'm either on or off. I'm a digital guy, I guess.

My cardiologist, who is usually dealing with difficult multiple-complication cases, says I'm his dream patient because I'm almost dead and then zap! and I walk out and have a completely normal life. But I'm on a short medical leash because I have to get my battery checked regularly. Every two to three years they have to implant a new unit because the battery runs down. That costs about $20,000, for which I used to be insured but now I'm not. To an insurance company I'm your basic preexisting condition. I've been booted off one plan and now I'm on my wife's union plan, but it's bankrupt and she's getting booted off that. So we're your standard American health-care-crisis story. But that's a different book, right?

We're talking about death and I do have an unusual point of view because of my situation. I'm perched on the fence and I have to say I enjoy it. I'm definitely not afraid of dying. This is typical of people who have had near-death experiences. Often they actually look forward to dying and I *do* look forward to going back. It's a wondrous passage and there is definitely something out there. But it's a one-way trip as far as I can tell. Others might debate that but, for me, I feel very lucky and blessed to be around for however much longer I have.

I have a certain feeling of patience and joy that I didn't have before. I used to be far more concerned about work, love, money, all that stuff. Things weighed upon me more. Now I feel if there's trouble, there's trouble, I'll deal with it. But it doesn't get under my skin and I don't feel the stress and strain that I remember having before. I feel more detached from things now.

Clinically this is a pretty typical reaction. Often people who've been brought back have a change in their emotional state where they don't feel as closely attached to things as before. For some people this becomes a problem in the family or with their spouse or loved ones. Maybe they suddenly become rather otherworldly. Some people drop what they're doing altogether and go off to do something completely different. Once they've faced death they realize they only have so much time and they want to do things they didn't do before. They might take up a spiritual path and pursue that. They might change their work or stop working altogether.

My philosophy and purpose in life were not greatly changed by my experience. I am all the more committed to my family and my work. I didn't make specific religious associations. I remain a universalist and value all faiths based in wonder and compassion. But I do have a feeling of . . . I don't know, maybe you could just call it a greater patience.

I came back before reaching the higher or further stages of the near-death experience that have been described by many people: meeting deceased friends and relatives, life review, voices from God or other kinds of spiritual guidance. I had just begun the trip when I was brought back. Others have been out for days and have awakened with quite fantastic visions to tell about, with far more profound experiences than I had. Something like that can really change you.

I went to a conference of the International Association for Near-Death Studies and there were endless testaments to the experience. And of course there are a lot of books and publications, almost a mini-industry around this now. I understand this because you feel you should share it or do something with it, you want people to know about it. Since I've been a composer and writer for many years, what I decided to do was to compose a music and visual piece recreating my own near-death experience, or NDE as they're called.

The piece, entitled *On the Way . . . ,* was produced as an audio work, a computer-generated sound field that gives a sense of distance and expanse without any foreground imagery—an ambient music. I would compare it to what you hear when you walk into an empty cathedral. There is no particular sound but your auditory perception encompasses that surrounding expanse, not just your ears but your whole body senses the space. That is what I tried to re-create in the audio work.

The visual component is a warm flowing light that covers an overhead screen and fills the peripheral view, to simulate the NDE "tunnel of light." It bathes the space while a projected stream of soft light-streaks and spots move forward around the center of vision in an effect similar to snow streaming at a windshield or to the star-stream of a sci-fi film.

One aspect of NDEs that I've included in this work but that I did not experience myself was what is called "the Void." This has been recounted in the research literature as one of the final stages of the near-death experience where, after you've had the light and the bliss, you have an experience of darkness that is referred to in religious literature as the dark night of the soul. It's been described as feeling lost and disoriented or even terrified. A small fraction of people have experienced a great sense of terror and come out of it emotionally devastated. At this conference I mentioned, one person after another was describing how the NDE filled them full of love and God and a sense of bliss. And then this man got up and said, "Mine was different. I was terrified and destroyed. It took me years to be able to stop shaking and get ahold of myself."

It's very much an open question as to what this is. Some people in the field surmise that this is an advanced stage of the process. Perhaps after you've had your blissful spiritual experience it all evaporates and you are left terribly alone. This man at the conference was heard, but there was really no way of reconciling it with all the other stories. Just as there's no way to erase the terrible grief and sadness that some people feel when they've lost someone, particularly to a tragic death. And of course there are people who believe death is a profoundly disturbing and terrifying thing altogether. I don't think these two views can be reconciled. Personally I think they are two sides of the coin. All you can do is try and balance it.

I did not reach the void in my experience but when we were working with the theatrical lighting to create the visual effect for *On the Way . . . ,* I was using dimmers that could produce a black center in the field of light. I realized that here was a strong sense of the opposite from the joy of the light, providing a wider potential experience and creating an image that had to be confronted, so I left it in.

I'm still working to realize this piece. There are lots of ways to go with it. Computer technology could be used to realize a continual version. A virtual-reality version would be interesting, allowing a person to direct the sense of motion or visions or events. But I'm most interested in doing it as an installation in a public space, a gallery or museum. I want to create a room where people can walk in, lie down, look up at the ceiling and it will encompass their entire field of vision so that they will feel that they are ''in'' it, not just ''watching'' it. The sound would roll over them in wave patterns like a low, slow rumble that would come up from the floor. I want to build a floor that would have speakers underneath, and as you lay there, you would feel the low-frequency waves, actually *feel* them. They would tend to cushion you as you're lying there. And that would give a sense of the feeling that I had—as if I was being carried along by a pervasive yet very gentle force.

This would be a meditative work where the sound or visual image is meant to be listened to or seen not as an object of admiration but as a tool for spiritual passage. It is like the use of mantra or mandala artwork, particularly in Hindu-Buddhism or other spiritual traditions, where the artwork is an opening or a door or a springboard to a spiritual experience.

Much of religious ritual has this purpose. If you can release your mind from its perceptual stance, you may well see and hear more than is actually presented because you are tapping into something inside yourself. There are a number of ways this happens, even in everyday life. Those who are deeply affected by music experience a sense of a wonderful yet invisible force when they hear a piece they love. The music triggers a reaction, a release. Psychedelic drugs also induce a radical shift from ''normal'' perception. Perhaps these experiences are intimations of what happens at death. In death, the body dissolves, drastically changing our perceptual stance. Maybe the NDE just opens up a perception of what's already there, but we're suddenly free to experience it.

These are open questions: Is the NDE merely the last firing of synapses deprived of oxygen or is it a transcendent release of spirit to other realms? Do fading brains imagine sound and light at death, or does death allow us to finally perceive beyond our eyes and ears, to get outside of ourselves so we can really find out what we are? The Tibetan Book of the Dead describes this state:

> Be not afraid of the brilliant radiances of the five colors, know the wisdom to be thine own. . . .
> With these radiances, the natural sound of the truth will reverberate like a thousand thunders. . . .
> Fear not. Flee not. Be not terrified. Know these sounds to be the intellectual faculties of thine own inner light.

Maybe it's *all* just light and sound and we may make of it what we wish.

MEINRAD CRAIGHEAD
Age: 59
Artist

∽

Death is the mother of religion, poetry, art, philosophy, all of it. It's all an attempt to address death. No creative work is very far removed from death. Creating art is like birth and birth carries death within it. The whole process of making something is about beginning with nothing; you have no idea what's going to happen; you have your material, you have your paint or whatever, but you have no idea what's going to happen. You're bringing something into being which has never existed before. As it comes into being you shape it; it is of you and yet it has a life of its own. It has its own work to do in society. Every painting, every poem, every piece of sculpture, every play, every song, has its work to do, has its own organic life. When it's made, the artist is depleted, exhausted, dead. To be part of that cycle, to be part of that creation, the artist goes organically into death without even thinking about it. You have to give yourself over to the death in it.

It seems to me that my painting, my imagery rises out of what I call the personal compost heap. By that I mean every experience you have, every dream, every piece of beauty, every piece of pain, all of the stuff that piles up in a lifetime, in layers of your soul, creates this personal compost heap; all of our transferred memories, all of the familial memories, the ancestral memories that we received. Even if we don't consciously remember, they're in us because they're part of our body memory. We are not only what we eat, but how we were made, mother after mother after mother and father after father after father and so on. For the artist, images rise out of this interior soul compost like plants rise out of the earth.

In my paintings there are images of the Divine Mother, whom I see as the ancient mystery, the matrix of the Great Mother who gives birth to all. She is like a door. The door opens and we come into life. The door opens the other way and we go back into Her body and we call it death. It's a threshold. On this side is what we know; on the other side is what we don't know.

You could say Her body is the cosmos and that we are born from it and ancestrally connected to it all the way back through time, through the animals, back into the first movements in the slime, in the ocean waters and so on. Our bodies are made up of stardust and also primordial water. Everything we see around us is just a huge, complete, organic manifestation of this matrix, of this source. We came out of it and we'll go back into it. My painting is an attempt to connect with that source. It's like prayer. It's being in the deepest touch with the soul of creativity which I believe lies within us, and in deepest touch with yourself as a creator. In many ways, praying and painting are the same thing, both an attempt to connect to that mystery.

Praying has always been a core activity in my life. The religious instinct is deeply imbued in me. I've been many places and done many things but when I look back I can see that serving the religious instinct has been the goal of my entire life. And I don't separate service to the religious instinct from service to the world as an artist. For me there is no distinction between praying and making art. Sometimes when I'm praying, or sometimes when I'm painting, it's like going into an altered state. When you make the connection with that source, you move into a different space. I think death may be a lot like that—maybe not so different from sitting under the trees in morning prayer.

JOHN GIORNO
Age: 57
Poet

∽

My personal belief is that death is like a mini-mini-mini nuclear explosion. I don't know exactly how nuclear fission or nuclear fusion work but I think it's sort of like that, something is released. There is a big change, down to the subatomic level. Something is released and you don't really know what it is, nobody knows what it is, but you feel it. At the moment it happens you can feel it, and in the minutes and hours after. If you happen to be with the person who dies, you really feel it. Some kind of energy is there that's more than was there before the person died. Everything has changed and it's very dynamic.

Usually nobody realizes this or even sees it much because they're wrapped up in their own thoughts, or their own grief (which is itself a great release of energy because loss is a powerful emotion), or they're full of fear, or some other emotion. But if you happen to be in a place where somebody dies, and you can look at it very clearly and calmly, you're gonna say,

"Wait a minute, what just happened?"

I'm a Buddhist and Buddhists believe that when you die your very subtle consciousness is freed from the gross body. And when your consciousness is let loose like that, it is out of your control, sort of like when you're dreaming. While you're alive you're in control. You can think something through or figure it out, and act. But when you're dead—you can't do that anymore. At that point your consciousness is directed by your karma. You're left with the sum of what you've done in this life and every life before, and you don't know what will arise. You continue to move in whatever way you have learned to move, through habitual patterns. It's like you've stepped over a threshold.

That's why people are afraid of death. And that's why everybody should be afraid of death, in a certain sense. Because after they die they have no control over their consciousness the way they have in life.

I think a good analogy is homelessness. The archetypical fear that you could become a homeless person, you could lose everything you have and be like a homeless person in New York City, carrying whatever belongings you can manage to pull in a shopping cart behind you. It's a primitive fear that everybody harbors, it's loss.

Well, that's literally what happens when you die. You can't take *anything* with you, you can't take your money or your power or your intellect or even your ideas about what you're going to do. When you're alive you have all these ideas and you might even think about death and say, "This is how I'm going to die." But when you die you lose that rational, thoughtful ability, and you have this shopping cart of karma that kind of turns around and starts pushing you along. What happens to you will be some result of everything that's gone before and you won't have any control over it. So that's why people are afraid, as well they might be.

People who are not afraid of dying are people who have tamed their mind, those who have actually *practiced* letting their mind rest quietly, in great equanimity. Then, when they die, they can do that and it gives them a chance to rise above their karmic predisposition and not be blown about helplessly. This is true for people who have done great meditation in any of the religions of the world, be it Catholicism, Judaism, Islam, Buddhism, or whatever. If you've mastered your own mind in this life, as great Christian meditators have done, as any great practitioner has done, then you can do the very same thing when you're dead.

My friend Terry Clifford was a great meditator, and when she died the room filled with light, great clarity and bliss, like you were on a drug. But nobody was on a drug, it was just Terry's consciousness leaving her body and you saw it and you felt it.

Terry was a devoted Buddhist in the Tibetan Nyingmapa tradition. She had meditated for many years and had done five years of strict retreat. She was a radiant, beautiful young woman. All of a sudden she had lymphoma, then breast cancer, then tumors in her brain. From being totally beautiful and healthy, suddenly she was dead in three months. About ten days before she died we were talking in her living room and she was just luminous, with a brilliant mind, and she said "John, excuse me for a second." She turned aside and lowered her eyes and sort of rested in meditation for a few minutes and then turned to me and smiled and looked in my eyes and said, "You have no idea what goes on inside my head."

One just had to be completely amazed. She was taking no pain-killers and dealing with the suffering that arises when these tumors grow in your brain and distort and create hallucinations and the whole thing, and was able to deal with it. That's an example of being able to detach, realizing the empty nature of all phenomena, and resting in equanimity.

One of the many people I've known who have died of AIDS was this friend Carl who was an artist and a junkie. He was only thirty-six and he pretty much just refused to die. Here's someone who lived three years longer than he should have and of course was nothing but skin and bones at the end. A living corpse resting in ignorance. He was really really sick and the doctors couldn't believe he wasn't dead already and one of his friends went into the hospital room and looked at his chart and said, "My God, he's getting the equivalent of thirty-two bags an hour!" It was like a dream come true for a junkie. He thought he'd died and gone to heaven.

He held on, he was very attached. A lot of people hold on inexplicably and you wonder why. Strength from past karma is what keeps them here, grasping onto this life. My friend Robert Map-plethorpe had a grand mal seizure at the very moment of death. A totally severe epileptic seizure so that he was vomiting blood, shitting blood, screaming, completely demented at the moment he was dying and he only stopped shaking and writhing after his breathing stopped. One looked on that as not a very auspicious sign.

Tibetan Buddhism deals more directly and specifically with death than does any other tradition, more even than other schools of Bud-dhism, including Zen. It's a lot like the Olympics—although this is not a good analogy because there is no competitive aspect—but you could call Tibetan Buddhists the Olympic athletes of death. They really focus on it and have lots of techniques and exercises to prepare for the event.

It's about practicing, you know? Like there's this dumb athlete who breaks his balls, or breaks her back doing all these dumb exercises from the time they are a child, just to win this one moment, the gold medal. You go to the event and you do this thing and you've done it so often that you get a perfect ten or maybe you get a nine, but the point is you've practiced for it. You're just doing it one more time, like you've done it thousands and thousands and thousands of times.

It could be a cloudy day or a bad day, or you're not at your personal best or something so you only get a nine or an eight and a half, but it's the same as a ten cause your mind is there. It isn't about the score, it's the process. So indeed, Tibetan Buddhists, practicing Vajrayana or Tantric Buddhism, are the only people who work with death the way an Olympic athlete works with his or her body.

Of course, there are very few people who decide to become Olympic athletes. I mean, think about it, most people have a hard time doing even just a little exercise, even though they know it's good for them. And then there are those who don't want to do anything and that's indeed their privilege. And if they live their life compassionately, for whatever reason, that's wonderful. If you've lived a really good life with good intentions, and not caused much suffering, that's the second best thing because at the moment of death, the sum of your recent karma will kick in.

Doing good actions is really the expression of compassion, and compassion is nameless—nameless and totally ecumenical. Compassion radiating and filling the world is what forgiveness and generosity and all these clichés are, it's a real thing, a real vitality. If you are practicing compassion, it will actually change your situation. It's a literal thing, not just an abstraction.

All the time one sees people helping others and doing wonderfully important, loving actions—AIDS health care workers and volunteers are just one example. They do it from loving kindness, and from the desire to relieve someone's suffering. They may not be interested in anything spiritual yet they function as if they were really spiritual people. When they die all of those things come into account. Then, especially if they understand about calming their mind as they approach death, it can be quite good. It's possible to calm the mind without meditation. It's difficult but you can do it.

The way not to do it is the way nearly every single person in the world does it, be they Christian, Jew, Buddhist, or whatever, and that is—to have no spiritual practice, to not pay any real attention to quieting the mind and to just have these token moments of so-called spirituality.

In other words, you live your life every day, you get up, have coffee, you're busy till you're exhausted and you go to sleep and then get up the next day and do the same thing. Then you go to church on Sunday for an hour and sit there and hear the sermon, or whatever the teaching is, but while you're there your mind is endlessly thinking about whatever problems you've had that day or that week and on and on, so there's no spiritual context for anything in your life. There is no quieting the mind, it just goes on and on, endless discursive thought.

Then, when death comes and you become a homeless person, you're wandering aimlessly. Even though you've gone to church every Sunday for an hour, you haven't really paid any attention to the way your mind works and to the nature of reality. And now you're dead and your mind is totally out of your control.

Generally speaking, the teaching says that whatever you're feeling or thinking at the moment of death, that will affect what happens to you. For example, if you're really angry, that's what happens at the second *after* death. It's like if I'm angry at you now, ten minutes from now I'm still going to have that adrenaline of anger in my mind, right? And the same is true at the moment of death.

If you're angry, you immediately go to a hell world, so it is important to be in a good state of mind when you're dying. That's why practice is important, so you can learn to be calm and centered even though you're scared or freaked out. They say—to be able to rest in great equanimity even though you are being pursued by forty murderers. To be able to see the empty nature of all things, recognizing all things as a dream. Dealing with your mind, watching your mind and working with it, learning to rest in great equanimity—this is the critical thing from a Buddhist perspective.

When you are with someone who is dying, it is really a matter of *just being with them,* rather than putting your own point of view on them in any way. No matter how strongly I might feel about the Buddhist approach for myself, I would never put that on someone else. I just rest in great equanimity with them. One wants to help them, not create an obstacle for them.

From a Buddhist point of view, the final moment of death doesn't happen when the breathing stops. That last visible breath is only one stage in the process. There are a number of other stages of physical and psychic dissolution that continue after a person has stopped breathing. So if you are with someone as they die it is very good to just sit with them for as long as you can after they have finished breathing and to leave their body undisturbed so that the rest of the dying process can proceed peacefully.

Everyone has their own death to experience—their own unique death. You can never make an agenda about dying because it happens differently with every person. The generalities simply lead toward helping. You use the generalities *because* they lead toward helping.

It's good to have as much experience with people who are dying as one can. It doesn't rub off, you can't get tainted, no vitality will be taken away from you, no negative force will affect you. None of that happens. It's good to help because you're generating compassion and that's only beneficial, to yourself as well as to the person. And if you're with someone when they die and afterwards, just be slow and easy, show loving kindness, and be gentle, as if he or she was still alive.

CAROLYN BURNS
Age: 36
Hospice Nurse

༄

Working as a hospice nurse, one of the things I'm often asked is "What's going to happen?" "What's this going to look like?" "Is it going to be horrible?" "Is he going to die screaming?" People don't know what it's like to see someone die.

I think this is an area where the hospice movement and the shift toward people dying at home will have a very good impact. Especially on kids coming up, who will now have actually—maybe—seen somebody die, in the home, with the family around them. And they will see it's not a horrible, horrible thing. It's a *sad* thing. It's sad for the people who are left, but it's not a horrible thing.

Hospice helps dying people to be comfortable and live as well as they can while they are dying. The program provides drugs and equipment, home health care, psychosocial support, and help for the family so they can manage having the patient die at home.

If somebody is in the hospital and they are terminally ill that's usually where they enter our program. Rather than put them in intensive care, the doctor might refer them to hospice.

Most statistics still show about 80 percent of people dying in hospitals, but that's changing. You can't just put somebody in a hospital and leave them there to die anymore. Hospital administrators don't want that. The utilization review people are on the case. They stay on top of the doctors. "How come this person's still here? They've been here *x* number of days, what are you doing for them? When are you going to get them out?" The discharge planner at the hospital works with the family to help get the patient back home or into a skilled nursing facility. Hospice referrals are up quite a bit as a result of these policy changes.

Sometimes family members will call us and ask, "How do I get my loved one into the program?" A social worker goes out and does a comprehensive interview and explains all the details of the program and answers any questions they have. There are various permission slips to sign and we must have a DNR, a Do Not Resuscitate order, when you come into the program. (A DNR means that if the patient's heart or respiration fail, we do not try to bring them back.)

If the family's calling us they will have already given it some thought, so they're usually able to understand the need for a DNR. If the doctor calls us, then we have to make the initial contact with the family. Many physicians don't handle that really well, so we've learned to be careful and ask the doctor, "Did you talk to them about a DNR?" We've gotten to where we can tell by how long it takes to get the answer, or how evasive the answer is, whether they've actually brought it up. A lot of doctors get very antsy around explaining a DNR. It's helpful to tell the social worker, "Okay, we're not real sure that Doc has talked about a DNR, so tread gently around that until you get in there and know what's going on."

The main job at this initial stage is to try and find out what the family's attitude is; what they want, what are their needs and wishes. Some people are fairly comfortable and accepting of the fact that dying is happening here and some people are way back there going, "No no, it's not time yet." We have to find out where the patient and family are on that spectrum. Then we can work from that point to move the family along toward being able to get the job done.

I never interfere with people's denial. To me it's real important to simply accept where they are. Now I have worked with colleagues who *do* try to get them out of that denial, but I think part of folks feeling cared for is this thing they do sometimes—it's almost like a test they are giving you. They'll say something like "I'm gonna beat this, right?" And it's like they're checking you out. Are you going to play the game? How are you going to be about this? In answer to those questions I usually say, "I hope you're right." I can get very noncommittal because—who knows? Things happen. But I think it's often like a test rather than a real question.

We try to let the patient be in charge as much as possible. They make decisions about pain medication, they make decisions about how often they want the nurse to be there, things like that. People relax more when they realize that they're in charge. If they want to stay in denial, if they want to leave the program because they think they're not that sick or they want to try this coffee enema or whatever they want to do, that's okay, they have control. When this becomes clear it gets easier, because they don't have to put all that energy into trying to convince us of something. We're just there.

You see varying levels of denial but, as disease moves through its course, that denial gets harder and harder to maintain and most people, by the time they get to active endstage, are ready to die. They're tired and they will be telling you they're ready. And, in one way or another, telling their family.

More often than not it's about families and family dynamics. The patient is, of course, the focal point, but as time progresses they're taking pain medication, they're not engaged or active anymore, they can become almost an ancillary part of the job. It's the family that you are going to be dealing with and often the family is very frightened.

All the horror stories they've heard about death, from cancer in particular—they come up and have to be dealt with. What they want to know is: "What is this going to be like?" "How will I know when it's going to happen?" "Will it be awful?" We get a lot of questions like that, mostly during what we call the "driveway consultation." Someone in the family will follow you out to the car and ask the real questions, especially where there's still some denial going on. Sometimes it's the adult kids who follow you out. Frequently it'll be the wife. Probably in the marriage she's been in charge of the emotional aspect of the relationship and now she will have to find out what this is going to look like because Dad's just going to sit there and not deal with it. That's the way the dynamic often works, especially in older families. But almost always somebody asks those questions and when they do I tell them what my experience has been:

Most of my patients just drift away. They begin to sleep more and be awake less. Soon they begin to breathe less, it's a gradual shift. To me, watching it, it looks like an ebbing of their life force . . . the energy's not there, it goes away. It's a natural process.

That seems to help families, if you can tell them that in the beginning. You can't promise anything, certainly, but you can say, "This has been what I've seen." "This is how I've seen it happen most of the time." It can help take away those fears of screaming and horror and agony.

One of the things I've found most comforting in working with people who are dying is the fact that someone who has already died will come for them. The patient will see them. *You* don't see them but the patient will. It could be a mother, a father, a spouse, a brother, somebody they trusted—it could be a *pet*—but it's someone who's trusted. I've had this happen so many times. The patient will get very calm, although sometimes we've seen them argue with the person who comes, or they'll tell you that somebody's standing in the corner and they don't want to talk to them yet . . . the details vary, but it happens a lot. They'll tell you the person is at the window or at the door. And you're looking and there's nobody there.

I had one lady who said her uncle was coming for her and he was outside her bedroom window. As the disease progressed, he moved further and further into the house. And she was real clear that when he got to the bedroom she would go with him.

I think there is definitely some kind of physical process going on. Doctors will tell you it's hallucinations or it's drugs or hypoxia or it could be their electrolytes going out of whack as they become more and more dehydrated. I think it must be part of the breakdown in the death of the cells if you will, or chemical imbalances that somehow allow this hallucination to occur and to be comforting.

But they all have the same "hallucination." Now why would they all have the same one? It's too common for it to be nothing. The nurses and social workers have all had this experience, and we feel that it is in fact part of the dying process. Maybe it's the brain cells breaking down, the life force ebbing away, whatever, but the hallucination is too common for there not to be something to it. And it does bring such peace . . .

If you see someone who's been really important to you, who says, "It's time to come with me," well, it relieves a lot of fear, and, amongst our group of workers anyway, we all just accept it. "Ah, that means it's getting time." It can start happening a couple of weeks before they die or it can be when it's very close. We hear it a lot. It seems pretty universal.

The most difficult deaths I've seen have been with people who are very controlled. These folks have a really hard time letting go. One patient said to me: "I don't have any specifications. I don't know what to do when I get there." And he had a struggle. He was trying so hard to die but he couldn't get there because he didn't have a map, he didn't have instructions, he couldn't just let it be.

A scientist friend of his came to get him, appeared to him in the way I described. I had reached the point by that time where I said to myself, "Boy, I hope so," because nothing else was helping him. But what finally worked, now I'm thinking about it . . . he had a granddaughter and she wanted him to read her a story about a butterfly. It was her favorite story and so they read it and they read it and they read it, over and over, and of course, it was metamorphosis. And somewhere in the process of this child and this man reading this book together, he did get comfortable enough that he could leave. But he had a real hard time letting go.

I have seen people do it "well" and I have heard stories. My personal experience is that a lot of the dynamics and issues between couples and between family members have to get resolved, so it's not a Hollywood ending, or a pretty little picture where everybody stands around the bed and smiles and goes gently. But I've seen cases where people got together and worked out what they needed to work out and mended whatever fences needed to be mended. And I have seen people who just simply had such a strong religious belief that this was the will of God that, well, this *was* the will of God. But it almost seems to me that in order for it to be a "good" death you have to not need a map. You have to have faith.

One of our doctors uses a quote and I don't know whether it's his or he got it from someplace else, but he always says—"When you've gone to the edge of the known light, you must have faith that either there will be ground beneath your feet or you will be taught to fly." I love that because, to me, that's what this is. You've got to make the assumption that something is going to happen and it'll be taken care of. Those folks who are able to do that are able to be at peace. They're able to say good-bye, to get their affairs in order, to plan their funeral, to do all those things. Then they're able to say, "Okay, I'm tired now, I'm finished." And they'll proceed on down the road.

That's the patient's job, you might say. The family has a different job. They have to let go in a different way. A lot of what I hear from families is, "I'm really scared about this, I'm afraid I'll do it wrong." My response is, "There's no wrong way to do this. There's no manual here that will tell you right from wrong. Whatever you do is right." You give people permission to do it their way.

I've done visits where I never saw the patient. I sat down and had coffee with the husband, or looked at family pictures with the wife. The patient was sleeping. The patient didn't need me. Often the caregiver needs somebody who is safe to talk to, to say, "This really hurts, this is really hard, I'm afraid I can't do it." Or, "My family is telling me this isn't right. I need to put him in the hospital or I need to put him in a nursing home." And you come in and you say, "You know, you can do whatever it is you want to do and I will help you do it. Obviously nothing illegal, but you decide. You want to put him in a hospital? We'll move him as close to endstage as we can figure. We'll do it however you want, but I think you can keep him at home and I think you can do this. We will be here." My job is building trust and supporting what they want to do.

I'm often in awe of people. Many, many times, people with no education as our culture recognizes it, not particularly sophisticated or upper class—whatever word you want to use—they really rise to the occasion. Let's face it, nurses, social workers, we come in like this authority figure, we come in with all this expertise, but when we turn that back to them and say, "This is your house, this is your family member, you know what you're about, I'm here to advise, period," people do beautifully. Bless their hearts, they will blow you away.

I had a man who put on his wife's makeup every morning. She was in a coma. He had started helping her before she actually became unconscious because she could no longer do it by herself. She never got out of bed in the morning without her makeup. It had always been really important to her. So even when she was in a coma, every morning he would comb her hair, put on her eyeliner and powder and lipstick and all that stuff. It was such an act of love. And bless his heart, it looked horrible. I mean, *horrible*. I thought to myself, "Good thing she can't see this, she'd have a fit." But that's always stuck in my mind as being one of those awesome things that one person can do for another. I loved this man dearly. He said, "Well, it's important to her." Okay. Now would you come in and say, "You'd better not do that" or "You might put a pencil in her eye?" No. You just let people do. And they will do the most heart-warming things.

Then there is a point in the process when there is nothing to do. Prior to that point you have all these chores and things to do, but at the end, when the patient is actually dying, it's time to stop doing things. For most people, that's the hardest part.

Usually the patient is unconscious. Sometimes this will happen several days before death and sometimes it's only in the very last hour or so. Because of the ebbing of the life force that we talked about, most people will get so weak that they go to sleep, or what looks like sleep. They may rouse or you may be able to shake them awake, but they're not really sleeping, they are in the process of dying.

At that point families may try to wake the patient. "This isn't really a coma, see? I can wake him up." We try to tell them, "Don't wake him, don't try to feed him, don't cut back on the pain medication, don't try to bring him back, just let it be."

But it's very hard because suddenly all the tasks are done, all the busy-ness is done and there's nothing for the family to do but sit there and watch, and that's when they really start getting very, very anxious—when there's nothing to do.

It's a very hard time. It's when you get those crash phone calls and you just get in your car and go straight to the house. I always think about it as putting my shoulder into the family's back so they can't slip backwards at this point. "This is what we've been talking about, now it's happening. You can do it." And you're there to keep them from backsliding.

"Gosh, there must be something we can do."

But there really isn't.

"Maybe we should call 911."

If you 911 at that point, what would you bring back? Nothing. You just bring them back to do it again. But it's a real temptation and that's the point where you see all of your teaching and education pay off. If you can get them past that period where the actual death is taking place, once they come out the other side they feel very strong. And, I have to say, very proud of themselves in a way. It gives people the feeling they've done the right thing, they've seen it through. Statistics show it helps with the grieving process as well. For most people, it's really worth it in the long run. But they do get so frightened and I don't blame them, it's a point where you have no control.

When someone is dying, they're going to quit breathing when they quit breathing. For the person who's doing it, dying is an active process, it's not a passive process, people have to work. They had to work to be born and they have to work to get out. There is the physical change, the physical deterioration . . . some people have horrible tumors and difficult situations and some don't, but whatever the circumstances, it often seems to be a job. Especially when we get to endstage and there begins to be a breathing irregularity or apnea.

The brain stem controls our reflexive respiration and as the brain stem dies you may go fifteen, thirty, forty-five seconds without a breath and then—about the time you think there's not going to be another one—there'll be another one. You'll have these long spaces and then they'll take a big deep breath and there'll be another long space, then all of a sudden they'll come back and breathe regularly again. You can almost see that there's some kind of struggle going on. It's not a passive slipping away so much as—you gotta get out. And *they have to do it themselves,* there's nothing anyone else can do for them at that point, except wait.

Most families manage to do it. There are a few that can't and that's okay. We bring the patient in and he dies in the hospital and the family gets to be engaged as much as they want to be without doing the hands-on care. Some families need to do it that way.

Because that waiting is hard. They want it to be over, but when it's over . . .

From my own experience, I feel hospice work is a calling, definitely a calling. Not just anybody can walk in off the street with a nursing diploma and do this. Most of the nurses I work with are very gifted, but the ones that don't have a calling are having a very hard time and probably will move on. It's because of the losses, they can't keep doing the losses.

You have to be able to establish a relationship with a family, knowing that you're going to lose. That's the way it is. For me it's possible because I learn so much from these folks. They have faced reality, in their own way.

Like the guy who put on his wife's makeup. It would never enter most men's heads to do something like that, and this guy would no more do it for anybody else than he'd fly. It wasn't a "manly" thing to do. But in the crunch, he did the thing that he felt she needed him to do. Not because he cared about it for himself but simply because it was important to her, and she couldn't do it for herself anymore.

When someone is dying it's a time of great intensity and great intimacy. It is an enormous privilege to be allowed into a family or family group, however that group is operating, at that point in their lives. I've had experiences where I can see a family member a week after the death and they do not recognize me. It's so intense and so concentrated, and then it's over, it's done. You are no longer in that circle. But I carry the experience of that intimacy and I have learned something from all of these folks.

It's an honor to be included in this process and welcomed into this situation. I think everyone in hospice feels that way. People can be very open. Some of them aren't, of course, but most of them are. The truth is, when you get down to the nitty-gritty, there's no time for bullshit. You have to be who you are. It's an incredible experience, it really is.

RABBI SHARON KLEINBAUM
Age: 36
Reconstructionist Rabbi

⸈⸉

In Judaism we don't believe we can really know who or what God is. We can know attributes of God, we can know what it is to act in a godly way, but we can't be God, we can't control things. We don't have choice in this, it's just the way things are. We're human and our definition of being human is our lack of control, especially over this business of dying.

Given that we don't have choice about dying, the question then becomes—how do we live in the face of that reality? We don't wallow, and I take this from my history, from my tradition as a Jew. We can't focus on the ways the world is stacked against us. There are many ways that things are stacked against human beings struggling to live a long and decent life. We can focus on those things and become, I think, a victim of our own sense of being victims. Or we can try to come to terms with our lack of control. We can say, "Look, this is what we have. How do we transcend death? How do we deepen ourselves as human beings and reach higher to some kind of transcendence?" Despite the way the deck is stacked.

In the Jewish tradition there is a very clear focus on life, to the extent that even the Kaddish, the mourner's prayer, doesn't mention death. Its goal is to help guide the mourners back to life, not keep them focused on death.

In the same way, while there is a wide range of Jewish belief about the afterlife, the primary sense is that Judaism is not overly concerned with that question. Although there have been schools in Jewish thought that have focused on it at different times in history, in some ways we leave that question unresolved. Our job is to live in this world.

There is absolute agreement that it doesn't all begin and end with the human experience, or what we know to be our experience.

There is a belief in an afterlife but again, as with God, there is the feeling that we can't really know what it is. There's an understanding that there is mystery in the world, and some of these mysteries we will not be able to solve.

Now that's very humbling and I think that's good. Human beings could use some humility. We are not in charge; we don't know everything there is to know; we must live our lives as fully as possible in the face of this mystery.

All of the various customs we have can be said to be aimed toward this same goal. We have the funeral as soon after death as possible. Burial is within twenty-four hours if it's reasonable to do that. It's considered a dishonor to the dead person to delay unnecessarily. Also, it's felt that prolonging the burial makes it harder on the family and friends. Of course there are exceptions, and funerals are not held on the Sabbath or festivals.

Barring extenuating circumstances, there's no embalming, no makeup, nothing done except a ritual cleansing, called *taharah,* that's done in that twenty-four-hour period. It is said that just as a baby is washed and enters the world clean and pure, so do we leave the world cleansed by the religious act of *taharah.*

This is performed by a special group that says prayers over the body, recites psalms, and then wraps the body in a simple shroud made of white cotton or linen, plain, very simple. This group is called Hevra Kaddisha or Holy Society. They are lay people who are trained to do this service, this ritual. Men do a man and women do a woman, so you have two different groups, usually about five people in each group. Many synagogues have their own Hevra Kaddisha.

The night before the person is buried there is a guard, a *shomer* or "watcher," who recites psalms and stays by their side, so that the body is never left alone from the time the person dies until the time he's buried. More orthodox communities take that very seriously and people sit up all night reading psalms. In New York funeral homes they have someone on staff whose job it is to sit by the body. It's part of having a Jewish funeral.

The ceremony or the service itself is very simple. There is no attempt to gussy up the situation. The idea is that in death we are all the same. There should be no distinction between rich and poor. We confront the equality of death—the equality of death and the practical result of that. So everything is kept very simple.

Traditionally in Judaism, cremation is not acceptable. There is a sense that the body has to return to the earth to complete the cycle of life. For me personally, I don't officiate at a cremation. I'll do a memorial service, but not the cremation itself because I find the idea of a Jew voluntarily choosing cremation, less than a generation after millions of our people were cremated in Hitler's ovens, an abhorrent idea. I feel very uncomfortable with it. I agree with, and feel strongly about, the Jewish tradition that the body should return to the earth—the sense that from dust we come and to dust we return.

Customarily the casket is just a plain pine box. It should have no metal in it so that it can become a part of the earth again as simply and as quickly as possible. In Israel they don't use a coffin at all, just the shroud or a linen cloth. It's actually much more traditional to just bury the body in the ground. Here it would be culturally unacceptable to do that, so what we do is—holes are drilled into the casket to make sure that there's contact, so the earth can immediately come into the casket. Some people use earth from Israel because it's considered especially sacred. They take this bag of earth and place it underneath the person's head so that person is buried with some of the sacred earth.

I urge my congregants always to use the simplest, most traditional forms. Both because there's something very elegant in the simplicity of an unadorned pine box, but also because I object to the consumer-for-profit business of death. Judaism provides religious support for not spending a huge amount of money, and I completely support that. I object very much to the attempts of funeral homes to take people at their most vulnerable moment and empty their wallets for them, which, to put it crudely, is what it ends up being. I always encourage people to go with the simple, traditional ways.

So the service itself is very modest and the eulogy is primarily designed to remember the life of the person who has died. There's a sense that healing doesn't really begin until after the burial. The idea is that people at that stage are in a heightened state of grief and anxiety and pain and we have a saying that you can't really comfort somebody in the moment of their grief. Words don't work. You're not supposed to try to distract with chatter, you're not supposed to talk about the weather or the baseball game or work. In fact you're not supposed to greet a mourner. You should wait for the mourner to greet you. And the only thing you should talk about is the deceased, because there is nothing else relevant in those moments to reflect what the mourner's feeling.

It's regarded as a great honor to accompany the casket to the cemetery, and again, at the cemetery there's no attempt to hide the mourners from the reality of the death. When the casket is put into the grave it is a Jewish tradition for the mourners to shovel the earth onto the casket. This is considered a final act of love to actually do the burying ourselves rather than leave it to the attendants. Most of all, we consider it a mitzvah of the greatest order, a blessing or gift, because you can't expect anything in return for it. You're doing this out of love and respect. It's a job the person can't do for themselves. They need you to do this for them, even though it may be hard for you. It is the last gift you can give.

Many Jews who have been influenced by our dominant culture can feel this is messy somehow—let's be neat and clean, let's not actually get *involved* in this. But I think it is a tremendously important custom and I have revived it here at the synagogue.

I always explain it. I don't assume that people standing there know we do this, or will understand it or have experienced it before. Even the immediate family may not have actually done this. People come from different Jewish traditions and they don't necessarily all do the same things. But I believe very strongly in the wisdom of this particular ritual. It confronts us with the finality of death. You hear the earth hit the casket and it's like a stab in your heart. You hear it again and again, over and over. You say good-bye with each shovelful of earth; not "I'll see you tomorrow," not "You're just sleeping," but "Good-bye."

It's very hard. I know it sometimes shocks people. To many people who have never seen it before, it seems barbaric. I feel exactly the opposite. My experience has been that however painful it is to do it, it is a very important piece of the healing work that has to happen. We're not talking about a minor little break, we're talking about death. We're not talking about a tiny little thing that people need to just—you know, get a grip, get over it. We're talking about the loss of a loved one. And the work people have to do is equivalent in size to the experience of their loss. And the first thing they have to do is to actually experience the loss, to acknowledge it.

People who don't come from a Jewish tradition or who didn't know about this practice, have told me how surprised they were at how meaningful it was for them, how helpful as part of that whole process of mourning and healing.

Of course some people really don't want to do it. They don't have to do it. It's not that kind of thing. I ask those who want to participate to come forward. My general experience has been that most people do, but nobody's put on the spot or made to feel badly if they don't want to do it. Usually we begin with the family and the partner and then the shovel is passed around. If there aren't enough people, we simply cover the casket, but the idea is for the mourners to participate, in one way or another, in this act of burying their loved ones.

I conducted a service on Monday for a man who had died of AIDS, and I was struck, watching all these young men bury their friend, of how it was a way for them to be involved. Here were these men in their thirties and forties, strong, young, and they couldn't do anything to stop his illness and they couldn't stop his death and they will miss him terribly; and for twenty minutes they could be there and work hard physically to complete that final act for him. At this point, they *could* do something for him. It was very moving.

It's done in complete silence, and when it's finished the mourners say Kaddish and then they begin a seven-day period of intensive mourning.

Judaism sees it in concentric circles of seven days, thirty days, and then a year after the death. The seven days immediately after the burial are considered the most intensive, most acute, where you really can't think about anything else, you really can't do anything else. You are in this very intense period of mourning. You're not

supposed to cook, you're not supposed to shop. People are expected
to bring you food. You're supposed to cover the mirrors in your
house to indicate how you can't think about things like your appear-
ance or putting on makeup or perfume. Men don't shave. None of
those things are done, because there's a way that you just have to
completely be there with the grief. You can't run away from it. You
have to be there.

During this time we sit shiva, which is saying the mourner's
prayer, Kaddish. People come and visit, they bring food, they help
out, and a couple of times a day they say the mourner's prayer. Some
people do this for three days, some people for seven. Different traditions and backgrounds do it differently.

We are expected to visit so that mourners are not left alone but
are surrounded by people who care and understand their loss. The
traditional rule of visiting a house of mourning is not to talk about
chitchat or try to divert the person away from the deceased.

However, sometimes I walk into a house of mourning and it's
like being at a cocktail party. People are so uncomfortable. They
know they should be there and they do it, but once they get there
they think they're doing the mourners a favor by telling them about
the latest thing at work or what's going on with so-and-so, did you
hear she's getting married to so-and-so, diverting their attention
from the loss. But it should be just the opposite. This is the time to
ask questions about the deceased, ask questions about relationships,
look at pictures, to really carve out time to grieve and not let other
mundane things get in the way.

When this intense mourning time is over there's a period of
thirty days, which is a less intense period and then, over a year there's
a gradual return to life. Often, at the end of the year, a gravestone or
monument is unveiled. This is a simple occasion with just the closest
family and friends and marks the end of the mourning period. After
that, once a year, on the anniversary of the person's death, you say a
special prayer and light a candle.

All the rituals around death and mourning are designed to make
us look at our own lives. What are we doing that we're proud of?
What are we doing that we want to change? What did this person

give us that we want to carry on? It is a chance to confront our mortality, directly, and ask ourselves the big questions that we actively avoid in the day-to-day rat race.

Being located in New York City and being primarily a gay and lesbian synagogue, at Congregation Beth Simchat Torah we are at the absolute epicenter of this current plague of AIDS. We have non-AIDS deaths, of course; we're a large population with a sizable non-gay membership, but AIDS has required everybody here to ask these questions in a way we wouldn't have had to do otherwise. Male or female, gay or straight, if you're a part of this congregation you have to deal with AIDS, which means you have to deal with death, which means you have to deal with life.

Like many human tragedies, this crisis forges our strength in ways we simply couldn't have figured out beforehand. Now I'm not saying, "God gives us difficult things in order to make us better people." I do think it's true however, that living with adversity of all kinds strengthens people in ways they could not have predicted in advance. And AIDS focuses those strengths. I don't think it's special in that way. I think there are unique aspects of it, but it's not special. Anybody who lives facing life-and-death questions, who lives on the edge of life in that way—their senses are sharpened, their needs are sharpened and their perspective changes. And when you're talking about a population of young people dealing with this, as opposed to older people who are dealing with death at the end of their lives, it sharpens it even more.

As a result, people here are even more committed to life. If you come here on Friday night for services, well, any of my colleagues would be jealous of the energy with which people participate. People come to our synagogue not to please their mother or their father or their grandparents. They're here because they're genuinely interested in asking of religion the hard and real questions posed by living in New York City in the 1990s, and some of that includes AIDS. The whys, the hows. "How come me?" "How come not me?" "Why do I live when so-and-so dies?" These questions are out there. People come here to ask and to challenge.

And let me say, I don't think there *are* answers. If there were, somebody in America would have figured out how to package it and make a lot of money from it. It's more complicated than that.

In the face of this suffering, I think it would be the definition of hubris for religion to say there is an answer. What religion can provide is a context for people to explore the real questions about what life and death are, away from the superficiality that's out there in America today.

But again, with the funeral on Monday, I can't stand up and say to that man's family, "I have an answer." I can't sit with his parents and his sister, who sat with him for the last six months as he deteriorated from an active, vibrant, involved young man to what he was when he died—which was about sixty-five pounds of absolutely nothing there—and say I have an answer.

It is so difficult. There is such suffering. People dealing with horrible physical circumstances, the severe deterioration of their body, debilitating cancers, thrush, blindness, dementia. I can't stand there and say I have an answer. I don't know why people die ugly, ugly deaths that lack any sense of dignity or profound transcendence. These are the ugliest moments I've ever witnessed. And then, despite that, people somehow are able to transcend it. That to me is the miracle—absolutely miraculous. I've seen people who are able to transcend even the worst of it, and their deaths mirror the way that they lived.

Then there are people who are very bitter, very angry, and you can almost see the bile in them contribute to the suffering. Now both of these groups of people die. It's not that anybody gets saved. Being gracious doesn't get you out of it. And it doesn't mean that people with that personality of transcendence are not angry, sometimes they're very angry. But there's a way that their spirit transcends and they're able to give meaning to their lives, and that meaning comes often in relationship with others. Or in relationship to God. That seems to me the key thing—a sense that there is meaning. Despite whatever the physical circumstances are, there is meaning.

In difficult moments the strength I get doesn't come from having an answer, it comes from knowing that I have to act so as to emulate the compassionate characteristic of God. One of the names of God in Hebrew is *Shechinah*. It literally means presence, to be there, to be a presence, to not abandon people. And that is where I find meaning. To make sure that in their grief and their rage and their terror, people are not abandoned by me or by Judaism.

To be truthful I have to admit I don't know much about God. But there are moments—when I see the kinds of acts I see around me here—there are moments when I feel connected to that Transcendence. When I see the kind of struggling and commitment, the love, the humor and joy, I am deeply moved. I think about the parents and the families that have watched a child in the prime moment of life, just about to really take off, in his work or his life, and they watch him disappear. And people have to struggle with the gay issue, and for some of them they find out about the gay issue when they find out about the AIDS. Imagine what that's like.

People have come through for each other; they sit at their side and take care of each other; and this from what we might think of as a spoiled, young population. We're not talking about people who are necessarily used to taking care of others. And here they are, they've learned about bedpans and what it means to be up all night helping and what it means to subsume their needs for someone else's, and to care.

I find God in the incredible courage and strength that people have demonstrated by being there, by being present through all of it, to the end.

WESTERN IDEAS ABOUT DEATH
CHRONOLOGY PART 8

✌

Death has become less a group proposition and more about personal loss. New social concepts of individual rights and freedoms reinforce the idea of the individual as separate from others. Now there is the sense that death is a rift or split dividing individuals, the experience of being torn away from a beloved other.

1800s   Infectious disease continues to decimate crowded urban areas.

In 1822, a yellow fever epidemic rages through New York City and 16,000 people die. Churchyard cemeteries are so overcrowded, they pose a public health hazard. A special committee of the New York City Board of Health recommends establishing cemeteries out of town, which helps to cut down on contagious infection. Rural cemeteries become a popular institution throughout the century.

In some urban areas, the survival rate for children under age ten is 50 percent or less. Sometimes, especially among the poor, children are not named until they are at least a year old.

Between 1830 and 1850, books on death and bereavement, known as "consolation literature" become popular. Titles include *Agnes and the Key of Her
Little Coffin, Stepping Heavenward,* and *Gates Ajar.*

Last wishes and confessions of the dying are given
great weight and recorded in letters, diaries, and
newspapers of the era. The "deathbed promise" is
held to be sacrosanct and binding. Mourning is extended in an effort to preserve the memory of the
deceased.

In midcentury, general anesthesia begins to be used
on a regular basis, easing many painful deaths from
wounds and injury and reinforcing the ancient association between sleep and death.

1861–65   More than 625,000 soldiers die in the American
Civil War. Dead soldiers are embalmed so they can
be sent home for burial, establishing the practice of
embalming that will become the basis of the commercial funeral industry.

Death has become much more private. No longer
the occasion of public ritual, the deathbed scene is
now a family affair.

The Romantic movement combines with the senti-
mentality of Victorian-era America to create lavishly
landscaped cemeteries where families spend Sunday
afternoons strolling in parklike settings. A major
change from the simple utilitarian graveyards of the
past, these cemeteries provide a place for communion with loved ones. People want to go and visit
the dead, who are romanticized as "the choir invisible."

At the same time, the growing influence of science and the Enlightenment begins to cloud traditional certainties.

Darwinism challenges the religious view of creation and with it the conventional view of death.

Scientific naturalism, a philosophical movement, describes death as a phenomenon that can be understood and controlled by unraveling nature's laws.

In 1899, a cultural essay entitled *The Dying of Death* reflects the changing popular attitude: *"Death is no longer regarded as a king of terror but as a kindly nurse who puts us to bed when our day's work is done. The fear of death is being replaced by the joy of life. . . . Full life here and now is the demand; what may come hereafter is left to take care of itself."*

We are about to undergo a dramatic transformation in our experience of death, a transformation that will radically alter not only our means of coping with it but our very sense of what death is.

ROBIN WHITE OWEN
Age: 43
Television Producer and Media Curator

∽

We had been at New Directors, watching a film, the night my father called to say he needed help. It was about twelve-thirty in the morning. He sounded really calm on the phone. He said, "Robbi, I think you better come down here. I'm having a heart attack, and I want you to take me to the hospital," but very calm, not agitated. I, of course, became immediately agitated, but I did have the presence of mind to say, "Just hold on, I'll call an ambulance, and we'll be right down." The ambulance was there by the time we got there. He looked pale. He said his heart really hurt a lot, and he'd been popping nitroglycerin every twenty minutes for the last three hours, but he was still being gracious. He really rose to the occasion. They couldn't find a vein to stick the IV into because he was so old, his veins were like paper. Finally he said, "Now listen fellows, you are really hurting my arm. Can we just stop this now?"

He got up, he got dressed, and they took him to the hospital in the ambulance. We went with him. At the hospital he told them, "I'm in pain, my heart hurts." So they put him on morphine. That was about two in the morning. I guess we left the hospital around four or five to go home, and the next day he was on a certain amount of morphine but not a lot because he was conscious and pretty clear, a little sleepy, but he was all right. We all went to visit and he seemed better.

Then, thirty-six hours after he first called me, he had massive heart failure. I don't remember the technical term for it but his heart collapsed, the muscle gave out. What had been happening was that less and less blood was getting to his heart muscle so, slowly, bits of the heart were dying off, bit by bit by bit and finally, when 80 percent of the heart was gone, the whole heart muscle stopped. And that's when they started doing all of these extraordinary measures.

Evidently they tried to call us. They called my sister and they got an answering machine. So without reaching a family member to say one way or another, they went ahead with all the procedures that they do. By the time they called me, he was already plugged into a million things. He was on a respirator. He was attached to an EKG and an ECG and all those machines and they had placed a balloon pump in his leg that was diverting blood to his heart.

My sisters and I mobilized, along with my father's friend Judy. We decided someone would be there twenty-four hours a day to see what was happening. I took the night shift, as befits the eldest daughter, and really, I'm the one that he was closest to. So I sat with him through the night.

He was mostly unconscious but when the morphine wound down, he was a little bit there. Not like let's-have-a-conversation conscious but conscious enough to be able to hold your hand. And he was crying. He couldn't talk because he was on a respirator with a tube down his throat, but he would open his eyes and shake his head no, no, no.

It was horrible seeing him all wired up and taped down. In cardiac intensive care, they don't cover you with blankets because they have all these attachments stuck on your body and IVs and catheters and those round things that attach to the ECG machine and everything. There's just this cloth spread over the groin area. It seemed cold to me. His body seemed cold. It was just heartbreaking, it was without dignity. He was completely plugged into all these horrible machines. His body was like an object to them, they were treating an object, not a person, not a person who was dying. It shouldn't be that way. It just should not.

What the doctors were saying was really difficult to deal with because it didn't make sense. Basically they told us that if they took out the pump, then the blood wouldn't get to his heart and he would die. If they left the pump in, and continued to divert the blood from his leg, the lack of blood in the leg would cause him to get gangrene and they would have to amputate, an operation he wouldn't survive, so he would die that way too. Clearly he was going to die no matter what they did. He wasn't going to get better and there really wasn't anything they could do, but he was being kept now in this kind of suspended state.

It hadn't occurred to us to talk it over beforehand, to say: "Well, what are we going to do if this happens or if that happens?" We didn't know anything we needed to know. We weren't told what might happen or what we should be ready for or anything like that.

He had just had his eightieth birthday a few months before. We had all decided to take him out to a snazzy lunch, pick him up in a limo and give him a big time because maybe that would be his last birthday. He even joked about it with us. But we never sat down and said, "Okay now, if this happens or that happens, what would we do?" I didn't even know he had a heart condition. He had always been a very independent man who kept his own counsel. He hadn't said a word, not a word.

At the hospital we kept asking the same questions over and over again. "What happens if you take the balloon pump out?" And they would say, "He will die." And we would say, "What happens if you leave the balloon pump in?" And basically they would say, "He will die." I mean it was really just like that. We kept asking until it finally sunk in that there was no way out of this situation. There was nothing to do. So we said, "Well, just take all this stuff out then." And they said, "Oh no, no, we can't do that. No, no, no, no, no."

But as it happens, the New York State Legislature had just passed a law that allowed hospital doctors to place Do Not Resuscitate orders on patients who were dying from diseases other than cancer. Up until that time, you could only put a DNR order on a cancer patient. So my father was one of the first patients in New York University Hospital to get a DNR with a heart condition. We had to fight for it, we had to negotiate. It took three days to get his doctor to the point where he would even consider this. We told him we wanted a Do Not Resuscitate order. Not only that, we said we wanted to take him off all these machines altogether because we didn't want this to continue. We had to insist, to say, "There is no point to this. He's in pain, he's miserable. Why are you doing this? The man is dying, let him die." The doctor didn't want to do it, but we told him he had to let us do it. This was our father, and this was ridiculous.

Finally, we go into this office at the hospital and they give us two forms to fill out. One was the pull-the-plug form and the other was the DNR form. We signed the DNR order and then, before I can pick up the pen to sign the other one, his doctor says, "Please don't sign that. I really don't want to let you do that. Please, don't." He said, "He'll die in a couple of days anyway even if you don't sign. Please don't." So I agreed, because I would have felt like a murderer. Not because I *am* a murderer, or because I would have *been* a murderer. The hospital had put him in this situation. They had taken away his natural right to die by putting in this balloon pump and putting him on the respirator. From one perspective, I would have been giving him back his natural right. I'm sure my father totally wanted them to pull the plug, I'm sure of it. I have no question about what he wanted. But this doctor didn't see it that way.

It was a scary thing because you really feel like if I sign this, he'll be dead because I signed it. Not because he had a massive heart attack six days ago, but because I signed this form. That's what *that* is about. You forget what is the cause of the situation because they complicate it. There is a cause which they negate, and then they create a new cause and it becomes something completely different. It was creepy to be in that position. It was intimidating and creepy.

After we signed the DNR order, we all went, each individually, and said good-bye. That was the last time I saw him alive, so to speak. He died the next morning.

Thank God we were able to sign the DNR and allow him to die before they stuck some other thing in him. Yes, everyone wants to save the lives of the people that they love. Obviously if doctors can save a life that's worth saving and give somebody more time and they're happy about being back, then no matter how invasive the procedures are, that's a good thing. But in a situation where it's so clear that there's no way out of it, it becomes degrading.

It's painful to see any human being be so diminished, really diminished . . . dwarfed in a sense by this inhuman situation, this equipment that just keeps pumping away and doing what it's doing, no matter what. And *for* what?

By the time it was over I was incredibly angry. The morning that he died, they were wiring his room, bringing in extra current so they could plug in more machines. It just pissed me off so much, because it was so intimidating. I was angry at his doctor for being such a pig-head about letting him go. I was angry at the hospital administration for not trying another number before they decided to stick the balloon pump in his leg, I was angry at my sister for not answering the bloody phone, I was angry at her stupid answering machine . . .

There was something fundamentally wrong about all this. And it happens all the time. I think that people who've had this experience need to speak out and be really vocal about how they feel. Once you've seen this you need to decide, is this what you really want? For yourself? For others you love?

I've learned that it's important to try and take as much control as you can over the process of dying, to consider, now, the possibility of your own death and the death of anybody for whom you are in any way responsible. Then maybe you have a shot at dying the way you want to die, or helping them to die the way they want to die. That is really a crucially important thing.

We don't have any control over the circumstances under which we're born, and it used to be that we didn't really have any control over the circumstances under which we died, and that seemed to be a pretty equal kind of situation. Hey, I come and I go.

But now it's more like democracy. If you want to have a democratic country, then people have to take responsibility for what happens. Now that we have options about dying, we have to be responsible and think about how we want to die and make those decisions. A massive education program needs to happen so that people are willing to think about it. Now don't ask me how to do that . . . I haven't got a clue.

One thing, though, I do think that experience is the best teacher and as more people are faced with the experience of watching loved ones die in hospitals, in uncomfortable and unnecessarily difficult situations, they'll think about it more and eventually they'll get around to doing something about it. Change seems to have something to do with a commonality of experience. The more people have the experience and the more people talk about it, the more acceptable it is to consider and explore it, and eventually a kind of common consensus will arise about how to handle it.

People who have been through it need to talk about it a lot. A lot, a lot, a lot. It needs to permeate through different layers of society and it needs to percolate and get experienced and get considered. Look at the struggle we're having over abortion. We can't even get to the point where we agree on a very loose national policy that allows people to decide for themselves what they want, which is the most humane policy we can have, the most democratic policy. I think if we can ever get to that point on abortion then it will be possible to get to that point on death. But it's certainly going to be a struggle, no doubt about it.

JONATHAN MARGOLIS
Age: 32
Quality Control Technician

∽

I was always close with my brother. Our father died when we were young and our mother had a real hard time. It was Ben who really held things together. He was sixteen and I was ten. We'd been through some tough times together. We were tight.

Two years ago Ben found out he had leukemia. It was a shock, really unexpected. He was a very healthy guy for the most part. He smoked, but other than that he took real good care of himself. He didn't drink much or anything, he did some sports. For a while there it seemed like he was getting sick a lot. Little things, colds, the flu, he was tired all the time. I didn't think too much about it. I remember one night I was having dinner at their house, with his wife, Cindy, and his little boy, Josh, my nephew. He's six now. He was four then. I looked at Ben and I thought he didn't look so good. I told him he needed a vacation.

Finally he went to a doctor who sent him to a specialist and they found out he had leukemia. They said he should have a bone marrow transplant, if they could find a suitable donor, which would most likely be me. I was tested and it turned out I wasn't a good match for him. They wouldn't even consider using me. I couldn't believe it. We were brothers. I thought for sure we would match. The doctor said it wasn't all that unusual, lots of times siblings don't match. It's four-to-one odds. But I felt terrible. I felt like I'd failed him, like I'd failed him when he needed me the most.

They tried chemotherapy next. That was rough and it didn't do any good. He just got weaker and weaker. He was really, really sick.

Cindy was having a hard time coping with it. She was trying real hard but the whole thing had been such a shock. At first she had big hopes for the bone marrow transplant. Then she had big hopes for the chemo and even when it was clear it was not working, she just couldn't believe Ben was going to die. You gotta remember, Ben was always the one who took care of her, took care of everything. He was definitely a strong, can-do-type guy. She married this he-man and now, five short years later, he's dying. I think she really went into a major denial thing. Or maybe she thought that if she actually *believed* he was getting better, then he *would* get better.

Personally, I thought he was going to die. To be honest, from the day I got the results of the matching test, I was afraid of the worst. For me, that was like, "Wait a second here. This isn't going to be all right." I had this pessimism deep inside. I didn't let anybody see it, I didn't let anybody *know* I felt that way, but I was definitely expecting the worst. I mean, it was *leukemia* for Christ's sake.

As Ben got weaker and weaker, we started talking about what to do about things. He laid out everything he wanted to do about his will and all that. We took care of business. Off and on we talked about what he wanted to do if it got to where it was too hard for him to keep on going . . . if he wanted some help to go on out. I was the one he chose to talk to. Cindy wasn't . . . well, she just wasn't the right one for him to turn to in this, she was too shattered herself.

Ben's best friend—this guy named Jimmie—he's okay, but he was dealing with it like, "Hey man, you're gonna beat this, come on, don't talk like that." So it fell to me to be realistic. I understood that. It was okay. Ben and I had been through a lot together, we didn't bullshit each other.

In fact, now as I look back, I think we were kind of proud about being so up-front about it, we were facing things square on. I read *Final Exit*. We talked about hospice, but Cindy just couldn't handle the idea of taking care of Ben at home. Basically, what she said was she was afraid she would do something wrong, screw up in some way that would hurt him. She wanted him to be in the hospital because she felt like they could take better care of him. She saw the hospital as this place where they knew what to do. She saw the doctors as being the ones who knew what to do.

I tried to talk her into doing the hospice thing but you have to stop treatment and sign a DNR order and all that and she just couldn't do it at that point. She freaked out. I could see I was only making things worse by trying to force her to face reality, so I gave up on that idea. And I guess, in my own way, I was hoping she was right; they *should* keep treating him; they *could* help him better than we could; the hospital *would* be better than home. I don't know. It's just so intense—what you're feeling when these things happen. There's a part of you that's looking to have it taken out of your hands. Even if you think you're not, you really are.

Those last weeks were rough. Ben looked so bad, and he was feeling horrible. He was in pain, he was so weak he couldn't move, he couldn't eat, everything was intravenous. He had all these infections, he had real bad fevers, at one point he went into septic shock. It was a nightmare, and they just kept maintaining him.

He was pretty out of it most of the time, but every once in a while he got clear enough to let me know he really wanted this to end. He told me he wanted them to "Take out the tubes, stop the antibiotics, everything, just increase the morphine drip." He talked to Cindy as well as he could. She seemed to finally accept that he needed to let go. He said to me . . . he said, "I'm done Jay. Let me go out."

When they removed the IVs we thought he was going to die that night. We all came to be with him. There was me, Cindy, Cindy's sister, Ben's best friend, Jimmie, and this guy he worked with that he was real close to. We're all there expecting Ben to die. He's out of it and not really conscious but he's not sleeping, he's agitated. He was having dreams or something, it wasn't what I expected. We were expecting to hold his hand and for him to just calmly pass away or something like that.

I went out to the nurses' station to tell them he needed more morphine or something and there was this one nurse there and I'll never forget how she looked at me. It was with sympathy, but also like . . . like I just didn't get it. She said, "Look, you can make the decision to take them off everything but they don't just die right away. It can take days and days. I'm not allowed to increase the morphine any more than I already have. You'll have to talk to the doctor."

I wind up talking to the doctor on the phone and he says, "You know he's going to die of thirst and all the complications, and I'm not allowed to give him enough morphine to make it smooth." He said, "This is the point where, if someone is going to help him, this is the point where they would do that." And I'm listening to this and I'm thinking, "Okay, this guy is being honest with me. That's good. It's up to me to pick up the ball here."

Early on, when Ben and I had first talked about this, I'd gotten in touch with a friend of mine who is a pharmacology intern and he said he could get ahold of some potassium chloride. At that time, Ben had said, "I want to be unconscious from the morphine and then I want you to give me an injection in the morphine drip." And that had seemed the best thing to do. So I called my friend.

Now it's the next night. We're back at the hospital. It's me, Jimmie, Ben's friend from work, and my friend I'll call Joe. Cindy couldn't do it. She said she couldn't bear to take part in this. She wanted it to happen, she told me she knew he wanted it. But she just couldn't be there herself. She said Josh was freaking out and she needed to stay with him and so that's what she did. As it turned out, I'm really glad she wasn't there.

At this point I'm fried. I've hardly slept in days. I know Joe's nervous because this is highly illegal what he's doing, providing this drug. He loaded the syringe and told me he'd hold it with me so I wouldn't have to be the sole one who did it, sort of like a firing squad. I wiped Ben's face and told him I loved him and finally Joe inserted the syringe into the IV. At the last moment Jimmie came over and put his hand on top of mine and Joe's and somebody squeezed and we all pushed it in.

At first everything was quiet but then the drug gave him convulsions. His body jerked and his eyes came open. He had spasms. He would seem to stop breathing and then he would gasp suddenly. Everyone tried to be cool but we were really just stunned. Over the next thirty minutes he had these spasm kind of movements coming at longer and longer intervals. Finally it seemed he hadn't breathed for a long time. I thought to myself, "This *must* be over." I reached my hand out to feel the pulse in his neck and just at that moment he took this heavy convulsive breath that shook his body. It shocked and scared me. I pulled back. It was terrible, like a scene from some horror movie. Everyone looked totally stricken. We were all in a state of shock I think, really like shock.

Ben finally died about forty-five minutes after we gave him the injection. Joe went over and closed his eyes. I'm just sitting there, dazed. Jimmie went out and told the nurse that Ben had died. After a while I gathered myself together and called Cindy and told her what she wanted to hear. I said Ben had died, quietly and peacefully, like he was sleeping.

For me the next weeks were a real nightmare of guilt. I felt like I'd really botched things. I couldn't talk to anybody about it. Finally, I went to see an old friend of mine. She and I broke up some time ago but we'd stayed friends. She helped me out a lot. I don't think I could've gotten through this without her. It was horrible. I kept having dreams about it. In one dream I had a gun and I was shooting up everyone in the hospital. It was like *Taxi Driver.* I was just killing everybody.

You know, you try to do the right thing. You have these incredibly difficult conversations with this person you love and you think you know what they want and what you're going to do and you've got your shit together. You've got a plan. It seems straightforward. When they can't take it anymore you're going to help them to die. But the plan is for a particular scenario and when the situation goes differently, you don't really have a plan B. You find you haven't been as rigorous as you thought you were. You didn't go over every possibility because it was hard enough talking about it in the first place. And if you get into a situation where everything that can go wrong does go wrong . . . I mean, I'm a systems control analyst for a company that contracts to NASA for Christ's sake, and I *didn't even ask the right questions,* let alone get the right answers. I didn't push for details, I didn't say, "What's this going to be like? What can I expect?" I let myself be shuffled along into making compromises all along the way and finally, there was this moment and I was doing this thing. . . .

Originally, when Ben and I talked about this it was like he would be at home, but he was in the hospital. It was like he would be completely unconscious, but they didn't give him enough of anything. He'd been taking morphine for months and months. He needed a bigger dose in order to have the effect we expected. That last night they gave him five milligrams of Valium. Can you believe that? *Five milligrams of Valium . . .*

In going over and over this thing I've been struck by the fact that the language used in the hospital is set up to be very ambiguous; the whole hospital situation is arranged so that nobody has to be clear, nobody has to bite the bullet; it's guaranteed to assure that responsibility falls through the cracks.

Later I talked to a doctor who deals with terminal AIDS patients and he was appalled at the behavior of Ben's doctor. He said that Ben's doctor had been the worst kind of coward, bemoaning Ben's pain and implying that we should take care of it. He said he sometimes "helps" terminal cases at the end, and the best way to do it is to open the morphine drip enough to deliver a lethal dose. He said if a doctor sees that as the best thing, then it's up to the doctor to do it himself, not to pass the responsibility onto the family. He was very adamant about that.

I think there are a lot of people who feel like they've got a handle on this. Educated people, they read books, they are up on the latest thing, they have computers, they use them. You know, it's like we think we're not racist anymore, we have sex before marriage so we're not prudes anymore, we have women doctors and lawyers, so all these things mean we've made progress, right? Yeah. Right. And we can talk about death, right? We talk about denial and how people are left alone in some cold institution or whatever and we think, "Well that's not how *we're* going to do it. We'll do it better, we'll exercise our right to choose, we'll do it with dignity." Yeah, right.

When I look back on it, I think the thing I didn't know about was dying. That's what I didn't know about. I mean, you think dying is natural or should be a natural thing. It's not supposed to be like buying a house or you've got to read *Consumer Reports* and somehow learn all this stuff to protect yourself from getting ripped off.

It's like when Ben and I had to put our mother in a nursing home, it was amazing what we had to wade through. We spent so much time trying to get up to speed on insurance, "custodial care" and the goddamned rights of the elderly; we had to work hard to find out how we could make it okay for her without going broke ourselves. That whole thing, you know what I mean? It's really fucked up. It comes up over and over in our lives, and we go ahead and do it. We read about it and we ask around; we become "informed consumers."

But when it comes up about dying, you don't buy *Consumer Reports* and weigh the cost/benefits ratio. You feel like shit. You're scared, you're full of pain, you're confused. It really pisses me off to think that you have to know all these secret things to make this okay for someone you care about.

Maybe death isn't natural. Maybe it's only natural if you're real old and die of "natural" causes. Maybe it's not easy or peaceful or okay no matter what. When that nurse shook her head and said, "It takes *time* for them to die," I felt like an idiot. I didn't know how medical people are about this, I didn't know about the system. But most of all, I didn't know anything about what it's like to die.

FENELLA ROUSE
Age: 44
Director, The Mayday Fund and
The Emily Davie & Joseph S. Kornfeld Foundation
Past Director, Choice In Dying

❦

As a lawyer I was always interested in the way law affects the lives of ordinary people. For instance, the law of domestic relations—when you get married, you don't really think of it as entering into a legal relationship, particularly if you're young; but then you want to get divorced and, low and behold, it's a whole different story. Or you rent an apartment and although you know it's a kind of contract because you actually sign a lease, it isn't until the landlord doesn't provide the water that you begin to realize how that contract directly affects you.

I went to work at Choice In Dying as a staff attorney. At that time the organization was called Society for the Right to Die and was known primarily for supporting legislation and distributing living wills in an effort to help people who were at the end of life. SRD did not take a position on suicide or on active euthanasia. We were solely concerned with the refusal of life-sustaining treatment so that people could die naturally.

I found this work interesting because here was an area in which the law affected ordinary people who hadn't done anything except to get sick or get old. They hadn't made an agreement or entered into any contractual obligation. They hadn't gotten married, they hadn't leased an apartment or bought a car, they had done nothing at all. And yet the law was controlling the outcome of their particular situation, the law was controlling how they died, and that was very fascinating to me, theoretically. It wasn't that I was personally dedicated to death-and-dying issues. I came into it from the legal side. It just didn't seem fair for people to be in this difficult situation through absolutely no fault of their own.

It was a very interesting time to be doing this work. During the eight or nine years I was there, a great wave of social interest developed in this subject. We went from being a small, relatively obscure group advocating use of the living will, to a 200,000-member organization, developing legislation and legal policy on issues that were being featured in newsweeklies and argued before the Supreme Court. It became rather a hot topic. We tried to make the most of the momentum and achieve what we could.

All the states now have law supporting patient's choices. On the federal level, The Patient Self-Determination Act was passed in 1991. This requires all health care facilities to ask their patients if they wish to refuse unwanted treatment; the expression "living will" is now widely understood. If people want to find out about their options at the end of life, most have a way of doing that now. It's not perfect but it's a big change in ten–fifteen years time.

At Choice In Dying, we were trying to take away the burden of thinking that decisions were made by the law. The theory was to free people up to make individual decisions. Now in fact the law permitted that anyway. Constitutional and common law had always permitted cessation of treatment. But there was a very common misconception that the law required treatment forever and so, in a way, extra law had to be enacted.

People think legislation is *real* law because they can read it— "black letter law" they call it—giving a positive grant of freedom to stop treatment. That freedom was already there implicitly but it needed to be spelled out. The legislation was largely public relations, public education. It was saying to people, "Look, this law is *really* here now, it's been passed by the legislature."

This is a very American approach but I'm not sure it goes to the crux of the matter. For example, when I used to go to hospitals, doctors would say "Oh no, I can't stop treating, it's against the law." And we'd say, "It's not against the law," and we'd demonstrate that it wasn't against the law, and then they'd say, "Well, I can't stop treating anyway." I think that the law was used, and still is used in lots of ways, as a kind of cushion against thinking through things.

We tend to resolve moral differences in court, it's that sort of system here in this country. When we have a moral difficulty or an emotional difficulty we often say one of two things: "It's against the law" or "It's a right." We tend to characterize those areas of moral uncertainty in quasi-legal terminology.

I think talking about death in this way is unfortunate. The idea that death with dignity is about control and individual rights avoids the whole point of death. The whole point of death is—you *can't* control it. It's finally uncontrollable and it's an illusion to talk about retaining control over the end. The important thing is to let go. I think the debate is couched in terms that deny the reality of death. When we talk about rights and control and choice, we're not *really* talking about death, we're talking about a phantom, a phantom idea—the idea that if we could only legislate it correctly, we wouldn't have to face death or experience it.

America was founded on an idea, built on the idea of the Constitution and individual rights. It isn't quite the same in Europe. Europe wasn't founded on an idea, it evolved and developed, rumbling along and just kind of getting to where it is. Europe incorporates its history as it goes. America isn't a country concerned with history, it's concerned with rights. Here we don't call on history or traditions when we need guidance, we call on the law. The language is couched in those terms; we tend to talk about these things in terms of rights.

I grew up in England in the fifties. In England we don't have a concept of individual rights in the same way. We have a sense of being given things by the state and being grateful for them. English people of my generation are a real product of the welfare state. We take things like the National Health Service completely for granted; we don't find anything odd about the idea of community and we don't find it particularly threatening or alarming for government to provide certain things. It simply makes good sense. We don't think there's a "right" to health care, we just think it's sound social policy to have it. Why not? It's so much more efficient.

Whereas here people say, "I have a right to so-and-so," which means, "I want it and I ought to be getting it." In America we're used to using the language of rights to assert a point of view.

There are many subtle differences between the way Europeans and Americans think about these things, about everything, for that matter. One has to guard against making gross generalizations, but I can be pretty sure that if my feeling about something or other is such-and-such, most Europeans will at least understand what I'm talking about, whereas the vast majority of Americans will hear it differently. It's a difference that's hard to articulate but it's a very common experience, and all Europeans who live in the U.S., and all Americans who live in Europe, know exactly what I mean.

For instance, in talking about somebody dying, it's very unusual to hear anyone in England say it was a bad death and fairly unusual to hear anyone here say it was a good death. Europeans rarely say anything except: "I'm so sad that Dad's gone but it was a wonderful death." Or "It was difficult and I miss him but that's the way it had to be." Very common, even when talking about a tragic situation, like somebody dying young of AIDS or children dying.

But here one hears, "It all went wrong," and "It cost too much." I don't know how much of this is because it actually *is* different or because the expectations are different or because of the cultural differences. One of the great talents of the English people is their ability to find the silver lining when confronted with the inevitable. It may simply be that kind of processing. But there's a real difference, an unmistakable difference.

Of course there's the difference in history, in experience, all those things, and again, these are generalizations, but Americans do tend to think more in terms of choices and options whereas Europeans don't have those kinds of assumptions. There was a columnist in the *New York Times* who wrote about how U.S. foreign policy decisions are based on television pictures. First there are the pictures of starving children and soldiers are sent to help. Then there are pictures of an American soldier being dragged through the streets and everybody gets upset and wants the soldiers to come home. As if soldiers don't die. But soldiers *do* die. All the time. That's what being a soldier *means*—being in danger of dying, violently. It is odd that we have this society where entertainment violence is everywhere but we can't seem to take the real thing. We're completely unprepared for the messiness of life and death. We can't take wars and we can't take people dying in hospitals.

Death isn't an option. We happen to live in a time when you can perpetuate biological life for longer than we've ever been able to before, but we still can't avoid dying. The only thing that's different now is—it's much more likely that we'll have to choose the moment. Sometimes, in the past, doctors had to make decisions about the moment of death, but now all doctors are asked to do it and all people are asked to do it.

We've never been confronted with that and it's a tremendous responsibility and a burden. It's about emotions and courage. It means that people have to make decisions which they're not used to making. I don't really think our current confusion is about a clash of values, or what is sometimes described as humanity against technology. I think the problems we have are the result of people saying, in one way or another, "I don't want to have to make this choice, for my patient or for myself or for my family member. I don't want to face this."

When people describe the "right to die" movement as a battle between humanity and technology, I just don't buy it. I take technology to mean hardware, machines, you know—stuff. Well, there's always been technology, since the wheel there's been technology. I don't see that a new bit makes much difference. The fact that it's a respirator or a feeding tube rather than a syringe . . . it's all technology.

The dilemma has to do with making decisions about how you use technology. And the questions that are raised are questions of personal responsibility and courage. I believe it's a fallacy to think that if only we didn't have the technology, if only we didn't resuscitate people fourteen times, they'd have good deaths. Many deaths are perfectly horrible and would continue to be so, even if all the technology disappeared tomorrow.

People die the way they live. Emotionally, families behave at the end the way they've behaved at Thanksgiving for the previous fifteen years. It's just human. I think we blame the technology because we don't want the responsibility of maybe making a mistake. It's a question of being prepared to make a mistake. People do make mistakes. Death is difficult. It's always been difficult.

There's a lot of nostalgic romanticism about the past and about how death was different then or easier somehow. To think there was a world, maybe a generation and a half ago, where there was this bucolic scene with a country doctor and people died somehow in a "nice" way—I don't think so. People didn't behave any better in Shakespeare's plays than they do now. That's why literature is important, it describes the way things actually were, the way people were and are. In Tolstoy there is no picture-perfect death. And you have Dante wandering around in the middle of his life saying "Where am I going? I'm forty years old, what happens now?" These are common experiences of humanity, not new to us or to this time.

Death is a point of common experience, the archetype of a number of things that happen to us all the way through life—universal experiences—but until they happen to you, you can't really get it. Having children is one of those things, a parent dying, getting a divorce, having someone you love die. One's read about it, one's seen it, one's friends have done it, but until it's actually happening to you, you don't know how you'll be about it. And you have to face it yourself. All the legislation in the world won't change that.

Actually, I think the way we probably will solve it—and this *is* an American theory—is to leave it up to individuals to come to terms with it as best they can. And that means a lot of things. It means making sure you've got a support system around you, which is very hard as you get older, but if you want to take care of the end of your life that's what you'll need, that's the reality.

If you're a woman, the chances are you'll be divorced, widowed, or otherwise alone, your children will be far-flung, you may be living in an institution. As unpleasant as this sounds, it's probably how it's going to be for most of us, so the answer is to start thinking about that. How do I want to set it up? It's going to be difficult but how can I make it as bearable as it can be? I think it comes down to those sorts of things.

For myself I've chosen an advocate and talked to him about what my wishes are, not because I have strong political views about it but because I want to know that someone's loving me, someone is taking care of me. And I can't be sure of that unless I choose someone to take care of me.

Thinking such things through is certainly as important as writing a living will. Speaking personally, I'm as concerned about not getting treatment I *do* want, as I am about getting too much treatment. So often over these years, I've heard people say, in this light, airy kind of way, "Oh I'm not frightened of death, I'm just frightened of dying." I feel just the opposite. Always have done. I'm not particularly frightened of dying. I think it will actually be kind of interesting now, especially as I've thought about it a lot. I am, however, quite frightened of being dead. I'm a Christian but I don't have a very strong belief in life after death, the kind of picture-book picture of it. I don't have any idea what's going to happen. I can't see how people *aren't* frightened.

Death has always been complicated and lonely and messy and if we want it to be different it's going to come down to us, as individuals, acting differently. I'm not discounting the value of changing the law and raising public awareness. It's important to do that. But in the end it's going to come down to us taking care of ourselves, which is a very American way of looking at things, isn't it?

A. J. BERMAN
Age: 56
Infectious Disease Specialist

∾

No matter how terrible they feel, most people don't want to die. The ones who go to Jack Kevorkian are the exception, not the rule. Most people go down fighting to the bitter end, in ways that would make your eyes pop out of your head.

In my experience about 75 or 80 percent of patients really want everything done, or think they do. They want extraordinary measures, want to be dialyzed if their kidneys fail, want to be put on a respirator, want every IV possible. And it makes no sense whatsoever if you stand back and rationally look at the situation from the point of view of the likely medical outcome, because they are not going to survive at that point.

What people want is to be back the way they were. Up and around, able to eat a decent meal and take a shit and walk from here to there. The likelihood that they're going to do that is: Big Zero. And they still don't see that. Then there are the family members who have irrational hopes. There are difficult personality and relationship dynamics. Some people understand, some people don't understand, there are fights, there's denial, there's this, there's that, and the reality of the situation falls through the cracks. Some little flicker of fantasy about what's going to happen keeps people hanging on.

Now I have participated in this. I've written orders for some obscene things in terms of keeping people alive, because that's been the expressed wish and need. There are illegal ways to get around it but doctors don't use those very often. Basically, if a patient says "I want that," we've been doing it. But with very mixed feelings.

I try to explain, "Look, I can put a tube down your throat but the likelihood I'm going to be able to get it out and you breathe again on your own is very, very small."

"I still want it, maybe there's something."

"Okay, okay."

Now I'm saying, "Okay, okay"—but as things change in how we allocate these resources, those decisions are going to be taken out of the doctors' hands. I think the involvement of technology in those last moments is going to be on the wane. It's going to be real interesting to see how that goes, to see how people react when these options are no longer available, people who are now used to all these technological wonders prolonging their fantasy of life, or their fantasy of getting back to life. Maybe there will be some calmer approach to things. Because every time we do this it's extremely costly in terms of dollars, not to mention extremely costly in terms of reality—the reality that says, "Hey, there's a point at which you're going to die, no matter what we do."

It's crazy to spend tens of thousands of dollars to keep someone alive for a few extra days that are, in fact, horrible days, difficult days for them. It's prolonged discomfort, not prolonged life. But that's what happens as a response to "I want everything, I want everything done."

When people say they don't want to live as a vegetable, they mean they don't want to be completely unconscious, as if they were dead and yet somehow were being kept alive in some creepy way. But that's not what usually happens, that's not a very common situation. What I see are people who are conscious, maybe drowsy, with a zillion tubes in their mouth, rectum, urethra, maybe in the chest, just about every orifice; IVs coming out of every part of the body where we can find a vein or an artery; behind them we have a computerized screen that's monitoring everything we can monitor, which is a lot: the basal body temperature, the heart rate, the blood pressure, the systemic blood pressure, the venous blood pressure, to name a few. On-line we can push buttons and tell exactly what your oxygen extraction is at any moment. It's amazing what we can do now.

However, in the middle of all this there's a real person, lying there, often conscious of what's going on, scared as hell, uncomfortable and agitated. When you put a tube down someone's throat they try to yank it out. That's everybody's reaction. It's reflexive. You want to pull the tube out because it feels like somebody's strangling you. Of course you can't talk with the tube in, so there's a panicked, inarticulate patient freaking out. Needless to say, they're restrained, either with physical restraints or chemical restraints. And then, when they wake up, their eyes are full of panic so they get sedated again. We're not talking vegetables, we're talking people who are alive, often very clear and usually frightened out of their wits.

So what is the general sense of death? People's sense of death is—going to sleep quietly. Now major electrolyte imbalances that develop slowly over time are actually good ways to die. Sudden electrolyte imbalances are not good and often cause seizures, but gradually progressing electrolyte imbalances cause a person to slowly move out of consciousness and to sort of go to sleep, quietly and peacefully.

There's the very real possibility that the human body, if allowed to follow a natural course at the endstage of many diseases, produces hormonal or other physiological reactions that prepare the body for death, or allow it to move more gently into the dying process. But we consistently interrupt that process and create a lot of very uncomfortable people. Take a walk through the medical intensive care unit. It's unbelievable. One bed after another of people with all sorts of high-tech things going on, most of whom are not expected to live beyond their hospitalization. Why are we doing this? We can't not do it. What is gained? Not much.

In many cases it just happens, without aim, as part of the system. It's a result of how the system works. For example, one of my patients, a sweet young man who was HIV-infected, hepatitis-infected, had bad liver failure. Liver failure is one of those things where, if you just let it go, people kind of go to sleep. I absolutely did not want him put in the intensive care unit because his liver failure was endstage—irreversible—and if we avoided aggressive measures, he would be one of those people lucky enough to die quietly, peacefully.

I went away on a Friday and came back on a Monday and there he was in the medical intensive care unit with this and that and the other thing going on. I mean I was pissed. I talked to him, I said, "How are you feeling in here?"

He said, "I feel terrible."

I said, "Well look, let's just stop some of this. You'll feel more comfortable. You're not going to survive this but you're going to be more comfortable."

And he said "Okay."

Now nobody had said any of that to him. They had panicked because he had a little bit of bleeding and they put him in the intensive care unit so they could figure out where the bleeding was from. It was irrelevant where the bleeding was from. The man was at the end of a terminal illness and if you let it go it will allow him to pass peacefully. Instead, what was being done was anything but peaceful. He eventually left the medical intensive care unit and died quietly shortly thereafter. But somebody, a person, has to say something, has to stop the automatic process that's built into the system. It's like a knee-jerk reflex. Do do do do do do do. Instead of—Let it go.

Because we deal with a group of patients who we know are going to become quite sick with a condition that is almost certainly going to lead to their death, we try to start talking to them early in the process. Talking about what can and can't be done, how much they want done and all that. Because you really don't want somebody making these decisions when they feel like they're drowning. When do you put a tube in to help somebody breathe? When they can't breathe on their own. That's *not* the time to ask them, "Do you want a tube?" "Yes, of *course* I want a tube, I'm drowning. Help me."

If I have a patient who states clearly they want to have a comfortable death and we reach a point where it's obvious that further treatment isn't going anywhere, and they let me know they don't want to continue with efforts that can cause them great discomfort, having that situation clearly understood by me, ahead of the time that is the real crisis, I would approach it as follows: We have morphine going, we'll up the dose, we'll give him a little extra, not announcing it, not saying "and now I'm going to do this," but basically just gradually, slowly put him to sleep. It's not done in dramatic increments. People become more tolerant of morphine as the doses are increased and it's done in the context of keeping the patient comfortable. We're much more humane about how we put animals to death than how we allow humans who are similarly ill to die.

Another thing I've done, in terms of allowing patients to die, is to permit various chemical imbalances, slowly and gradually, to get worse and worse and worse. I stop drawing blood and I stop checking and I stop trying to correct, and it takes its natural course.

As I said, most of what's done is real individual, real secret; it's very secret. I, for one, don't feel guilty, but I know some doctors do. Many have very, very mixed feelings. They don't discuss it with each other, or with their families or friends. It's all done very privately. They keep it to themselves.

That said, there is a strong shared sense of what "futile" is, in terms of intervention, and when that point is reached these measures do happen, these approaches do take place. But never, *never* against the wishes of patients or family members. I want to stress that. Never.

Mostly I just think it's a real tragedy that this can't be open and discussed, that articulation is discouraged. It would be a lot healthier for all of us if we were able to talk about it. However, in this country, assisted suicide has many hurdles. Even simply revising the system, so that people are "allowed" to die, will not be easy.

For starters, for Americans, and for people who have lived the "American dream" for any length of time, death isn't included. It's just missing. So talking about these issues is very hard. It means starting from scratch. I'm always surprised when I'm reminded of how ignorant people are about death.

Americans will have to hire outside consultants to write the rules. As a culture we're not anywhere near ready to face the facts, which include the fact that the medical system is driven by profit. Most people probably know this, if they stop to think about it at all, but they don't pay attention to what it really means.

There are tremendous profits being made by doing things the way we do them now. Profits from developing the technology, selling the technology, running hospitals like factories. The system creates its own excess because it needs excess to survive, to produce ever-increasing profits. What motivates the system, in a very subtle way, is: keeping the beds filled, keeping those nurses busy, keeping those catheters and lines going in, keeping our respiratory technologists busy. Keeping it going as is.

There's the profit motive and there's the power motive. Today medicine is being specialty-driven. The generalist has fallen by the wayside. What gets paid for is what's needed as defined by the specialists, and what specialists need is to hone their skills, to get better at this one thing they do, to get ever more specialized. I'm a specialist and I say this.

Specialists make a lot of money. I'm an academic so I figured out a way to be a specialist and *not* make a lot of money, but there are people out there making a fortune doing these very expert things that require tremendous technical skills and understanding. This has to be done in volume to be sustainable. So many livelihoods, so much money involved. It's not really about what's efficient or even about what's best for people's health, or their care when they're dying. It's about keeping this big machine going. It's a system that perpetuates itself big time.

Medicine is the only system I know of that is driven by the provider. In other capitalist or profit-making models, the consumer drives the market. You go into the store and you buy what you want. But in this market, you come to me and I *tell* you what you want, I order you to have this, that, and the other thing. I feed the system, not you. It's fed by the provider. It's a very odd economic model, that's why economists have a hard time working with it.

It's quite possible that caring for people who are sick and/or dying, just isn't supposed to be a profit-making enterprise. But in this country it's a business and it gets run like a business. Using all that technology brings in a lot of money, even if it's being used on people who are dying and don't really need it.

The numbers are very compelling. Some unbelievable percentage of health care expenditures are spent on the last months of life. In fact if you telescoped it down, it'd probably be even more shocking. Probably more than 25 percent of all health care expenditures are spent on the last six weeks of life, and most of that is absolutely futile. People say, "Well you don't know it's going to be futile because some people do survive," but, frankly speaking, with most people we know it's futile.

On the other hand it's futile to try to sustain a twenty-two-week-old fetus but boy, are they trying. It doesn't matter if the kid's blind and retarded. It's an example of how great we are that we can do that. And again, there is a lot of money to be made.

All this is amazingly new. As recently as fifteen years ago there were many fewer things we could do to patients. Then we could put in tubes, now we can put in balloon catheters and pumps and fancy respirators. We can control and monitor everything under the sun, perform dialysis with various kinds of membranes, place pegs in the head to relieve intracranial pressure. (Just when you think you get to be a vegetable, noooooooo.)

To pay for these developments you have to use them. So they get plugged into a system that's already set up to use them without discrimination.

Don't get me wrong, I'm not antitechnology by any means. There's an important place for high technology in medicine. Cancer treatment has become much more sophisticated. There are bone marrow transplants for people who need it, liver transplants are not a bad thing in certain kinds of situations. These advances are tremendously valuable. Many people are saved by them, people who have one or two things that go wrong and we fix them and they go off on their merry way and live a full life. That's great. But most of what goes on in hospitals, and particularly intensive care units, is expensive terminal care for people who would, in a developing country, be dead. Or even in Great Britain probably, where I think expenditures are more rationally meted out. It's as if the therapeutic advances carry some compulsion to use them in all cases. There's no discrimination. The problem is, discrimination is totally against the grain in a system that needs all this excess.

In order to change it, a line will have to be drawn beyond which point you just do not do things. But who's going to do that? I don't know who's going to make those decisions. I don't think doctors are prepared to make them. For the most part, doctors aren't any better about death than anybody else is.

JED MATTES
Age: 41
Literary Agent

❦

Something I have observed is that people often change their defini-
tions of what's okay and what's not okay when they are dying.
Someone can have been very clear about the dividing line between
wanting to live and not wanting to live and then later, their actions
will contradict that decision. I have seen a few people cross that line,
a line that they had discussed directly with me, very explicitly. I
knew firsthand what they had defined as acceptable and unacceptable
and, in a number of cases, things went clearly into the unacceptable
area, at which point they changed the rules.

I think I understand why this happens, what the process is. Basically their universe changes, their universe of experience and expectations and sensations and desires. It becomes much smaller and more
primitive, and as that universe becomes smaller and more primitive,
so do their requirements.

There was one friend in particular who had very frankly indicated to me a desire to commit suicide if his physical condition
deteriorated to a certain point. He was dying. It was very clear he
was dying. He went into the hospital when everything was falling
apart. He was in great discomfort, his throat was so raw, it hurt when
he breathed. He had no appetite and couldn't keep anything down
anyway. He was losing fluids, his kidneys were failing, he was just
falling apart. He had signed a Do Not Resuscitate order. He had a
living will but he remained conscious so it didn't kick in. At one
point I talked to him and I said,

"You had a very close call and you almost died."

He said, "I know."

I said, "We've talked before about how you want things to be,
and what your minimum requirements are. Do you think you've
gone beyond that?"

He said, "Yes."

I said, "Well, is there anything you want done?"

And he said, "I just want a few more nice days."

So it was clear that he was not wanting to die, but it was also clear he was not talking about going out to dinner with friends, seeing a movie, having a walk in the park or anything like that. If I had asked him to be specific, I think he would have said, "I'd like to drink a glass of water and have it feel good going down my throat." I think that's what he meant by a few more nice days. He wanted to eat a favorite dish and digest it. He wanted to have a solid bowel movement. I really think that's where his expectations and desires were. His universe was so diminished, his frame of reference for "happiness" and "meaning" so changed. And that's an example of something I've seen a number of times.

I think it's the same with belief. I think it's circumstantial. I don't mean that in a negative way, or as a judgment, I mean it literally. I think what happens is—we believe one thing and then the circumstances change and we learn more; we understand it differently as a result of the changed circumstances.

There are two situations in which I've seen this happen. One is with people who hold a very emphatic belief that death is the end, you don't transcend, you cease to exist, you are dead, that's it. And the other is with people who simply have not examined the question. They don't have a position one way or another, they have never focused on it.

In both cases I think it's understandable that, when faced with imminent death, such people find themselves reexamining and changing their position or finding a position. I don't see this as a last-minute revision of the rules, or denial, or some kind of wishful thinking as the Grim Reaper comes into the room. I think what is happening is they are now in a circumstance where their identity is ending and that does not jibe with their sense of reality, with what they feel to be real. Even the person who considered the question intellectually, when they assumed death was decades away, and came to the conclusion that "When you're dead, you're dead," now, when death is imminent and he or she is looking at the fact that this will happen in an hour or a day or a week, there is a new sensation. It does not *feel* like they are actually going to cease to exist.

Then there are a lot of people who don't acknowledge any kind of spirituality, even to themselves let alone to others, who nonetheless do live their lives with a general spiritual compass that's guided by a sense of how the world should be and how they should fit within it. They're guided by a belief in the Golden Rule and a sense of fair play. They don't want to have the feeling that the world is worse because they're in it and they hope it's actually better because they're in it.

When someone like that is faced with imminent death they can easily go from not thinking about it to feeling that something will continue when they die because, on some level, they always had a sense of something else. The difference isn't so much that they had one belief and now they're having another, it's more that the changed circumstances have caused them to acknowledge something that wasn't in their awareness before.

It's my experience that a lot of people stopped examining the idea of a life after death when they rejected the organized religion they grew up with. They felt it remote, it was contrary to what they experienced or valued, so they closed the door on any kind of examination that had overtones of a spiritual nature or the idea of life being part of something larger, and they kept the door closed. As death comes knocking, that door is opened and it reveals an urgent question that they've put on the shelf for years. They wind up reconsidering the question with new data and new urgency.

When it does become an *urgent* question, a compelling question, when it's suddenly in the present tense, it changes things. Just as, on the physical level, when someone gets down to those last, limited measures of life, they may find that what they thought wouldn't be bearable becomes bearable.

Being with someone when they're dying requires a certain sensitivity to these things, to the changeable nature of the situation. The dying person is dealing with things you simply can't understand until they happen to you. Maybe they're learning something as they come up against it.

I would say that there's a lot of advantage in allowing death to be mysterious and accepting that we can't know for certain what it is, we can't know for certain what we'll feel, and allowing ourselves some leeway in dealing with it. Most of all, I think there's a great deal to gain in treating death more gently than we do.

CARLA TORRES
Age: 29
Wife and Mother

✑

My sister was forty-one when she died last year. She was a captain for USAir. She started flying when she was very young and was one of the first women to become a commercial airlines pilot. She was really, really something—brilliant and incredibly courageous and brave. She had an amazing life full of adventures that would take me a whole other day to describe.

There were eight of us kids in my family. She was the oldest and I'm seventh in line. She started college when she was sixteen and I was only two at the time so for a lot of my formative years she was gone, traveling around the world and doing remarkable things. It was always exciting when she'd come home. She was also my godmother and that gave us a special bond.

When Paula found out she had lung cancer, she did tons of research and really learned about the disease and about all the different options for treatment. She was on top of things. She decided to take an alternative, holistic-type approach that involved a lot of vitamins, enzymes, and various kinds of nutritional and other treatments.

Her doctors in Boston wanted her to have surgery, chemotherapy, and radiation, and, even with all that, they said there was still only about a 25 percent chance she would live five years. That just wasn't good enough for her. She knew she'd be sick. She knew she wouldn't be able to pursue the intellectual and spiritual kinds of things that she was really into. So she decided to do this alternative approach, where she expected to stay pretty healthy for a longer time.

She had bought a house in New Mexico before all this happened and when she found out she had cancer she decided to go out there and live. She thought it would be a good place for her to heal, and if she wasn't going to get better she wanted to spend her time there.

Paula made a good living and this helped her to be able to do things this way. A great deal of her day was devoted to doing the treatment; it was very, very labor intensive and involved enemas and a complicated daily regimen. It may have seemed a little bit off-the-wall but I had so much respect and admiration for her that I probably wouldn't have doubted whatever she decided to do.

About three years after the diagnosis she started to be pretty seriously debilitated. She wasn't able to take care of herself anymore. She had tumors in her brain and in her bones and could not physically do her treatments by herself. I decided to move out there to help her.

It was scary when I saw her so incapacitated, so different from the dynamic, take-charge Paula I had known all my life. Up to that point I don't think I had really expected her to die.

I spent five weeks with her before the end. She was in bed pretty much the whole time. She was deteriorating physically, although mentally she was sharp as a tack, and I know it's because the vitamins and the enzymes and her treatment were keeping her body as healthy as it could possibly be, given the fact that she was so ill with cancer.

She made every kind of arrangement you can make for your death. She prepared her will. She told us she wanted to be cremated. There was nothing left uncommunicated about the practical questions around her dying.

Spiritually, she had practiced Siddha Yoga for years. She had always been exploring God and spirituality, and she felt certain about what was going to happen to her. I don't know exactly what she thought that was, but I know she wasn't afraid to die.

We were busy all day with all the various things she had to take and do. I don't want to get into the details of her treatment, but it was really hard work. It was exhausting for me physically and emotionally. And, well, I've been talking about how great she was. She could also be difficult. She had a pretty big ego and was a very dominant kind of person. It was not easy all the time, but mostly I was aware of what an incredible opportunity it was for me to be with her—to know that she needed me, that was pretty amazing.

Seeing her die was incredible. I certainly didn't expect it to happen so quickly because she had been so sharp and had even continued to look beautiful. But I guess the cancer got to a point where all the good things she was doing for her body couldn't keep up with it anymore, and she just started to shut down. Her body changed right before my eyes. I saw the different parts of her dying.

She wasn't exactly in a coma but she was only semiconscious. I would talk to her and she would open her eyes once in a while and look directly at me and I knew there was a connection, but she wasn't speaking. I hadn't really given any thought to how she would look or what it would be like physically; like I said, she had stayed so beautiful until those last days. Now her fingernails and her lips became sort of purplish. She had a tumor on the right side of her brain and she was having tremors up and down that side of her body and her right eyeball turned yellow. That was pretty awful. She didn't look like my sister anymore, she looked sort of like a creature. It was really scary to see that change. Inside I was completely freaked out and panicked. I just wanted to stop time and get some kind of grasp on what was happening. But of course I couldn't.

Also, though, I really want to tell you how, at the same time, it was a good experience. It was humbling to see what happens to a body that's dying. It's a natural process, the decay of the human body. I'm sure it's different for different diseases but this experience made me so aware of what we are and what's going to happen to every single one of us including me and everyone else that I love. It was a really dramatic and important lesson.

I know that she was in some pain, she had been moaning almost constantly for a couple of days. And then, maybe eight hours before she died, that stopped. She became very calm and quiet and her breathing was much more shallow for a while. Then she suddenly took this really deep labored breath. It was startling because she'd been so quiet. She took two more of those labored breaths and her eyes were open and she was looking out her window at the incredible view and then she just stopped.

A hospice worker and a friend were with me when she died. After a while they went downstairs and it was just Paula and me. I really felt like she was there with me for some time, for a couple of hours. I felt reassured, almost comforted. It was awful hard too . . . it was so much bigger than sadness, it was pain—anguish I suppose.

Feeling her present after her body was done—that was something. *She* wasn't gone. It was just the body that was finished. And then there was a point where I *felt* her leave and I knew she wasn't there anymore. It was amazing. We kept her body there for a whole night and the following day, and I sat with her a lot, and now it was really just the body.

My parents had flown out from Boston. Before they got there we dressed her in some clothes she really liked and fixed up the bed and burned incense. It was nice. My parents came and they saw her, and then, while we were all out of the room, a smile appeared on Paula's face. She hadn't been smiling when she died. I understand that's rare but it can happen—a person's facial muscles can change after they die, not often but it is possible.

Personally, I think that she was pleased with the way we were handling things. I choose to think it was a small sign. Maybe her spirit hadn't quite left all the way, and when it decided to go it left with a smile. Who knows?

My own spiritual belief has been evolving over the years. I don't participate in any organized religion, but I definitely believe in reincarnation. Other people in my life have died, although I've never had the experience of actually being with someone and watching them deteriorate. The whole experience with Paula's death confirmed, as much as it can, what I had believed about death. And one thing that it really, really confirmed for me is how ultimately unimportant our bodies are.

Later I read *How We Die,* by Sherwin Nuland, and I think it's so neat the way he talks about dying—how people have the idea that when death comes it's going to be this beautiful moment where the person quietly smiles and goes to sleep, and he says how it's just not like that. It was so good for me to read that because when people ask me what Paula's death was like I almost feel I'm supposed to say it was this really transcendent moment with angels and violins and it wasn't like that, it just wasn't. It was real.

At the same time it was something I could handle. In fact I gained a great deal from it. It was *okay* that it wasn't pretty. It was real. It's a shame that we cultivate such an unrealistic image of death. I think it keeps us from dealing with it in so many ways.

All during that time I was grieving but I also felt like I had gained something. I somehow *understood* death, after going through that experience. I felt like I understood it in some way that I can't even articulate well. I have a very strong feeling that it's okay, maybe even something to anticipate. There's just no way I can believe death is bad anymore.

I've never envisioned my own death, but my gut feeling is that I would probably prefer to be alone, unless the people who were with me were unafraid of what was happening to me. I wouldn't want people with me who were freaking out. I felt this with Paula a few times over those last couple of days when I did some freaking out. That was really bad for her. She didn't need to be hearing that or experiencing it. I don't think I would want that around me either. In her case she had a serenity and peace of her own because that's what she'd explored for years and years.

For my part, the experience of being with her has changed my life completely. I feel more comfortable in my life now than I used to. My whole perspective is clearer. I've decided to go to graduate school and get a master's in social work, because I want to be a hospice counselor. I saw how important it is to have someone with you who isn't afraid—to have someone there, in whatever way the dying person needs them to be there. That's the most important thing.

WESTERN IDEAS ABOUT DEATH CHRONOLOGY PART 9

✌

At the beginning of the twentieth century, modern medicine is struggling to define itself as "scientific." Life expectancy at birth is approximately forty-five years.

1900s   Blood grouping is discovered, allowing for the trans-
           fusion of blood, saving millions of lives which would
           otherwise be lost from accidents and surgeries.

           The parlor, a formal room usually used for funerals
           and wakes, and referred to as the *doed-kamer* or
           deadroom by Dutch colonialists, becomes the "liv-
           ing" room. The word "parlor" is given to funeral
           establishments.

           Life insurance payments provide money for com-
           mercial burial services, replacing the assistance survi-
           vors had received from the community and the ex-
           tended family. This decreases personal involvement
           in rites and rituals and increases the role of funeral
           professionals. In rural areas most families still take
           care of their dead themselves or with the help of
           their church or community.

World War I (1914–18) results in so many deaths in Europe that some governments discourage traditional bereavement practices and public grieving because national morale suffers with so many in mourning. This influences attitudes toward public grieving in the United States as well.

1920   Many Protestant sects have modified their teaching on death to emphasize scientific understanding and a more pleasing picture of everlasting life. This helps to associate Protestantism with the trend toward materialism and "modern" views of death.

1940s   More than 400,000 Americans die in World War II (1941–45). Nazi death camps and the German government's genocidal slaughter of over six million Jews establish horrific new levels of methodical mass death. Cultural observers, social historians, psychologists, theologians—everyone asks the same basic question: "How can human beings do this to one another?"

1945   Penicillin becomes commercially available. Its wide use, coupled with improved public health programs, drastically decreases death tolls from infectious disease.

              Streptomycin is developed and used to treat tuberculosis successfully. The idea of the "miracle cure" becomes instilled in popular culture.

              Average life expectancy reaches sixty-five. Infant mortality declines to an all-time low. A child's death becomes extraordinary rather than commonplace.

1950s   By midcentury, infectious disease is said to be eradicated. As a result of medical advances and public health programs, death is no longer a threat in the prime of life. It is likely that the average individual will reach forty years or older before experiencing the natural death of a spouse, parents, or close friend.

More and more people die in hospitals instead of at home. In the past the family home has been the center of a multigenerational life. You were born in the house, married in the house, had your children in the house, and died in the house. Now the family farm is sold, the extended family breaks up, everybody gets a car and heads out to meet the future.

Science replaces the church as the dominant religious institution in the culture and the idea of death as failure becomes established in medical terms. With the advent of scientific materialism comes a tendency to see death as something to be hidden, something shameful.

ANDREW WEIL
Age: 53
Physician, Author and Lecturer

❧

From the doctor's point of view, to see death as the ultimate failure is very, very common. Every time a patient dies, that is a stark reminder that in fact you are not in control of the process. At the same time, doctors tend to be very pessimistic in their prognoses. In practice, I find doctors regularly predict that patients will not get better and, in one way or another, they *tell* patients that they're not going to get better, which on the surface seems at odds with the notion of "miracle cure" Western medicine.

I've really looked deeply into where that contradiction and that pessimism come from, because it seems to me it's very destructive and very counterproductive and it's not what doctors should be doing, especially since patients invest them with such great power. I think you can find superficial reasons for it: Doctors don't actually study healing and remission, they study disease and complications; they only see a very skewed sample of people, only very sick people, and that affects their view, contributing to their pessimism about healing.

But I think underlying this is something much deeper, which is not immediately obvious, something that has to do with the psychological motivation for going into medicine in the first place. It's said that people go into medicine because it's a way to make a lot of money or to have prestige or autonomy or to help people, but I think underlying those reasons, in many doctors, is a feeling that medicine provides the illusion of control over life and death. I think people who are very afraid of death may be drawn to medicine as a way of giving themselves the sense of being in control.

At the same time, in practice, doctors can protect themselves psychologically by coming out with these negative predictions, because then if the patient does get better, they're an exception and that's great; but if the patient dies, you're not surprised, you predicted it. This maintains the illusion of a kind of control . . . and a kind of power.

This is never talked about, it's not written about, and I've come at it from the angle of hearing these stories of patient after patient being told that they're not going to get better in one way or another, even while they are being treated by the miracle-cure medical establishment. I think, in a certain way, this pessimism is related to the idea of death as failure. They go together. Predicting failure is a tried and true way of distancing yourself from failure.

Most doctors just don't know much about death. I was given very little training in death and dying when I was in medical school and while I haven't worked in a modern medical establishment in a long time, my impression, from working with medical students today, is that their training in that field is still very deficient. Actually, there are many areas in which doctors are ignorant because they've simply had no training. Nutrition is one of them, and most doctors are not very well informed about human sexuality. They're certainly not informed about death and dying. I know it doesn't get discussed very easily between doctors and patients.

When I was in medical school, in the sixties, we generally did not tell cancer patients their diagnosis. One of the scenes that I remember very vividly was being in the room of a cancer patient with a team of doctors making rounds, and we would use code words to describe cancer and malignant processes, so that the patient wouldn't understand. That was horrible. We've progressed somewhat since then.

Now, there appears to be a little bit of a shift. It's becoming somewhat easier to talk about these subjects, the ethical questions are being debated. There's some opening in the culture, which is a long way from how things were when I was in medical school. And whatever you may think of Dr. Kevorkian and his style, I think he's a great hero for having raised these issues and made it a matter of national debate.

I have been asked by many older patients if I would provide them with materials they could suicide with. That brings up a lot of ethical issues for me that I don't really know how to resolve. I'm not comfortable with providing them with medication and I don't know where to refer them. It's a very difficult situation that became a personal one for me when my father, who had Lou Gehrig's disease, read that book by the head of the Hemlock Society, *Final Exit,* and as a result, made a botched suicide attempt.

He was in a hospice program here and the service that he received from hospice was otherwise excellent but I was very bothered by the fact that the people taking care of him were unable to answer questions about self-deliverance, or to help. The woman in charge of his case, who was a head of the hospice program here, got him to make a written agreement that he would not make a suicide attempt. I think that was none of her business and I really was bothered by it. But I think that's typical of what happens in hospice. They don't want to be associated with that.

This experience with my father also made me aware that I had no expertise in that area, I had no training in it; I was completely unprepared for how to deal with this, and the fact that I was a doctor made no difference. I don't know where to steer people, I honestly don't. I think I am as uninformed and untrained as most people in our society.

As it happened, my father had a great death, as peaceful a death as I can imagine. He was very lucky in that way. But it was hard for me. I mean, there were moments in the dying process when it was just agonizing for me to sit there with him. Because it was long and it was—just—difficult. I wanted it to be over and I was scared and . . . there were lots of things. It was very clear to me what he wanted and why, but it was very, very difficult.

It was also—I don't know exactly how to articulate this—just a very, very powerful moment. For all of having worked in medicine, I'm not sure that I'd actually seen a person die from beginning to end, before that. Even in medicine I was fairly insulated from that. And there was a feeling at the moment of death—there was a moment in which his spirit left his body. It was obvious that's what had happened.

For me, the way I experienced it was a wrenching feeling in my chest and then suddenly a feeling of terrific loss and sadness and I realized that he was not there anymore, that this was just a body. It was a very powerful experience.

Afterwards a number of people, friends of mine who knew about this, asked if I would please be there to do that for them if the need arises. I don't know that I want to do that.

Many doctors *do* do that. There are ways, especially in situations where, say, cancer patients are on intravenous drips of morphine for pain control, it's relatively easy to up the dose of morphine to the point where a person's breathing stops. But when to do it, whether to do it, who should do it? I don't know what the answer is. For me, it was a very intense, draining experience and while I would hope people would have that option available, I don't know that I want to be the one to provide it. Maybe it would be better to have some other class of professionals who were skilled in doing this, who could assist with suicide if that were an option.

I do a lot of work in Japan, where there is a great national debate going on over the question of prolonged life, especially around the issue of organ transplants, which at the moment are not done in Japan. There is great medical pressure to do it but there's a lot of cultural resistance, a lot of argument over the matter of not being able to define the moment of death.

There is a trend in Japan for Buddhists to set up hospices and I would welcome that here. I'd love to see Buddhists or people who, like Buddhists, have thought a lot about the significance of death and dying, in charge of hospice programs and perhaps providing counseling services to people in advance of dying so that they can make some plans as to how to do it. I find that Buddhist psychologists and thinkers do more creative thinking about death than other kinds of people that I've met. And on a practical level as well, they're approaching it with a certain kind of attention that is not known here.

Buddhists place a great deal of emphasis on the state of consciousness at the moment of death. Now, in allopathic medicine, there is absolutely no thought given to the importance of your state of consciousness at the moment of death. And since a major theme of my work has concerned states of consciousness, I think this is tremendously important. Personally it's one of the great concerns that I have and people I know have. It's such an important question: "When you are dying, what do you want your state of consciousness to be?"

There used to be traditions in Europe that focused on teaching how to die. There was a whole series of books called *The Art of Dying*. This was something that was written about and talked about. People were given instruction and practices to do so that when the time came for them to die they would know how to do it well. *Ars Moriendi*. I would love to see that revived, that whole idea of the art of dying.

STEPHANIE SEREMETIS
Age: 42
Internist and Hematologist

❦

I remember this from when I was about seven. There was a pint of wonderful-looking strawberries in our house, luscious and red. I picked one up and it looked beautiful too but then I saw there was this thing, like a growth on the side of it, a kind of creepy vesicular growth. I focused on it, checked it out, looked at it from every angle, and then responded to it as if it were something that was going to kill us all.

I decided the only thing to do was take it out to the backyard and bury it. Actually, at first I threw it in the garbage and that wasn't enough, so I took it out to the backyard and dug a hole and buried it and that wasn't enough. I had to dig it up and stomp on it and burn it and *then* bury it, and finally that was enough.

It was probably some insect pod or something but to me it was— *Disease*. It was not just something *on* the strawberry, it was going to somehow seep *off* the strawberry, get me and my family and everybody around us and take over the world.

I think in retrospect it was cancer I was afraid of. My grandmother died of cancer around that time, and I didn't understand what cancer was at all, it was kept very secret from me. Her whole death process was kept secret from me, so I think I had a fantasy about what death was. Maybe it was something from a strawberry . . .

Even during that period I knew I wanted to be a scientist and when I went to college I trained to become a biologist. Then, in graduate school I got involved in the early women's movement and with a collective of people who were writing about women's health issues, and that inflamed my interest in medicine. I made the decision to go to medical school and I've never regretted it.

Most doctors' experience in medical school doesn't touch on
death much at all. Usually students do premed, they do their science
stuff, then they go to medical school where there's two more years of
grinding away at the books before they begin even limited clinical
experience or patient care. But I had some rather unusual experiences, right from the beginning. I went to Stony Brook, which was a
bit of a different place. As a new medical school it was trying to do
things differently. This was the 1970s, there were forty-eight students in my class and 60 percent of them were women, many of
whom were looking to change things. There was room to push your
education a little bit.

We had just gotten there, had our little "Welcome to Stony
Brook" picnic in August, and right away, even before we started our
classes, they initiated a program where each student was assigned to a
health care professional, just to tag after them for three weeks and
sort of get a feel for what they were doing. I was assigned to a nurse
practitioner who was involved in discharge planning. (Discharge
planners help patients figure out what they need and how they're
going to handle things after they leave the hospital.) So everybody
else was doing these glamorous things and they said, "Oh, discharge
planning, yeck." But this nurse practitioner happened to be a really
wonderful woman and she took her patients very seriously, the way
she dealt with them made a big impression on me.

The very first patient we saw was a woman with breast cancer
who was very sick and had kids and it just totally blew me away. The
nurse talked to her about what arrangements she was making for her
kids if she didn't survive chemotherapy, and it looked like she wasn't
going to. The nurse was lovely with this woman, basically just addressing her needs, but it was the way she did it, she was a very
calming sort of influence. I remember seeing that and being very
impressed with it but also being very frightened. I had no idea how I
would cope with seeing people like that every day, watching them
deal with the possibility of their imminent death. This nurse took
the time to talk to me, talk me through it, listen to my concerns, and
she recommended that I read Elisabeth Kübler-Ross. Now this is

even before I started taking anatomy or physiology. It was like—
zap—right into it.

So I read Kübler-Ross and became very interested in a lot of
what she had to say. I mean it was very simple, schematic stuff but
still, she talked about death and dying, which were both, at the time,
quite taboo.

Then later, in the Introduction to Clinical Medicine course, we
did videotaped interviews with patients in the hospital, which were
then replayed so that the student could go over it with his or her
faculty and understand where they had made mistakes. I was assigned
to this elderly gentleman who had agreed to talk to a medical student
with videotape going.

So again, this is the very first time I'm doing this. You read all
this stuff and you go in shaking in your boots. And here's this guy,
he's in his eighties, had probably lived a pretty good life, had a loving
family and was obviously a very nice man. So I'm taking this history
as best I can, knowing nothing about how to take a patient's history
. . . you know, "Hi, what's your name?" that sort of thing. I finally
said, "So, why are you in the hospital?" And he said, "Well, because
I had some pains." And I said "Well, what has happened since
you've been in the hospital?" and he said, "Well, they've done some
tests." And he's talking in a normal tone of voice all this time and I
said, "Well, have your doctors told you anything about what the
results of the tests were?" Immediately his voice drops and he whispers, "I have cancer." I couldn't hear him, I had to lean forward,
"Excuse me, what did you say?" He barely whispers, "I have cancer." He couldn't say it. This was his diagnosis, this was probably
going to kill him and he simply couldn't articulate it.

As I realized he was upset, I got upset and the whole thing
deteriorated. I didn't know how to get out of it because at that point
he was totally silent, looking down at his hands . . . completely
silent in this kind of contrived space with these video cameras rolling. It was an incredibly difficult experience. I didn't have the skills
then to get beyond that point. To say: "Tell me how you feel about
that," or "Would you talk to me about why it's so hard for you to
say that," or anything. It was really hard, but having been through

that experience I know much more deeply how important it is to get to the next point in the conversation with a patient. How important it is to give them back their voice, to help them to be able to say the word, to be able to say it and take it in, understand it and then say the next thing.

I will be forever thankful for having had those and other early experiences that began to teach me how to work with people who are dying. It was unusual, it was more exposure than most people had elsewhere in medical school. It was very important, in terms of how my approach to patients developed, and I think that was the whole point of introducing us to patients early, before we were bludgeoned by medical school.

Also, I have to say, all this was in the context of an incredible and very clearly articulated fear of death on my part. You are not talking here with a person who is comfortable with the concept for herself by any means, and I think that a lot of this, besides allowing me to learn how to be a doctor with patients who are dying, was also my way of trying to get through my own fears if I could.

Some of it was: "I'm really afraid of death, how am I going to deal with people who are sick enough to die?" Some of it was simply being scared about facing that great unknown, that enormous fact of human existence—we're all going to die. It just seems so impossible and so out of whack with everything else one knows; it's out of kilter with loving life, with existence. And it's scary. Also, I came from a family where illness and death were concealed from me. That makes it worse. So my effort to confront dying was counterphobic, an attempt to face my own fear head-on.

I'm much better now, but it wasn't so much from my counterphobic approach as it was from years of psychoanalysis— actually sitting down and talking about all that stuff. And maybe it helps getting older, having a kid of my own. Death isn't an over-whelming reality that colors everything for me now. The awareness of mortality is there, it's definitely there, but it's not something that affects everything I do.

Everybody is so different about this. I have patients who are really quite sick who *seem* not to think about the fact that they're probably going to die. It's not part of their reality until they get very very sick, in which case it's really hard for them, because then they have maybe a couple of weeks at best to sort it all out, as opposed to people who've been gradually acclimatizing themselves to the idea.

In my specialty I see a lot of people who have diagnoses that you would call lethal, whether it's going to be tomorrow or five years from now. Some of them never even acknowledge that. I'm not talking about *accepting* it. I'm talking about simply taking that first step of *acknowledging* their diagnosis, never mind the next step of accepting it or not, fending it off, denying it or whatever. On the other hand, some people do acknowledge it but then just go about their daily business until they come into the hospital and die. That just happened a couple of weeks ago.

A very interesting guy whom I really liked a lot, very bright guy, HIV-positive from blood products. Forty years old. He had come to me four years ago, to ask me to write a letter supporting his and his wife's proposal to adopt a child. He needed it specifically from a doctor who would say that there was no medical reason for him not to adopt a child. And I said, "You understand you're HIV-positive and you could die." He said, "I understand this is not something I'm going to be able to beat. The reason I want to adopt a child is I want my wife to have somebody after I'm gone." And with that in mind I wrote a letter that said there was no medical reason for him not to adopt a child. I just wanted him to understand what we were saying. And they adopted a child, and he had two and a half years with this great kid and it was the center of his life, the child, the family.

Now he worked, literally, until the day he was dragged by his wife into the hospital and died a week later. I mean he worked twelve hour days, it was amazing. I'd ask him how he was doing and he'd say, "Oh, pretty good." Meanwhile he was a complete wreck, fevers, had lost a hundred pounds. It was, "Oh, pretty good."

I asked, "What are you telling the people at work?" Because he hadn't told them he was HIV-infected. "Oh, I'm telling them I have some undiagnosed autoimmune disease." I said, "So you think everybody in the world is stupid?" And he said, "I just don't want to deal with it."

Finally he came into the hospital. At that point he did tell the people at work and they were extremely supportive, but he was dead a week later. I think part of his energy required that he not accept what was happening to him. And he didn't. He was also getting kind of demented at the end, which was too bad in terms of helping him cope, but the last sentient thing he said to me was, "I don't think there's anything more we can do, just help make this more comfortable for me." So we did what we could.

I'm far from being that twenty-two-year-old person in the room getting videotaped with the poor man who was losing his voice, but it's still hard to always know exactly what to do. It's very complicated. My own feelings about my own death are in evolution and will be until I die. I've grown to understand that that's true of everybody. It's not a black-and-white thing, and I have to learn to pick up the rhythms of whoever I'm dealing with and try to work with where *they* are about it. For me, part of making it more comfortable is talking and listening, hearing, engaging and communicating. But that's not what everybody feels. . . . No, that's not what everybody feels.

KAREN MILLERTON
Age: 39
Hospice Administrator

∽

When I tell somebody what I do for a living, I usually get a very predictable reaction. You can see them glaze over and close down. There's the usual question:

"What do you do?"

"I'm a hospice nurse."

"Oh."

Then there's usually a physical pulling back.

"That's people who are dying, isn't it?"

"Yes it is."

Then they'll take another step back and say,

"Don't you find that depressing?" And before you can get that answer out you see the curtain coming down and the end statement will be "I couldn't possibly do that." I should have money for every time I've seen that happen. Everyone who works in this field has seen it. So I just don't deal with it in society much. I used to want to, but it finally got through to me that nobody wanted to hear about this. It's a little dent in their sense of invulnerability, so people move away.

I used to be a hospice nurse and now I work as an administrator. Altogether, I've worked in hospice, in one role or another, for over eight years. Now I'm at a crossroads because I'm thinking that maybe I need to not do this anymore, or not do it for a while. There's so much pressure. We have 125 patients and a staff of 50 and it's unremitting pressure. With all the health care politics, the downsizing and all the political stuff that's going on, it's really hard.

The danger is, you get very removed. It can happen to people in the field as well. If you've only had the patient a couple of days that's one thing, but when you've had them for months—and the patient dies and you see the nurse come in and say, "Well, I can take a new one now," it's like there hasn't been any process.

I have nurses you can spot. You can see it coming. They're the ones who give out their beeper number or their home phone number. There's no boundary. They get sick regularly. I had a nurse break down and cry last week and she said to me, "You know, if I lose three patients you just give me three new ones and it never stops." I said, "You're right, it doesn't."

I admitted to her that before I came in from the field they had begun to seem like numbers. If I didn't have them very long, if I didn't have a chance to really get into the family dynamics and know the family that well, it was literally, one in, one out, one in, one out. I have to admit, after a while, it was: "Well, take a deep breath, ring the doorbell and start over again." It's not that I didn't care about that family, or didn't know how important it was, it was just . . . hard.

I think everybody who's involved in the work goes through this at some point or another, and I'm not sure any of us necessarily handle it well. We get sick, or we leave the field, or we overeat, or we do whatever it is that we do, but we don't confront it.

Several years ago I was diagnosed with breast cancer. That was very frightening because it was the first time I'd had my own mortality bang me on the nose. I think it was probably the first time it ever completely got through to me that, in reality, I too will die.

I projected ahead to the cancer deaths I'd seen other people go through. As a health care professional, you automatically know a lot of things about what might happen. You start thinking about chemotherapy and how awful that is and how people vomit all the time and their hair falls out and all these horrible things that you've seen, which the layperson would not necessarily know about right up front. As a nurse you think about the people you've cared for who died of breast cancer. You project ahead.

On the other hand, I think a lot of it is the same for the professional as it is for the layperson. I can remember getting the diagnosis, sitting in the doctor's office and watching my surgeon's mouth moving, but I cannot tell you a word he said. Fortunately my husband was there and he did remember. For me personally, I heard the diagnosis and I went directly to the funeral. But I think everybody does that, I don't think that's just the professional. Everybody who hears this does the quantum leap to—*terminal*—because that's the connotation of the word "cancer." The laypeople I've talked to, it didn't sound like it was much different for them than it was for me.

It's a very chaotic time, so a lot of the emotional work gets delayed because you have all this immediate biological and medical stuff you have to get through. A lot of what you're feeling gets put aside. And of course your family have all their fears and you try to keep yourself together so that they don't freak out, which also causes you to delay your own emotional process. I've been thinking that maybe what I'm feeling now is the grieving, finally. The loss.

Recently, I went to a breast care conference in La Jolla. One of the speakers there was a psychotherapist who does a lot of work with cancer and bereavement issues, and she said, "What you've really lost is your invulnerability." And that's true. I've lost my invulnerability. Of course it was always an illusion, but hell, it worked for me. I felt good about it.

I think hospice workers feel they have a magic charm. As long as they are working in this field they feel like they're protected some- how. Myself included. It's always a big shock to any health care professional, but especially a hospice worker, to be diagnosed with something that is life-threatening, because it's supposed to be: "Uh, excuse me, Mr. Death, I'm doing this work here and that means you leave me alone." It's not really conscious or anything, it's just this unexamined thing that's there. That has always kind of amused me and still does. Hey, whatever works . . .

Last month it was four years since my surgery, so I had begun to feel safe again. Then I went for my annual visit to the oncologist and he found three lumps in my other breast. I have to admit, when he found the lumps, it was almost a relief in a way, like now I don't have to wait for it anymore. It's recurred, so okay, now we'll deal with it.

I had the biopsy done and the surgeon removed all three lumps, and they were benign. There was almost a sense of disappointment that this wasn't the time to deal with it. This was a false alarm, then you go to the next false alarm and the next, until the real alarm comes.

There's a part of me that believes a real alarm is an inevitability. I've talked to my surgeon about a prophylactic mastectomy. For me that seems like a more comfortable alternative. I guess that shows how deep the fear is. He'll do it if I really want it, but he definitely doesn't think it's necessary. Personally, I think that once you've had cancer, you're cured of it when you die of something else.

I don't know how to describe what I feel. I'm going to say depressed—although I'm not sure "depressed" is the word for it. I'm definitely feeling flat emotionally. I'm guessing it's in response to this recent incident. Clearly, I haven't sorted all this out quite yet.

Working in a field where I see other people die is, in some ways, a double-edged sword. For the most part it makes you feel more comfortable about the inevitable, but on the downside, there are situations that are so horrible, you wish you didn't know about them.

When somebody gets to the point of being a hospice patient and they're going to die and you know they're going to die, nobody can really predict how it's going to be. Some people have a relatively easy time and you can control their pain and you can do all this great stuff. But some people don't. When you start having pathological fractures where you roll over in bed and your back breaks, those kinds of situations . . .

One thing I know about all the people I work with—they all want a massive M.I., a quick heart attack, dead before they hit the floor. I don't know how other hospices are, but everyone I've ever worked with has, at one time or another, said "Man if they diagnose me with this, get me a couple bottles of morphine and close the door, 'cause I don't want to deal with it." I feel that way too. It's not that we're uncomfortable with death, we see it all the time. But sometimes the process can be so difficult. You look at it and think, "Well, I'd just as soon not do that, thank you. Let me sign up over here for something else."

When I had the recurrence scare, I think these thoughts slithered back there, in the shadows where you can't see clearly. I didn't have to look at it real close but I think that if I pursued those thoughts very far I would have gotten to that. I would get a bottle of morphine and a bottle of vodka and do it.

The medical professional probably gets to those thoughts quicker because you know the stages and you can set parameters. You set limits beyond which you do not intend to live with it anymore. Like I said, the pathological fracture stage, that's as far as I'm going to go. Whereas the layperson doesn't know ahead of time that those kinds of things can happen.

On the other hand, we've heard of nurses in other hospice programs who have become terminally ill, have refused hospice care, had chemo, the whole thing. On their last breath they've still been fighting. Classic denial. Go figure.

One of the worst deaths I've ever seen was a good friend of mine who died some months ago. I don't think she ever actually dealt with her illness. She got breast cancer and she said to her husband, "You will now make all the decisions please." She just went away. She went far away behind a glass wall and you couldn't talk to her. I had the impression she was almost rigid with fear.

As the illness progressed, every time God provided an opportunity to get out easy she went for one more treatment. She could've left with septicemia—they did IV antibiotics; she could've died of kidney failure—they put stints in the kidneys. They left no easy way to leave. So when it finally came time, it took three days, and it was bad. It was bad.

I wanted to be with her but the doctor threw all of us out of the hospital room, which I do not approve of, but he didn't ask me. Then her husband would not let anybody be there. I called him and I said, "Look, I will go by myself and sit, I just don't want her to be alone." He said no and basically told me I couldn't do that because if I did he would feel guilty. She finally did die alone, which haunts me still.

I thought, ultimately it's their story. They wrote it and so it has to play the way it plays, but it was a particularly difficult death. There wasn't enough pain medication, there wasn't enough of anything going on, and there'd be these long periods of apnea and no palpable blood pressure, but still she'd grab another breath, and it just went on and on and on . . .

You know, I told you how people back off when they find out you're a hospice worker, but there's another side to the whole thing. When something like this happens, they all expect you to take care of it somehow. It's like, when they absolutely can't avoid it anymore, then they'll try to avoid it by turning it over to you.

A graphic example of that was when my friend had her last surgery, and a group of her friends were waiting together with her husband to hear the results of surgery. The surgeon came out and you could tell from what he was saying that this was only going in one direction and that was bad. Everyone was sad and hugging everyone else and everybody who hugged me said softly, into my ear, "I'm so glad you're here to take care of her." And every time I had to pull back, make eye contact and say, "No, excuse me, I don't do friends. I am not a hospice nurse here." But that's the feeling, into my ear, "You're going to fix this, you're going to take care of this." And then they'd call me and say, "Why don't you get them to do this? Why don't you get them to do that." For a while there I was supporting about five people, I was worn out. That was the feeling I had when I came in out of the field, like I just couldn't carry all these people anymore.

The work itself is a real privilege. In a lot of ways it's a very joyful specialty because you do learn so much, and folks often have amazing experiences. There is so much going on with the family, with the situation. It's very dynamic. You meet some really neat people and you get to know them at a time when they have things to teach. People have dreams and visions. It can be incredible. No matter what I do, whether I stay in the work or I go to some other aspect of it or I take a break or whatever I do, it will always have been a real important part of my life.

But it was like, when my friend died . . . all of my training didn't work. There was nothing to do. Now I find I cry where I didn't used to. . . .

One thing I know—I'm no longer one of the group that can go ahead pretending death doesn't happen to them. Now I'm one of the group who has seen that it can . . . who has seen that it will. I've lost my magic charm.

ROBERT E. SVOBODA
Age: 42
Doctor of Ayurvedic Medicine

❧

All humans have at one time or another dreamed of becoming immortal. Despite our knowledge that everything which is created is eventually destroyed, each of us secretly cherishes the hope that death might, in our one case, make an exception. India's ancient *rishis* (or seers) studied this question and addressed it in their hymns, collected in the oldest compositions of the human race, the Vedas, which are the foundation of Indian culture.

Because every embodied individual is composed of a body, a mind and a spirit, the ancient rishis organized their wisdom into three bodies of knowledge: Ayurveda, which deals mainly with the physical body; Yoga, which deals mainly with the spirit; and Tantra, which is mainly concerned with the mind.

In Tantra there is considerable interest in the philosophy of death. Having a good death is considered to be as important as having a good life. In fact, from some points of view, the main purpose of living is to have a good death so that you will have a good progression toward the next life you are scheduled to run into.

A "good" death, in these terms, would be first and foremost a conscious death, one in which the individual has had an opportunity to settle all his or her affairs, and ultimately, one in which the individual focuses, not so much on death itself as on whatever he or she sees as reality. You could call it God, or you could call it whatever you want to, whatever your version of reality is. But the rule of thumb is: The more focused you are and the more open you are to whatever is going to happen at death, the better off you'll be.

Ayurveda is less concerned with philosophy and more concerned with whether the patient is likely to die or not. The Ayurvedic physician would presume that an individual had been taught how to deal with death emotionally and psychologically by his or her religious preceptor.

Ayurveda is a science in the sense that it is not limited to a specific way of interpreting spiritual reality. Its origins are in India and, speaking in general terms, Indian culture believes that a human life is one stage in a very large ongoing evolutionary experience for the soul, but from a medical or therapeutic aspect, there's nothing in Ayurvedic practice that says you must believe in reincarnation. It's basically nonsectarian. At the same time, classical Ayurveda believes reincarnation is the best way to explain a lot of things that otherwise would have to remain inexplicable.

As it exists today, Ayurveda has been influenced by a group of disciplines that were interested in investigating the potential for living a very long time, becoming, effectively, immortal—living for hundreds of years or longer in the physical body.

Throughout Indian tradition there have been stories of people who have become immortal and are still living, and now and again people will claim that they've met them. So within the tradition of Ayurveda there is included that idea of immortality, or relative immortality, as a goal. It's not the sort of goal that the man in the street thinks he or she is going to be able to achieve, it's a normative goal, something that's built into the system. Yes, theoretically, if you really got into it, you might, with some luck, become immortal. It's like, in America, you have a goal to become a millionaire. The average person does not really and truly believe he or she is going to become a millionaire. But it's something like—"I'm an American, I should become a millionaire." Or maybe it's—"I'm an American, I should become immortal," since America is the place where material perfectionism is the ongoing religion.

So, in the Ayurvedic tradition, the idea of immortality is possible. Not very probable, but possible. However, immortality is possible only for people who are ready to die. So the first thing you have to do is to have no particular interest in becoming immortal and if you should become immortal then that's fine, you're not attached to it. Being attached to the fruits of your actions has never been regarded as a good idea.

In the Ayurvedic paradigm human beings are viewed in terms of the five elements—ether, air, fire, water, and earth. The air element feeds the fire, which in turn keeps the water warm enough to circulate throughout the system, just as when you're boiling something convection moves the water around, keeping it active and mobile. This in turn keeps the earth element soluble. The earth element is basically like a rock, when you leave it in one place it stays there. Water keeps it soluble. The body is 75 percent water. When it's kept warm and circulating, heated, moving, then the body is alive.

Prana, the life force (equivalent to *chi* or *ki* in Oriental medicine), sustains the body's function. One of the jobs of *Prana,* maybe the *main* job of *Prana,* is to feed the fire. Fire needs oxygen in order to burn and when you blow on a fire it gets hotter.

When *Prana* is no longer able to stimulate the movement of things through the system, the air stops moving. When the air stops moving, the fire doesn't get fed and the fire goes out. When the fire goes out the body gets cooled and the water stops circulating— ceasing to do its job of salivation and flowing. Now the earth element is no longer able to maintain itself in the dynamic equilibrium that is characteristic of life, and it simply drops to wherever it is. You've reached the end. Cold, unmoving, the body is no longer alive.

In Ayurveda there is a principle called *Ahamkara. Ahamkara* is your assemblage point, the thing that coheres you as an identity, the thing that organizes your individuality. *Ahamkara*'s job is to aggregate together everything needed for a living being to live. So she aggregates together the body, the mind, the spirit, all the thoughts, all the sensory impressions, all the self-identifying qualities like name, address, phone number, likes, dislikes, preferences, aversions, what have you. . . . All the different parts of you that you identify with are held together by this force called *Ahamkara.*

There are many combinations of things that can cause the departure of *Ahamkara* from the individual. As we age, there is usually a gradual buildup of obstructions and disease which decreases the strength of *Prana,* weakens the digestive fire, and interferes with the process of tissue nutrition. This leads to a breakdown in the system which ends in the dissolution of the organism, which in turn forces *Ahamkara* to leave.

Or there could be a sudden complete and total physical obstruction that no longer allows the *Prana* to move, causing the physical body to cease to be able to function as an organism, which, again, forces *Ahamkara* to leave. This could be a major trauma such as an accident.

Death can get started in any of a number of ways. It could begin because *Ahamkara* no longer wishes to connect herself to the body for emotional reasons. People actually *do* sometimes die of fright, for example. The fright is so much that *Ahamkara* flees. And once she's fled there's nothing to move the *Prana* around and there's nothing to inflame the fire, which allows the water to get solidified, which then causes the earth to drop and coalesce, etc.

As long as *Ahamkara* remains connected to the body, as long as she remains aware, and as long as she's in control and causing everything to run, then the body, mind, and spirit complex that is an individual being will continue to work. As soon as *Ahamkara* loses, for whatever reason, her ability to identify herself with what's going on, loses her ability or her interest in identifying with the individual, the individual will die.

As long as she can, *Ahamkara* will continue to identify herself with your body, your mind, and your spirit. As you die, and it starts to become obvious that that's not going to be feasible anymore, she will begin looking for something new to identify with. After you've died, when she eventually finds that new thing to identify with, then you'll get reborn in that new place. So death is a big transition between *Ahamkara* identifying with you as you are now and *Ahamkara* identifying with you as you are going to be in the future.

Right now pretty much all of *Ahamkara*'s attention is stuck on the physical body and the mind, the self-definition, the self-image. When that self-image is disconnected from the body, then you still have that image of yourself as you used to be but now you're looking for a new way to project it into material reality. *Ahamkara* is looking for the thing that is most copacetic to it, the thing that is going to be most congenial for it. When it finds that location, then automatically that thing acts as a conductor for it and she connects to it. When *Ahamkara* leaves the body she is looking for a milieu in which she will feel comfortable.

In a way, it's just like electricity, which will flow into the thing that best conducts it. *Ahamkara* can be compared to a very sophisticated form of electricity that can only be conducted by certain things, which are dependent on what sort of consciousness you have. Your consciousness will determine what *Ahamkara* will be drawn to and be conducted into. This is where the law of karma comes in.

That's why they say whatever you're thinking of at the end of your life is where you're going to end up going, because that will leave the strongest residual impression on *Ahamkara*. When she leaves the body, she will only remember the last thing she experienced just before she was launched. Now you're hurtling through the bardo stratosphere and seeing all sorts of things that you may not have experienced during life, and looking for something familiar. As soon as you find the thing that resembles very closely what you were thinking of at the time of death, that's where you head.

When death comes suddenly and unexpectedly, sometimes *Ahamkara* can become confused and then you're stuck. A friend of a friend of mine died in a car crash about a year ago. After he died she had a very vivid dream of him. He told her what he thought about how she was living her life, and he also told her that she shouldn't be worried about him. She asked him, "Where are you now?" and he said, "Well, mostly I like to drive down the highway at eighty miles an hour." Now in that case, *Ahamkara* is still very much attached to the thing he was doing at the time that he was killed.

After someone dies, a number of things can remain "alive" in many subtle ways. Ideas are also alive. As my mentor used to say, "The person who owned the *nam* will die. But the *nam* [the name] can go on indefinitely." Jesus is an example of this. Jesus died two thousand years ago but the name of Jesus is still going on and is still affecting many, many people in a very positive way. So there's tremendous power in things that are very subtle, things that do not necessarily have any kind of identifiable, material existence.

English is not the ideal language for talking about this kind of thing because in English there is the assumption that you are talking about discreet, self-limiting things. In Sanskrit it is frequently assumed that you are also talking about the nonmaterial aspect of a thing, so various terms and concepts are assumed to have different meanings depending on what level or mode of existence you're referring to or what application you are making, etc.

For example, Ayurvedically speaking, from the point of view of objective reality, death is termed a process. From the point of view of subjective reality, it's a deity.

Objective reality is the reality you and I agree on. We're both sitting down on two chairs across a table. In the world we live in you can go to sleep and wake up tomorrow and the chairs will still be there. They'll be there for a good long period of time before they gradually deteriorate and fall apart. This is objective reality in the sense that we all agree on it and it's independent of our need to actually *believe* in it. You don't have to believe in a rock in order to be damaged by it when you kick it. That's the external world we experience when our senses are pointed outward.

When the senses start pointing inward, like they do when you're asleep or when you do a lot of *sadhana* (spiritual exercise), you start moving into subjective reality, moving with your volition into the reality that's inside you. Subjective reality is something you have to create and maintain.

For example, let's say you visualize something and that visualization becomes more and more solid inside. As long as you maintain it, it will have a certain momentum. But if you stop visualizing it, it will gradually stop existing. So the subjective reality of death is something that's experienced in a very different way than the objective reality. The objective reality is something that takes place mainly in the physical body. Whereas subjective reality is something that takes place mainly in the mind. Because they're on two totally different planes of existence they will be very different experiences.

If a person has become advanced enough spiritually to feel comfortable about dying while they're still alive, then the physical process of dying may, because it's such an unknown thing, temporarily nonplus them. But if they can remember that, yes, death is what they're headed toward and if they can stay focused on the subjective level, they'll be fine with it and everything will be calm.

Sometimes I work with people who are dying. In some cases, if a person is particularly ill, they will want to hold on to the idea that they are going to be saved at the last minute. I usually don't tell them that, in my opinion, that's not going to happen. I usually say, "Yes, but you should be prepared for both eventualities. You should be prepared for not succeeding as well as succeeding. Then you will have no problems. Whatever happens, you will be prepared."

There's the general rule of thumb that the *Prana,* the life force, starts to leave the body about six months before death happens. If the person is even slightly aware, they will start to accept the idea of death about six months before it happens, whether they are Westerners or anyone else. It's a physiological thing.

I think that people who do not possess the concept of *Prana* will probably not think of it in that way, but you run across Westerners who, some months before they die, become convinced they are going to die and let go of the idea that they need to hold on to life. They begin to relax into death. So this suggests to me that this is the same sort of thing. It may not happen conterminous with the actual turning of the *Prana* out of the body, it may be precipitated by that. But at least a certain group of people, a certain percentage of the population seems to be sensitive enough, on a subconscious level, to realize that death is becoming imminent and therefore it's wise to accept it.

Here in the U.S., people seem to try to avoid being aware of death and since they don't spend much time around it, it *is* pretty easy to forget about it. In India people sometimes die on the sidewalk. In a place like Benares (a city where pilgrims go to die), you see corpses being carried down the street, three, four, five or more per day. Death is available everywhere.

Here there's no death except on TV. And everyone knows TV is unreal. If you never expose yourself to death, you can develop the notion that there isn't any. You're not at all exposed to reality. If everyone in North America was taken to a slaughterhouse, even for half an hour, there'd be a lot more vegetarians than there are today.

It's the same sort of principle. It was Bismarck, I think, who said that making governments and making sausage are things that should be done in private. But, in fact they should not be done in private. And death should not be private either, it should be public. In India, my mentor suggested I go and watch corpses be cremated. He said, "It's always good to live with reality, otherwise reality will come and live with you." I've found this to be true.

From the point of view of most varieties of Indian philosophy, the only certainty we can rely on is this: Everything that is born is going to die. If you approach Ayurveda, or any other discipline, in order to prolong your life, perhaps it will help you. But whether you live for a hundred years or a million years, that still does not negate the fact that at some point you're going to die. Therefore it is wise to accept it.

JUDITH CAMPISI
Age: 40
Molecular Biologist

❦

I think death is the end. I don't believe there's anything afterwards. I think once you're dead, you're dead and at that point nothing matters. Dying is the hard part. Dying is often painful and even if it's not physically painful it's emotionally painful, saying good-bye forever. I think there are many, many people who cannot accept how hard it is, who cannot accept that when you're dead you're dead. And they will evolve all sorts of creative ways of saying it's not true, even if that requires a total suspension of rationality.

Religious belief is the traditional way to reassure yourself, of course, but there are also people who think science will fix it, which is very much the same kind of thing. The idea that science has the potential to perpetuate the human body indefinitely is wishful thinking on the part of those who have taken the advances that have been made in the past and extrapolated as to what might be possible in the future. As a scientist I find these kinds of futuristic expectations embarrassing and annoying. They try to make science like religion. God can move mountains, science can move mountains. But that's not how science works, it's not religion, it has its limits. Science has done wonderful things for us and will continue to do wonderful things for us, but it's not going to make us live forever. At least not in our lifetime or in any foreseeable future. There's no evidence that this will occur.

You can replace a liver, replace a heart, replace a kidney, but aging is much more than your heart failing or your liver failing. It's not one organ or one tissue or one process that gives rise to what we recognize as aging. It's a slow degeneration of all systems, and therein lies the complexity in understanding how it's controlled. To add to the complexity, there is a genetic component and an environmental component, and the two together determine the rate of aging in any organism.

If you look at the genetic component alone, you see that the problems inherent in gene manipulation are immensely complicated . . . immensely complicated. We don't know enough about how complex organisms integrate *normal* function, never mind attempting to manipulate them.

In my work I'm not trying to help people live forever or eliminate death. I'm a scientist working on an intriguing biological problem. I'm intensely interested in understanding the many genes that put the brakes on cell proliferation. I think those genes will tell us a whole lot about how to control cancer and maybe a whole lot about how to control aging. But I can tell you we already know that, even as we understand what those genes are, there are going to be limits as to what we can do.

I look at very, very basic cell mechanisms, focusing on a few particular genes and the process of cell senescence. Cell senescence is a fundamental process that limits the number of times a cell can divide. To illustrate: Your body is made up of billions and billions of individual cells. Some cells never divide in the adult organism. Of those that do divide, each has a genetically determined limit to the number of times it can do so. When it reaches that limit, the cell just sits there; it can't reproduce anymore. You can see how this would be one reason why, for example, wound healing becomes less efficient as people age, because you have fewer cells that can repopulate if you incur a wound.

Now, why is this so? Why would we evolve a system where each individual cell cannot simply divide forever? The reason is, every time a cell divides it runs the risk of becoming a tumor cell. Mice die around three years of age. If you do an autopsy on them, they are riddled with tumors. It's the same with humans. Anyone who lives long enough will show hyperproliferation, early signs of cancer. So as we developed longer and longer life spans, we've had to evolve ways to cut back the rate at which cancer might occur. But that very same protective mechanism means that at some point you have tissues that can't regenerate anymore. The forces that have slowed down the rates of cancer are the same forces that contribute to aging. That's the trade-off.

Genes tell cells what to do. When a particular gene that tells a cell to divide and reproduce is expressed at too high a level, the cell may become a tumor cell. When a cell senesces, that is, when it reaches the point where it can no longer divide, one of the things that may happen is that same gene may shut off. If you imagine, in your wildest dreams of genetic engineering, that you could take that gene and switch it back on, you could make the cell continue to reproduce itself. But you have a problem. Now you have a potential tumor cell. If you allow that gene to shut off, you've also got a problem, you have a cell that can't reproduce.

Now, it may be possible in the future to find ways to fine-tune things. You give a little or take a little, cut back on the rates of cancer without compromising cell senescence too much and vice versa. But in the end you're going to have to make that basic decision about which way to go. It seems to be that that's the way the organism is set up, that's the way the genes are set up.

I think that the promise of this part of biology, transgenic technology and gene therapy—actually changing the genes that are expressed by an embryo before it is mature—is going to come to fruition. But I think it's going to be most useful in correcting very specific defects.

For example, mice don't get atherosclerosis (clogging of the arteries), that's one of the things they don't die from. For years people said you can't study human atherosclerosis in mice because they don't get it as part of their normal physiology. Well, it turns out that if you take the human genes that predispose to early-onset atherosclerosis and make a mouse express those genes, you now have a mouse model where they *do* get atherosclerosis—a transgenic mouse. Now you can start testing drugs to see what might help, slow down, or cure atherosclerosis.

In this area there's enormous potential for intervening in individual disease processes. But whether that's really going to get our maximum life span extended—I think it's too early to tell. While it's true that transgenic technology has advanced wonderfully, it's like trying to predict what the stock market is going to be like in 1999. Who can predict?

Yes, the technology exists to create transgenic mice, mice that express particular genes, or don't express particular genes, or express foreign genes or even their own genes at the wrong time. You can make entire mice that have these genetic abilities by manipulating DNA within an embryo and then allowing the embryo to develop. It's possible to create strains of mice that contain virtually any mutation you want as long as you have the cloned gene in hand, and we have quite a few in hand, although quite a few more to clone.

But what happens if you make a mouse that underexpresses a particular gene, or expresses it all the time? Well, it's been done and many of these mice are in big trouble. In fact, most don't have an extended life span, they die earlier because they've got too much or too little of something early in life. I can tell you this for sure: One thing we've learned from making transgenic mice is—there's lots of ways to screw up a mouse.

Myself, I don't like to kill animals so I try to work with cells as much as I can. Cells have a genetic program which allows them to divide. They also have a genetic program which allows them to differentiate, that is, to express those proteins that make a skin cell a skin cell and a blood cell a blood cell. Although every cell has every gene that is capable of making an entire organism, not every gene is expressed. Your blood cells express hemoglobin but your skin cells do not. Your eye cells express lens protein but your tongue cells do not. That's what is called differentiation.

We have learned that differentiation is a bit what we call plastic. You can make an already formed fibroblast change to a muscle cell. But you can't make a fibroblast become, for example, a neuron. There are practical limitations. The less differentiated a cell is, the fewer the limitations. Theoretically, because every cell has all of the genes needed to make every single part of the body, *theoretically* you could re-create yourself from your DNA. You could take the nucleus of a cell, put it into an unfertilized egg, give that fertilized egg a signal to divide and literally create an embryo, and eventually a fully formed baby, containing the DNA and all of the genes encoded by that nucleus.

The problem is, even if that experiment were *practically* possible, that baby would be no more related to you (or the you that you think you are) than it would be related to the next person. All of the information, the neurons, the history, the memory, all of that is gone. That does not get re-created. So what you've got is a bunch of DNA and a bunch of genes, that's it. You *might* get a baby that looks a lot like you, although if that baby ate differently or had different parents or had more sunshine or less sunshine, he or she may not even look the same way.

Another of the many, many practical problems is that by the time you're a fully formed adult, your skin cells are programmed to be skin cells, your blood cells are programmed to be blood cells, and if you take a little bit of skin tissue and ask it to make kidney, liver, heart, lung, brain, you're asking too much. Those cells have already made up their mind what they're going to be. You have to do it prospectively, not retrospectively. You can't do it fifty years later.

When you're talking about extending life expectancy, theoretically many things are possible. But the application problems are so complicated that, while it may be amusing to speculate, practically speaking it's a little silly. Not to mention the ethical implications. But that's not a question for scientists. Scientists have no business deciding ethical questions at all. Except, of course, personally, as human beings themselves. If it's your child or someone that you love, you have your opinions and your feelings about what you want. But professionally, scientists should discover and educate, not set guidelines for the appropriate use of the knowledge they give society. It's society's job to do that. The health care professionals, the ethicists, the lawyers, etc.

For example, it's society's job to decide how to apply scientific technology when someone is dying. The problems you have now in that area are ethical problems, not scientific problems. But I think it's much more complicated than that. There is a problem *within* the society. Our country is absolutely schizophrenic about death. Totally. We have the death penalty but you can't have abortions. You send young troops to Iraq and you bomb the shit out of Iraqis but you can't let some poor woman with Alzheimer's do herself in because she's had enough. It's totally schizophrenic.

Frankly I think religion is a big part of the problem with this. The major argument against allowing assisted suicide is the so-called ethical argument, but when you really read those arguments they're religious arguments. Being a committed atheist I will maintain that religion does more to screw us up societally and psychologically than maybe any major force including politics. Even though we have a stated policy of separating church and state, we don't do it. And until it's possible to separate religion from the realities of life, if ever, I think we're going to remain schizophrenic as a society.

Think about what religion says. Religion says that biology doesn't matter. It doesn't matter that your body is falling apart and you're going to die. Your soul is going to go on and you'll go up to some cloud or you will pass on to something better or you'll be a king or queen or whatever it is, and that has enormous appeal. It makes you feel better about the fact that your body is falling apart and you're going to die. It makes people put up with lots of stuff in life. If you can honestly hold these beliefs, you are going to feel better about some of the very, very troubling aspects of life on earth.

There is a theory of aging which says that from an evolutionary point of view organisms evolve to maximize their reproductive capacity; that basically we're all on earth to make more babies, to make DNA and keep that DNA being passed on. But one of the antagonistic by-products of that vigorous ability to get your genes passed on is that those same genes then act in a deleterious way later. Evolution has optimized us for reproduction but that very optimization makes us die sooner.

It's a theory; it's just one way that some biologists look at the problem. You see this whole continuum of genes turning on and turning off and programs of genetic expression being timed just right, and part and parcel of that continuum is a peak and a decline that's just intrinsic in the system like it's intrinsic in a circuit to have an oscillating wave. From that point of view you could say that in order to assure survival of the species, we have to die. That's the trade-off.

I think this concept is basic. As you delve into anything in enough depth, you begin to understand that there are certain trade-offs that have to be made no matter what it is, whether you're cooking a meal or building a house or creating a biological system that is complicated and has to go on for a long period of time. There are trade-offs and that's just the way it is.

Now, if you believe in God, then you can say God cut us the best deal he could. As an atheist I just think that that's the way it is. You enjoy what you've got while you've got it. Recently I bought this house which is sitting right on the Hayward fault here in California. It's absolutely inevitable that this fault is going to blow sometime in the next thirty years, but I love this house and I want to live here. What can I do? Just enjoy what I've got while I've got it.

ROBERT FULLER
Age: 57
Educator and Writer

✑

I started off as a scientist, following in my father's footsteps. Now, looking back, I can easily see how I was seduced into science by the glamour that it had in the fifties, in the aftermath of the atomic bomb and the transistor and all the significant developments of that era. Being a physicist meant you were part of a whole culture, a whole way of looking at things. It was aggressive and full of hubris and fun and childish and—invincible. A kind of robust scientist's identity that can take on anything and solve it and if not, come back and solve it next week.

I was good enough to succeed at science but in the process I left behind my real questions. Now I see my real questions had to do with identity. After traveling through a number of identities in the course of my life, I found myself interested in the construction of identities in general; in the nature of this thing we create for ourselves called "identity." Lately I've been spending a lot of time thinking about the death of identities, about the birth and death of identity in the same body.

When most people think of death they focus quickly on the death of the body and that makes a lot of sense because without the body there is no mind and there is no functioning identity. On the other hand, we may very well be among the last members of our species ever to die. It seems very probable to me that we're literally, as a species, going to outmode death as a waste of education. First we're going to discover the aging genes and the growth genes and so on and double and triple the life span and then get rid of bodily death altogether.

We intrepid souls here are like that last soldier to be killed in the Vietnam War. No one wanted to be that last guy killed in Vietnam in 1975 when they were all getting out, you remember? But we knew that some poor devil was going to be the last guy.

Well, we're all the last guy who's going to be killed in Vietnam. We living five and a half billion folks are all among the very last animals called *homo sapiens* that are ever going to croak. And we are all going to croak. There's nobody alive today who will make it into the new era, although it's possible that some one- or two-year-olds, the very youngest, might squeeze in. They *might* fix 'em, but probably they'll decide it's better to birth these immortals outside of wombs and in laboratories with all the genetic defects removed.

Now this could be the cause of some terrible final wars on earth because there's going to turn out to be some carrying capacity for the globe—how many bodies are going to be allowed, how many people can be produced. And it could be that there'll be some awful liquidation occurring.

But if we have any sense at all we'll do it through attrition, and manage it. I would bet that that's what happens because you can't get smart enough to do these kinds of things without also being wise enough to do fairly well. I have the feeling they're going to go together this time. Which would be a first in a way but . . . it's the globalization thing that makes me think that. We're getting so drawn together as a human species that everything we do affects everybody else and by the time we can eliminate physical death perhaps we will have developed an awareness of our interconnectedness in that way.

Or maybe that's just my inborn optimism or wishful thinking, I don't know. There's no doubt that physical immortality would be a disaster and lead to nothing but stagnation unless we find a way of letting identities perish instead. Old identities will die and new ones be born within the nice, perfect twenty-five-year-old bodies which will go on and on. The body continues but the "somebody" dies. Now we identify with our bodies because we're so aware that everybody loses them. We're so concerned with physical aging and death because we will *experience* physical aging and death. But once you don't lose the body you won't identify with it that much. You'll identify with your identity.

Now everyone can whine all they want to about how we

shouldn't play God and this is terrible and all that. And that's fine and maybe those groups who say that will manage to convince one whole country not to do it, but then some other country will do it. It's *inevitable*. And it's fine, it's just fine. If you want to talk God-language you could say God made us the way he did precisely so we would develop these techniques. He gave us these brains and these brains have figured this stuff out. For all we know, that's just what he wants.

Forty years ago, they didn't know any of it. While I was a student taking freshman biology at Oberlin, Crick and Watson were deciphering DNA and they didn't even mention it in my biology class and now forty years later we have all this stuff happening and forty years from now I think it's going to be pretty well solved and then genetic engineering and the whole biotechnological culture is going to come down the pike.

And that's enough said about that. Death is a topic that shouldn't be distracted from by science fiction-y kind of talk. The importance of the vulnerability of people who are dying, the final months and days before death and how people are so afraid of it they shut their own parents up in old-folks homes. Since death has had this really nasty characteristic of killing our bodies, it's all mixed up with aging, decrepitude, and sickness. It provokes our distaste for bodily functions because it gets real messy at the end there and people can't stand that either. These are critical matters that we live with here and now and they need our attention here and now.

But I really think we're going to solve this genetic biochemical machine in the next century and remove from death all that ultimately irrelevant baggage having to do with chemical degradation and so on . . . and then focus on the kind of death that we really live with moment by moment, as we change inside.

Once you begin to feel the minute-by-minute death of your own personality, the death of the body is almost a diversion. If you let yourself, you can fall for the illusion that you are really there, stably there, reliably there. But it's not real. I know that my identity, and the identities of all my acquaintances as well, are dying every few years, if not every few days. They're constantly changing.

When you realize that, then you discover that a lot of the spiritual principles which have been, in my view, inaptly or incorrectly stated as applying to the body, work exactly correctly as applied to the identity. For example, the famous Christian idea that you have to die to be reborn. Applied to the body, I've never known anyone who died and was reborn. People say Jesus did but I'm not interested because it violates my sense of the nature of the world.

On the other hand your identity damn well has to die to give birth to another one inside yourself. So a lot of the spiritual stuff works perfectly when it's reinterpreted as applying to identity. Take the whole reincarnation idea. I find it completely uninteresting as applied to bodies, highly implausable, and, in any case, not worth discussing. But, if you take it as applying to the identity of someone—their body dies and their identity *seems* to die, but the unsolved questions that that identity was carrying will sure as hell appear immediately in someone else in the group who'll begin pushing those very same questions because they were unsolved and they remain behind.

So in *that* sense the "spirit" hops from one body into another one, if you define the spirit as the thing that's questing after a certain truth. And that quest will not die with the death of the body that has been manifesting it. The quest will continue, often in a child. Notice how often children seek out the aborted radicalisms of their parents, the things that we flirted with, say, when we were twenty, but then we gave up investigating, for one reason or another, because we had to bring home the bacon or we were scared or we just got seduced into some other line of work.

There's this unfulfilled and unexplored secret area and children have a tremendous nose for just what that is, because they can feel, in their parents, what it is their parents don't know, and they gravitate right to that. It's maddening for the parents, of course, but it's what children have to do. That's their job, to figure out the answer to what their parents *don't* know. What their parents *do* know, the truths their parents *have* found, children absorb with their mother's milk and have no attention for because the stuff works. The true part works, it's what doesn't work that draws our attention. That's the pocket of ignorance, it's full of questions and those questions give the children their quests, and those quests generate identities. What drives us is what we haven't figured out yet.

It's the same reason that news is mostly bad news, because that's what interests us. That's where there's danger, that's what isn't working yet, that's what we still need to figure out. "How come there's all this violence in the society?" A big question. So of course news is about violence because we need to figure it out. I don't want to hear "good news" news, it's boring. Every ten years somebody comes up with an idea for a good-news newspaper. It always fails, and it fails because no one's interested. *That's* the stuff that's working. We've done that. We're drawn to what isn't working, we pay attention to what needs our attention.

Our human computer was designed that way because it was linked with survival a million years ago. And we're moving right along here, changing constantly. It's like that ancient idea of the river, you know, what they say about how you can never step into the same river twice. Our identity is like that, it's constantly changing, constantly moving, constantly dying. At that level death is clearly embraceable, healthy, and as necessary to anything new happening as the cocoon stage is for the butterfly.

HANS MORAVEC

Age: 46

Principal Research Scientist

Robotics Institute

Carnegie Mellon University

✍

I wrote a book several years ago where I described the fact that robots are getting better and better. I tried to project the foreseeable future and show how, over the next fifty years or so, they are going to recapitulate the evolution of animals on Earth, at a much faster rate, of course. They will acquire all the capabilities that we have and more. They're essentially overtaking us evolutionarily and we're going to become obsolete. That's just the bottom line.

After describing this likelihood, I went on to speculate about what we might do. One possibility proposed in that first book was to join them. But we can't join them by remaining biological beings the way we are, because that's the primary problem. The biological form just isn't that malleable and has very strict physical and other kinds of limits. So we need to change our form.

There are many possible scenarios for doing that. One would be to turn yourself into some kind of robot, piece by piece. You can hypothesize a situation in which biological life extension works as a stopgap until we get the robot techniques down well enough so we could jump into a robot. It's just a matter of holding on for probably, oh probably less than a hundred years. There's even the possibility of this generation hanging on that long.

Or you can put it into purer form and contemplate things like matter transmitters that take you apart at a receiving station, analyze your construction, and then transmit a description of your construction to another receiver which assembles you from different atoms, and then the new you walks out.

You can speculate about any number of potential scenarios. One would be a kind of portable computer that included a program that makes it an excellent mimic. Then it's programmed with the universals of human mentality, your genetic makeup, and whatever details of your life are conveniently available. You carry this computer with you through the prime of your life; it diligently listens and watches; and soon it can do an impeccable imitation of you. When you die, the program is installed in a mechanical body that smoothly and seamlessly takes over your life and responsibilities.

Another way to do it would be a total body scan that simply reads out our essentials—you can imagine some kind of brain and body scan—encodes those essentials in some more transferable form, maybe as a computer program, and then installs that program in a more durable kind of physical body.

But people don't like this. They say, "It's just a copy. It wouldn't be me. I'll still be dead after you throw away the thing that you scanned." And then, even if the original were unconscious when the scan was done, they'd have qualms about killing it or destroying the original, even though the copy is totally functional. So as an alternative, as a kind of ploy to get the dialogue going, I thought of this other process, where the brain is actually excavated as it's being simulated and the original is destroyed in the process.

This would be a kind of brain transplant done by a machine with millions of tiny, microscopic fingers, all organized like a tree, branching and branching and branching. This million-fingered hand would reach into the brain and feel around for the boundaries of individual neurons, or maybe smaller components, and taking all the measurements that are necessary to characterize the cell that it's touching at that moment and then doing this for each individual cell. This robot brain surgeon has enough prior knowledge, an immense amount of prior knowledge, so that those measurements would be adequate for it to construct a simulation of the cell, which it would then do. So basically the cell is replaced by a simulation of itself. High-resolution magnetic resonance measurements would create a three-dimensional chemical map, while arrays of magnetic and electric antennas would reveal the pulses flashing among the neurons. These measurements, combined with a comprehensive understanding of human neural architecture, allow the robot surgeon to write a program that models the behavior of the scanned brain tissue, which is then installed in a waiting computer and activated.

I imagine this done as a kind of brain surgery during which the patient is conscious. (Brain surgery is usually done with the patient conscious, partly so that surgeons know if they're doing something they shouldn't be doing.) So the skull is open and this proceeds incrementally. The surgeon's million-fingered hand contains electrodes that can override the normal signaling activity of your neurons and activate the simulation. You are given a push button that allows you to turn the hand's simulator on and off, testing the accuracy of the simulation by comparing the signals it produces with the corresponding original signals. Any discrepancies are highlighted on a display screen. The surgeon fine-tunes the simulation until it is accurate. As soon as you are satisfied there is no difference between you and the simulation, the simulation connection is established permanently. The old brain tissue still receives inputs and reacts as before but its output is ignored. Microscopic manipulators on the hand's surface excise the cells in this tissue and pass them to an aspirator, where they are drawn away.

So this million-fingered hand is eating its way into an actual brain and replacing the parts it's eaten with simulations that work just as well. You don't lose your train of thought, you retain a complete sense of continuity and identity, even though at the end of the process there's no brain left and it's all simulation. Eventually your skull is empty and the surgeon's hand rests deep in your brain stem. The computer simulation has been disconnected from the cable leading to the surgeon's hand and reconnected to a shiny new body of the style, color, and material of your choice. The person's continuity of awareness and thread of thought has "migrated" into something else, rather than being "copied."

So you can do it as a scan that copies the original and then have something left over that you have to destroy, or you can do it incrementally and have only the copy left at the end.

Personally, I don't think there's any real difference between simulating and transferring, in this regard. If you made ten copies of you, they'd still be you. But a lot of people are uncomfortable with it. This feeling is an old instinct, an evolutionary hangover from the one-copy past. You just have to get used to the idea that it's easy to make copies of people. Then it becomes a legal question as to who, legally, is the "original" person. But I think it's entirely arbitrary, because both the original and the copy feel exactly the same way and are capable of exactly the same thing.

For me, I've thought about this long enough to be comfortable with simulation, with making a copy. I think that's perfectly fine because I know I am not the physical atoms that make up my biology. Those change all the time anyway. Old cells within our bodies die, break up, and are expelled and replaced by copies made of fresh materials as we eat and excrete and so on. The only thing that's really maintained is the pattern, the relationship of the parts to each other. It's as if you were a steady eddy in a flow of liquid. And that eddy or pattern is retained, is encoded into different forms by this matter transmitter idea or the body scan or the transplant idea—all of them.

As soon as you stop identifying yourself with the physical body and identify yourself with the pattern, all of these things become perfectly reasonable, including making copies. If you have a book it's still only one book, even if you have a million copies of it. The book is not the physical thing, it's the ideas that are in it, the pattern that's encoded. In the same way I don't think we are our physical stuff, our body-identity, I think we are the pattern encoded in our biological selves. And that pattern is preserved when you make these kinds of transfers and simulations because the pattern is what you're extracting in the scan, or what you're copying. I think it's more a matter of terminology than anything else. Basically we're talking about a process going on in the head and body, it's the essential organization that makes you what you are. If you want to call that pattern a soul, then you might say the soul has migrated into the simulation. You've made the path very smooth for it.

Thinking about computer simulation can lead you to ideas and propositions that are parallel to a lot of very traditional philosophical and religious ideas. As can contemporary quantum mechanics. And mathematically there are simply so many possibilities that the simplest one, the idea that the world is exactly the way it seems—a purely physical thing—becomes highly unlikely. I find it hard to muster up belief in the notion of extinction at death because I can think of too many alternatives. Here's one of the simplest ones.

Say we continue evolving along the path that we're on and there are superintelligent robots in the future, I mean *really* intelligent. I did some calculations on the physical limits of the exponential growth of computer intelligence and they're so astronomical compared to where we are now that it's just mind-boggling. You will have these truly godlike entities, converting most of the mass of the universe into thinking stuff, thinking stuff at the most efficient physical level. This is really a very mundane possibility, it doesn't require any exotic ideas about the universe, it's just a straight extrapolation.

So, you have these entities and they're not only able to think very fast, they're able to observe astronomically well. So for instance—and I'm sure this is Mickey Mouse compared to what they could really do—you could imagine them taking something like the Earth and scanning it in three dimensions, like a CAT scan, only at very high resolutions so that they can resolve down to individual atoms. And their ability to deduce will be beyond belief. You know how Sherlock Holmes could figure out a lot from just a few hints. Well, these entities can reason on an astronomical scale and the information they start from is so detailed that they should be able to, among other things, re-create the past. And they'll do it with incredible accuracy, probably down to essentially atomic precision.

Now the past would be of some interest to them because that would be their history, right? *We* would be where they came from. So think of how archeologists work today. They find some place that's a bit eroded down and find a handful of artifacts. They dig a bit and pick up a few basketfuls of stuff. But *these* entities would scan the whole Earth down to atomic scale. They'd know everything.

So they would sometimes think of us and when they thought of us their thoughts would be in such detail that we would be re-created. They would be simulating us in their minds. And we, being re-created in their minds, would feel just as we do now. In fact, if they're thinking of us this very moment, we couldn't tell the difference. Because this very moment would be the internal logic of the present moment, not the fact that they're thinking of it.

Again, it's the pattern. Subjective experience is the internal relationship of the interactions, it's the pattern, so if the pattern is being re-created we couldn't tell the difference between that and the original. We couldn't tell.

In a loose way of talking, the amount of thinking that would be going on in this future is, well, it's some heavy thinking. In fact, there are some arguments that the amount of thinking these supercomputers could do would be subjectively infinite as they think faster and faster toward the end of the universe. Whether that's the case or not, it's a lot of thinking. Given that, there should be plenty of time for them to think of us quite often, a thousand times, a million times, a billion times, 10^{20} times. And sometimes they'll think about this present moment, so this present moment would be re-created in their minds billions of times.

So, if you cared to distinguish between them re-creating this present moment and the original physical occurrence, the probability is overwhelming that it's a re-creation, rather than the original, because they think of us many more times than it actually happened. Basically, the possibility that we are a re-creation is extremely high. In fact I think it's almost ridiculous to think that this is just exactly what it seems to be. Like I said, I can't muster any belief for that possibility anymore.

And again, you see, there's really no reason to separate original existence and these various re-creations of it, because to the entities being simulated, living the reality, it feels exactly the same. So it doesn't matter if this moment is re-created a billion times. The moment isn't any different because of that. It's just like the idea of a mind being copied or the content of a book. The fact that there are copies of it doesn't make any difference. It's the encoded pattern, the internal logic that matters, and really, that's *all* that matters.

Based on the implications of modern physics, there's a lot of likelihood that the experience of that internal pattern may be possible in an astronomical number and variety of forms.

Personally, being a thinking type, I don't feel emotionally devastated by the possibility that I might just die and that would be it. After all, not existing would not be painful, not existing would not be a problem. But frankly, it's difficult to see how to achieve it. Maybe, if you worked really, really hard, you might arrange some probability such that, after you physically die, you don't exist at all anymore. But, at this point in my own thinking, it's very hard for me to imagine how you could do it. It's much more likely that we are, in some form or another, immortal.

WESTERN IDEAS ABOUT DEATH
CHRONOLOGY PART 10

✺

The space program, microelectronics, and microcomputer technology fuel breakthroughs resulting in a staggering explosion of medical advances. Multinational corporations redefine cultural values. Death moves into the marketplace with a vengeance.

1950s   Chemical embalming and makeup are used to create a "lifelike" corpse and a funeral service that discourages realism. The cost of a funeral becomes one of the biggest expenses a family must meet.

Extended mourning is frowned on. It is assumed you will "get on with your life" with as little fuss as possible.

Watson and Crick discover the molecular structure of DNA, paving the way for the science of genetic engineering.

The hospital is now the center of medical care, and the place where we die—often alone. Death has ceased to be the occasion of ritual ceremony attended by relatives and friends. Few have the time or patience to attend a final moment that has lost its meaning.

1960s   *The American Way of Death,* Jessica Mitford's ex-
                 posé of the funeral industry, helps encourage federal
                 regulation and prompts a growth in "memorial soci-
                 eties," cooperative organizations providing inexpen-
                 sive and simple disposition services.

                 While there has always been interest in and adher-
                 ence to Eastern or Asian death paradigms among
                 Americans, during the 1950s and 1960s there is a
                 new surge of attention, particularly to Hindu-
                 Buddhist models (including the concept of reincar-
                 nation).

1970s   Organ transplantation begins to be a surgical com-
                 monplace. Respirators, dialysis machines, and a con-
                 stant evolution of new therapies and equipment are
                 utilized in intensive care units as heroic treatment
                 efforts stave off death, raising the question of how
                 and when someone should be "allowed" to die.

As miracle cures and miracle detergents are mass-produced in triumph, questions begin to be raised about the long-range efficacy of
modern science as applied to the dying process. Some medical professionals and social psychologists begin to notice new problems.
The dying have become pariahs, left alone at best and, at worst,
actually feared. The bereaved have little support and are often required to repress even the most basic expressions of grief.

1971   Elisabeth Kübler-Ross publishes *On Death and Dy-
                 ing,* describing the mechanistic treatment of the dy-
                 ing, urging medical professionals and the general
                 public to reconsider the value and importance of
                 dealing more directly with death.

1974   The first hospice care program in the United States is
                 established in New Haven, Connecticut, trans-
                 planted from England, where facilities provide care

for the terminally ill. In the United States, hospice develops primarily as a program designed to assist families to care for the dying in their own homes.

1976   The New Jersey Supreme Court rules that Karen Ann Quinlan's respirator may be removed at the request of her next of kin. Artificially fed and hydrated, she remains in a persistent vegetative state before finally dying nine years later. Removing life support becomes a subject of public contention.

1980s   The phrases "Death with Dignity" and "The Right to Die" enter public parlance as assisted suicide becomes a widely debated controversy.

The AIDS epidemic re-creates communities of people experiencing the frequent death of loved ones while in their youth.

1990s   Average life expectancy continues to climb. Genetic engineering is looked to as potentially controlling all disease including congenital diseases and anomalies.

The state of Oregon passes a law permitting physicians to prescribe lethal medication for terminally ill people.

Books recounting near-death experiences, providing instruction on suicide, and describing clinical details of the dying process become widely popular.

A California jeweler colorizes a Victorian photo of a deceased infant and creates "Dead Baby" necklaces, which become a big hit on college campuses.

Cases of drug-resistant strains of tuberculosis and other infectious diseases reappear in major urban areas and begin steadily to increase worldwide. Whether this will result in a resurgence of past pandemics, or will motivate the development of new healing modalities, remains to be seen.

The defining value in the culture is now explicitly monetary, leaving issues such as health care and death care to be determined by the profit motive and "the bottom line."

Nostalgia for traditional approaches and beliefs is widely manifest. New immigrant populations continue to establish themselves and contribute a profusion of creeds and customs.

As we enter the twenty-first century, the potential exists to evolve a new paradigm for dying in the midst of the longest and healthiest life expectancy in human history.

JENNIFER
Age: 14
High School Student

&

I've never seen anyone die for real and no one in my family has died yet, so I haven't had to deal with that. It never comes up. I don't think about it but for sure I don't want to die. I know some kids get suicidal sometimes but I don't ever feel that way.

If I really had to say, I guess I'd have to admit I'm afraid of death. I wish I could live forever, or at least for a long, long time. They're doing lots of things now, you know, DNA and gene-splicing, stuff like that. Maybe they'll have figured it out by the time I have to really worry about it. I heard about some kind of cell-regeneration thing, where they can give you new, younger cells when you get old. That's what I'm interested in.

I think science will make it really different in the future. I mean, I know it doesn't solve everything but science has done amazing things. I think we'll be able to live a whole lot longer in the future. That's what I want.

ROBERT A. F. THURMAN
Age: 55
Professor of Religion
Columbia University

℘

Fear of death is universal. It's not just a Western thing. Everybody is afraid of death. People shouldn't feel like, "Oh, I'm a Westerner so I'm more frightened of death," that's not true. People in Eastern cultures are very afraid of death. They're luckier because they're more familiar with it, which keeps them more immediately aware that they'll be dying, which makes them realize they have to deal with it. This, in turn, gives them more incentive to work on ways to overcome their fear, and they have developed many methods for trying to do it. That's what people in other cultures have had better luck in doing.

I think what has happened in *this* culture is that people have indulged their fear of death too much. Our tremendous materialistic power has allowed us to succeed in keeping death out of our sight, so you can put it out of your mind that you're going to die.

Add to that the materialistic idea that there is no afterlife, so we have no responsibility to the person who has died, and the messiness, the unsanitariness of death becomes easier to put off as well. By sheer, habitual repression we lose all familiarity with it. Therefore it holds an extra special freak-out for us. Also, on the other side of that coin, it holds a weird, morbid fascination, if you look at the popularity of violent death in movies and the like. It's one of the imbalances in Western culture.

These imbalances show up in science and medicine. The materialistic ideology that there is no soul—no spiritual reality other than the material reality of the physical individual—poses the possibility of a kind of mechanical immortality by becoming a machine in a way, with interchangeable parts. That's another result of the denial of death. If your actual scratching, clawing, physical, sensory, waking life is all you have, it's easy to understand the tremendous imbalance in the medical industry, where you get the possibility of having a new heart, or even the fantasy of having a new brain.

We can also see from this a certain cultural tendency in the West not to deal with consequences. There's always the techno-fix fantasy, "We can dump this radioactive waste in the middle of the campus because by the time people are starting to get bone cancer we will have invented something to neutralize bone cancer." It's that type of completely cuckoo way of behaving which is very reinforced by a world picture that says, "Well, if it all gets too crazy I can just kill myself." And killing myself means—become nothing.

Because of the strong orthodoxy of materialism within the educated culture, the idea developed that it was mature to face up to the annihilation of the individual at death. Humanists think that "acceptance" of the view that there's no life after death is a sign of cultural maturity, a sign you've overcome these childish fantasies about immortality and have accepted that you are going to be obliterated at death and therefore you put your all into whatever you can achieve in this life.

This is a positivistic theory or worldview. Of course they don't present it as a worldview, they present it as fact. They have the whole thing organized to show that thereby they are the most grown up, you see. But from a Buddhist or Hindu or an Indian philosophical point of view, the person who denies the afterlife is actually considered to be among the most childish and self-indulgent of persons because they are counting on an easy out, an out that can't be proved to exist at all.

It's ironic, you know, it's an interesting confusion, because the materialist thinks that the person who believes in reincarnation is saying, "Hey great, I can come back and have another chance, so we can just hang out and be lazy in life." But that person is *not* thinking they're going to have an easy out. On the contrary. That person is frightened of the negative states into which you can be reborn if you're not developed, if you're not ethical, if you don't have wisdom, if you don't have a high degree of self-awareness. So they put a lot of emphasis during their life on working to achieve a greater self-awareness, increasing virtue and merit and goodwill, being more open to the universe and less prone to fear, less aggressive and violent, because being violent and filled with negative emotional conditions or habits will lead to negative rebirth.

People who believe in future life are not at all looking forward to it. It's not at all a sop to them or some way of disguising the reality of obliteration to them. They feel that obliteration would be an *easy* way out. Obliteration is like anesthetic, an *escape* from the consequences of what you've done, which is considered very childish actually.

From the Eastern point of view it's the materialists who are kidding themselves. By holding up the dogma of no future life they are saying, "Hey I can just slide right out into nothingness and it'll be no problem." In Eastern psychology that person is being very immature.

You have a different level of commitment when you have a view of yourself as embedded in a continuity of time. Not in some rigid immortal way where you're always white and you're always middle class and you always have a hankie, but in a way where the form of your sensibility is completely malleable—transformable into anything. And what causes it to be transformed into something good is how good you are, and what causes it to be transformed into something bad is how bad you are. That's a very different level of being committed to what you're doing.

The scientistic picture of a random universe, full of completely unpredictable things, wherein the network of causality is unpredictable, where you can't count on a good effect of a good act, or a bad effect of a bad act—this picture definitely leads to people behaving erratically. It creates a situation where the level of commitment to good ethical action is very low, especially in situations of emotional stress.

From the Eastern psychological point of view, it would be considered no surprise that the twentieth century, where a large percentage of educated people have come to such an attitude about death, is the greatest era of holocausts, of vicious horrible technologies that have polluted vast areas of earth and destroyed whole species, an era of the unlimited and uncontrolled use of individual self-centered power, irrespective of the wreckage caused to others—from the Eastern point of view this is totally predictable, absolutely predictable. Because when a world is governed by such people, there is a level of commitment to causality and to consequences that's very low.

This is another diabolical aspect of materialism, from a spiritual point of view. A materialist will treat other beings as if they are nothing, because ultimately they believe they are nothing. Like Stalin, they'll send millions to the gulag, or like the Khmer Rouge—"Well, let's wipe out this generation because they're miseducated, we'll start with the next generation"—it's like a scientific thing. You just throw out this batch and mix up a new batch. Then you're being a tough realist to say that the sense each person has of being a unique individual is an illusion, it can be discounted. You needn't take each person into account. It's really a very, very serious difference with serious consequences.

In fact, I think the view proposing no continuity to individual consciousness is a highly counterintuitive, extremely unsensible idea. There's nothing anyone can point to in nature that would indicate that *something* can become *nothing*. It's even, on a simple philosophical level, an incoherent statement to say "become nothing," because nothing is nothing, so nothing can become it.

If we reify our notion of absence into a sort of place where you go in, and then you don't know you're there or somehow you're *not* there—it's still something, not nothing. The radical materialist will say that consciousness becomes nothing after you die because it is nothing now. They'll say that what you think of as your consciousness is some sort of illusion created by your body, some sort of temporary aberration that the body is creating for itself. But this is actually completely counterintuitive and contradicts all of our commonsense experience.

What is much more commonsensical is the idea that things continuously transform and change into other things. The laws of physical matter, the law of conservation of energy and so forth, speak directly to this question. The physical part of your body, the part that everyone can see, becomes something else. If it's buried it becomes compost, if it's burned it becomes ashes and heat, thermal waves, etc., whatever. All the material elements transform into something.

Now, awareness, consciousness, that which is the subtlest level of the human being, that is *something,* clearly. Why should it be privileged, of all things in the universe, to become nothing in fact?

At the point where an orthodoxy becomes so extreme as to counter experience, it bangs itself up against reality. I believe the materialistic orthodoxy of our culture has banged itself up against reality. The fantasists of the nineteenth century who thought they were going to make stainless steel people with interchangeable hearts and interchangeable brains and everything, are losing ground. There are still a few out there, and ironically they still have a high command of resources through big foundation and government grants, as a result of the technoscience-like superstitious awe and reverence that they generate in semieducated people, but really they're a small minority of rather weird folks.

The majority of people have totally lost faith in the march of progress. They've lost faith in science's ability to deliver immortality, freedom from pain, even a clean environment, or *anything* really. They've lost faith in the promises of big corporations and of government. They've lost faith, in a way, with the whole promise of Western materialist scientistic culture.

What people are realizing is—"Gee, we're *on* the planet, we're interconnected with things." We need to figure out what it is we're interconnected with, what makes sense here. We better get a new level of reliance on our common sense. Let's challenge the experts. Let's not accept every medicine the doctor gives us. They give you thalidomide, they do radiation experiments on people without telling them, they give you stuff that turns your bones to plastic, all these scandals. There's one thing after another. So there's a tendency to lose faith, and in the light of that to go back to what might be called common sense.

The larger mass of people are saying: "All these systems and all these experts are full of it." "I can't just buy everything they're telling me, I have to think it through, figure out what works for me, I have to face these things, I wanna see somebody."

And when they're putting electric jolts into my elderly uncle who's dying, instead of letting him die, I have to question: "What are they doing here?" "Is it worth the torture he's going through?" "Where do I draw the line?" "Can I pay this bill?" "I speak from the authority of my common sense: This is crazy." These are machine systems that are going to crush me as a person like they're crushing him. So I'm going to take the risk, I'm going to say, "Turn it off." "Cut it out." "Pull the plug."

Part of this process includes coming back around to the fact of death as a reality. Death is reintroducing itself to us. Medical science developed inoculations for smallpox and polio and eradicated infectious disease, but then we get epidemics of cancer and AIDS and viruses coming out of the rain forest, other things. You can tinker with the external environment but you can't control it. We tried to hide death but we're being forced to face up to it again, at least a little bit.

The current problems we face in dealing with death and dying are difficult but they're part of something that's very good I think. When people start to react and challenge the authority systems, they begin to take responsibility for themselves, they look around for what makes sense, and when they look for what makes sense they begin to realize that many native peoples have a wisdom about how life and death work, how the river flows, why it's important to not just go in and move the river around, but to respect the way the river flows. These native peoples we used to crush, to genocide. Now maybe we'd better pay a little attention. We're coming up against other civilizations that had equally great and vast literatures as ours, and we're beginning to realize that maybe they have some better views about things than we do.

Westerners look and see that in the East there has developed an interior science that can help them psychologically and philosophically. There are sciences of the mind that are every bit as sophisticated as the Western sciences are sophisticated in building automobiles and airplanes and rocket ships. And maybe they should

take advantage of these sciences just as they take advantage of the
Western one that allows them to fly to Chicago for Thanksgiving
dinner. Maybe they should take advantage of the Eastern science to
learn how to fly around in other ways, you see?

So I think it's no accident that now, as we face real problems
with the materialistic approach to dying, wisdom is being sought
elsewhere; wisdom is being sought in any cultural quarter where
there is wisdom.

All of this is very good because the whole complex of these
experiences, and these reactions, allows us to come back in touch
with our own life cycle, to become aware that death is very much a
part of life, it can't be put away, it is inevitable. When people think
about that they begin to realize that investment in their body, in
possessions, in objects, in material things—that this is a futile place to
put your chips. They begin to look to see if there are other things
they might invest in, if there are other dimensions to their being
perhaps.

This leads to a consideration of mind, of consciousness. It leads
to the fact that the main aspect influencing the quality of your life is
the quality of your mind. They realize that the way in which you
react to things determines the degree of pleasure you get from them,
more than the actual thing itself. If, for example, you have a true
sensitivity and appreciation of flowers, you can really enjoy the smallest, most modest flower. Whereas you could have the very best, most
extraordinary flower in the world and if you had a mind that was so
impatient or so tied up in its own notions that it couldn't actually
spend time and look at the flower, or appreciate the flower, even the
greatest flower wouldn't be of any use.

They began to realize that it's the quality of the mind, the quality
of the sensibility, that determines the experience of life.

Then they realize that this quality is something that can be developed, that it's not just innate. They see that if they cultivate certain
habits they're going to have a good time and if they develop certain
other habits they're going to have a bad time.

They begin to start to work with themselves, to develop themselves, to realize that the more subtle dimensions of their being are

actually the more important dimensions. They find that developing their consciousness is a valuable thing. That, in fact, their consciousness is the *most* valuable thing. This in turn leads to an exploration of what happens to this subtle dimension, this subtle consciousness when the physical element changes at death.

Wisdom lies in the contemplation of death. The ancients have always said that you must face death to really experience life. I think we're going to see larger numbers of people recognizing this to be true. I think part of it will happen from within the culture and part of it will come about by taking help from outside the culture, without this silly pride about how we have to be the greatest, you know. To help them face death, people will take what is useful from where ever it resides. This will be a very good thing.

THE HIGHEST COMMON
DENOMINATOR

When I began this book I wanted to know how death works as a
common denominator in this nation of ratings and demographics.
What do we really believe about death, and what does that say about
us as a people? What I found was a great discrepancy between the
American doctrine on death and what individuals actually feel and
need when facing it.

The dominant doctrine says: "Defy death," leaving individuals
to cope on their own when they come up against it. The voices in
this book show how, despite the harsh standard of that American
ethos, we are trying to find ways to love and care for one another in
the face of our common mortality.

Fortunately, we are a wildly diverse and ornery bunch who will
seek meaning and solace wherever we can. We struggle continually
with the tension between the dictates of the group and the needs of
the individual—whether it's about sex or speed limits—reflecting a
universal conflict as old as human history and most stunningly expressed in the paradox of death itself. While death is the only thing
that happens to all of us, everyone dies alone. But we die alone in the
world we make together, we die alone with others.

Unfortunately, in the world we've made together, the denial of
death is much more than a pop culture commonplace. It is, truly, the
fundamental paradigm for how we live. It is the root cause of our
inability to accept aging, to abide in the natural world, to tolerate
what we don't understand. It has allowed us to proceed unchecked

with a merciless, mechanistic, profoundly flawed mythology of progress, and has undermined our best efforts to address resulting societal and ecological ills. We have put aside an ancient and fundamental truth—the one that says coming to terms with death is how you come to terms with reality. In doing so we have put aside our ecumenical compass, the one sure thing we can count on.

Our pending death is our common ground. We have traditionally explored, pondered, and debated that common ground in the realms of art, literature, theater, poetry, and philosophy. But in a materialistic society those realms are dismissed as marginal and given little credence and no currency. We lose the answers and ideas that come from a communal discourse, we lose the connection that comes from it.

Furthermore, without the experience of death in our lives, we lose perspective. With no experience we have no authority, no grounding, no common sense. If we've never seen anyone die, we don't know what makes a "good death" or a "bad death." We don't know what's normal and what's not. We become prey to all sorts of projections and fears because we don't know the reality of the thing. Being naive about death, we are suggestible, gullible, ready to buy into anything that promises to take care of it. We become suckers.

For many of us the structures of religion and community we once depended on to provide guidance, have given way to the structures of materialism and technology that seek to provide control. But dying is the antithesis of control. When we are dying we are more vulnerable than at any other time of our lives except during infancy. This requires nothing less than letting go all pretense of control and depending on the goodness of others. The dominant American ethos doesn't allow for letting go or being vulnerable, but encourages competition in all things. The result is battalions of defended institutions that take the reality of death and manage it out of existence, leaving us with nowhere to go when we are dying.

Today there are two demographic exceptions to the majority experience or, rather, inexperience of death: ghetto youth who are living in a war zone, and gay men and many minority men and women who are living through a pandemic. These two conditions were universal in the past when religious conflict and political turmoil often leapt the boundaries of class and power as readily as did pestilence and plague. Now, however, they are often conditions relegated to the impoverished, or exacerbated by cruel and ignorant political and economic policies in communities deemed marginal by the dominant culture.

As a result, these two particular communities have been forced to address death in a way that others in America have not. In some cases they have successfully adapted traditional ethnic and religious practices into updated, relevant rituals; and in some cases they have created whole new support systems, even new conventions within the subculture itself.

Most Americans, however, are not forced to do this. Living with the expectation of a long life and a natural death, we have a chance to ponder our condition from the safety of favorable statistics. We have a chance to turn and look at death from a distance—air it out, open it up, see if we can allow a little space around it. This is an unprecedented opportunity, and the promise of life lived without fear of death is so great, we'd be nuts not to take advantage of it.

Today, the potential exists to rediscover some respect for death, some reverence for the magnificent reality of it. As many of the people I spoke with show, we are, even now, creating new paradigms, within our extended families and within our hearts.

A dialogue has begun, reflecting our deepest feelings and beliefs. More and more frequently there are conferences and support groups on the subject; people are asking questions, looking to address their grief and face their fears, seeking the comfort of age-old wisdom, a deeper comprehension, a more compassionate approach, a combination of ancient knowledge and new science.

As revealed in the voices of this book, there are many important reasons to do this, but in the end, the most important reason of all is our dying. It is simply too cruel to treat the dying with fear and aversion. Dying is a sacred act, the moments of death are profound moments, and those who have reached the dying point in their lives are deserving of our respect, simply because they are doing it. Dying is okay. It is not a flaw. It is not a failure. Natural death is not an external visitor that comes from a distance and happens *to* us. Death is inside us. It grows within us and will come to fruition when it is ripe and ready to flower. To deny it is to deny ourselves, and saddest of all, it is to turn our back on the freedom that lies within the fact of impermanence.

Like children rebelling against rigid rules that no longer serve our changing experience, we have thrown off death's dreary omnipresence. But still, we die, and that remains the one sure thing we can count on. Now we must reacknowledge that certainty and discover death for ourselves.

BIOGRAPHICAL INFORMATION

❧

Anyone under the age of twenty-one at the time of his or her interview is designated in the text by first name only. The interview designated as "Jennifer" is a composite drawn from conversation with two teenage girls in a southern California shopping mall. When a pseudonym is used, it is at the request of the interviewee.

Isabel Allende—Born in Peru and raised in Chile, Ms. Allende worked as a journalist for many years until forced to leave Chile after the military coup of 1973 killed her uncle and threatened her family. She is the author of many best-selling novels, including *The House of the Spirits, Eva Luna,* and the memoir *Paula,* which traces her life through the death of her daughter.

Laurie Anderson—Often described as the penultimate performance artist, Ms. Anderson is noted for her use of cutting-edge multimedia technology in music, film, and video production. Her albums include "Big Science," "Mr. Heartbreak," "Strange Angels," and "Bright Red."

Marta Arqüello—Born in Nicaragua, Ms. Arqüello was raised in the United States. She was a gang member from the age of thirteen until, at sixteen, she became involved in community outreach programs and has since been active in working with youth and their families in the greater Los Angeles area.

A. J. Berman—Pseudonym

James Blake—Professor Blake has been a counselor, teacher, and member of the faculty of the Borough of Manhattan Community College in New York City for more than twenty-five years.

Carolyn Burns—Pseudonym

Judith Campisi—Senior scientist and acting head of the Department of Cancer Biology at the Berkeley National Laboratory, University of California. Dr. Campisi works primarily on the basic science of cell proliferation.

Meinrad Craighead—An artist, Ms. Craighead lived and worked in Europe for twenty-one years, including a fourteen-year period as a nun in a Benedictine monastery in England. She now lives in New Mexico, where she paints and teaches art and spirituality. She is the author of two books: *The Mother's Songs: Images of God The Mother* (Paulist Press), and *The Litany of the Great River* (Paulist Press).

Lee Cullum—A syndicated columnist and television commentator, Ms. Cullum appears regularly on the *NewsHour with Jim Lehrer* and National Public Radio's "All Things Considered." An award-winning television journalist, she is a member of the Council on Foreign Relations and the National Conference of Editorial Writers.

Hobie Davis—Mr. Davis makes his living as a carpenter and has a fascination for the unknown; the unknown in the Holy Trinity, the unknown in his wife, Lee; and the unknown in three-dimensional form.

Lee Davis—Ms. Davis works as an elementary school teacher. She is married and has a grown son. Conscious living, voluntary simplicity, deep connections with God, people, and nature are the major themes of her life.

Larry Dossey—Dr. Dossey is an internal medicine physician and former chief of staff of Humana Medical City Dallas Hospital. He is the author of numerous books including *Recovering The Soul; Meaning & Medicine;* and the *New York Times* best seller *Healing Words: The Power of Prayer and the Practice of Medicine.* He is the former co-chair of the Panel on Mind/Body Interventions, Office of Alternative Medicine, National Institutes of Health, and is executive editor of the journal *Alternative Therapies in Health and Medicine.*

Margaret Fielding—Pseudonym

Robert Fuller—While teaching physics at Columbia University, Dr. Fuller coauthored *Mathematics for Classical and Quantum Physics* (Addison-Wesley, 1970; reissued as a Dover Classic, 1992). As president of Oberlin College he led his alma mater through a series of educational reforms, many of which drew national attention. During the 1980s Fuller became active as a "citizen diplomat," traveling all over the world working to find "a better game than war." His writings have appeared in the *Utne Reader, Harvard Magazine,* and *Whole Earth Review* among other publications. He is currently working on a book about identity.

Father Gary Gelfenbien—Parish priest of St. James Church, Chatham, New York, Father Gelfenbien received his Ph.D. from Rensselaer Polytechnic Institute, where his dissertation featured the study of light in Byzantine and medieval art. He recently returned from Italy, where he has been studying theology, art, and architecture.

John Giorno—The originator of *Dial-A-Poem,* the first automated call-in service, and a progenitor of performance poetry, John Giorno produces albums, video compilations, and films through his company, Giorno Poetry Systems. His work has been anthologized in *High Risk* and *The Norton Book of Experimental Poetry.* His most recent book is entitled *You Got to Burn to Shine* (Serpent's Tail, 1995). Mr. Giorno has been a Buddhist in the Tibetan Nyingmapa tradition for thirty years. His teacher is H. H. Dudjom Rinpoche, whom he invited to America in 1975.

Bob Golden—Pseudonym

Fleur Green—A practicing Gestalt and Transpersonal psychotherapist since 1972, Fleur Green specializes in dreams and the deeper psyche.

R.I.P. Hayman—Mr. Hayman's compositions and media events have been presented in venues across the Americas, Europe, and Asia. He is a founding editor of *Ear Magazine,* a new music journal. He is also a sinologist and consultant in Chinese cultural affairs, has taught at the National Language Institute in Taipei, and lectured on American music and new music technology at the Conservatory of China in Beijing.

Jennifer—Composite interview drawn from conversation with two teen-age girls in a Southern California shopping mall.

Rabbi Sharon Kleinbaum—A graduate of Barnard College, Rabbi Kleinbaum was ordained by the Reconstructionist Rabbinical College in Philadelphia. The spiritual leader of Congregation Beth Simchat Torah, she was recently selected by *The Jewish Week* as one of the top forty-five Jewish leaders in America today. She lives in Brooklyn with her partner and two children.

Marilee Longacre—Working as a waitress at the time of this interview, Ms. Longacre was preparing to travel, with her daughter, to Europe.

Charlie Lord—Past headmaster of St. Timothy's School and the Holton-Arms School, Mr. Lord joined Children's Express in 1992 as the founding director of the Washington bureau, then moved to the national office as director of Special Projects. His board service has included the vestries of Episcopal churches in Panama, Guatemala, and Toledo, Ohio. Currently he serves as a trustee of the National Cathedral School in Washington. He and his wife, Gay, have three grown children.

Jonathan Margolis—Pseudonym

Lorena Martinez—A doctorate student at Claremont Graduate School, Ms. Martinez continues to work within her community, organizing on behalf of families and youth in the southeast region of Los Angeles.

Jed Mattes—In addition to a long career as a literary agent, Mr. Mattes has been extensively involved in gay and lesbian political and social organizations since the early 1970s. He serves on the boards of the Paul Rapoport Foundation (as president), which funds gay and lesbian and AIDS organizations, and the Hetrick-Martin Institute (past president and current vice-president), which addresses the needs of gay and lesbian youth.

Karen Millerton—Pseudonym

Hans Moravec—Director of the Mobile Robot Laboratory of Carnegie Mellon University, Dr. Moravec is the author of *Mind Children: The Future of Robot and Human Intelligence.*

Alan Moyle—Screenwriter and film director Alan Moyle labors in Los Angeles, where he lives with his wife and two dogs. His films include *Times Square* and *Pump Up the Volume,* among others. He is an admirer of the work of Terence McKenna and describes himself as the last person on earth who still reads *Seth Speaks.*

Wes "Scoop" Nisker—Philosopher, journalist, and Buddhist meditation teacher, Mr. Nisker is a regular faculty member at the University of California Extension Division and at Esalen Institute, and an affiliate of the Spirit Rock Meditation Center in Woodacre, California. He is the founder and co-editor of the international Buddhist journal *The Inquiring Mind,* and author of the books *Crazy Wisdom* and *If You Don't Like the News Go Out and Make Some of Your Own.*

Robin White Owen—A television producer and media curator with a special interest in children's programming, Robin White Owen lives with her family in New York.

Fenella Rouse—From 1984 to 1991 Ms. Rouse worked as a staff attorney and then executive director for the Society for the Right to Die and Concern for Dying, nonprofit organizations protecting the rights and improving the care of the dying. In 1991 the two organizations merged to form Choice In Dying, where Ms. Rouse served as executive director through 1992. At the time of this interview she had taken up her current position as executive director of The Mayday Fund, a private foundation working to improve the treatment of pain, and executive director of the Emily Davie & Joseph S. Kornfeld Foundation, whose mission includes projects to educate the public and professionals about informed choice in the face of death.

Stephanie Seremetis—Graduating medical school in 1978, Dr. Seremetis trained as an internist and hemotologist at Mt. Sinai Hospital. She undertook an extensive research career and now works as director of the Hemophilia Program and the Women's Health Program at Mt. Sinai.

Ron Short—Musician, storyteller, and playwright, Mr. Short tours widely throughout this country and Europe as the artistic director of Roadside Theatre, an adjunct of Appalshop, a multimedia production organization in Whitesburg, Kentucky. A common thread through all his work is the importance of faithfulness to place.

Korby Siamis—A writer and producer of more than 250 half-hour comedies for television including *The Cosby Show, My Sister Sam, Murphy Brown,* and others, Ms. Siamis and her husband, Bruce Janousek, have recently retired in order to raise their children, Wylie and Kasey.

Frank Snepp—During his eight years in the Central Intelligence Agency, Frank Snepp served as one of its chief strategy analysts in Vietnam during two tours of duty from 1969 to 1971, and again from 1972 until the fall of Saigon in 1975. He resigned a year later and wrote *Decent Interval: An Insider's Account of Saigon's Indecent End,* which won notoriety as a landmark Supreme Court case when the CIA sued to silence him. Today he works as a journalist and is currently writing a novel.

Reverend Barbara St. Andrews—An Episcopal priest with training in comparative spirituality, Barbara St. Andrews did extensive pastoral work with AIDS and cancer patients, and co-founded and served as executive director of Medicine and Philosophy for the California Pacific Medical Center. She became the first woman to serve as guest chaplain in both the U.S. Senate and House of Representatives. She was killed in an auto accident in April 1994.

Shirley Stapleton—Pseudonym

Robert E. Svoboda—Dr. Svoboda received his Bachelor of Ayurvedic Medicine and Surgery degree from Tilak College in Poona, India, where he was the first Westerner to become a fully licensed Ayurvedic physician. He is the author of *Pakruti: Your Ayurvedic Constitution; The Hidden Secret of Ayurveda; Aghora: At the Left Hand of God; Kundalini: Aghora II,* and *Ayurveda: Life, Health and Longevity* (Arkana/Penguin Books); as well as coauthor of several other works. He travels extensively, lecturing and conducting workshops in this ancient medical tradition.

Terry Tafoya—Trained as a traditional Native American Storyteller, Dr. Tafoya is a Taos Pueblo and Warm Springs Indian who has used American Indian ritual and ceremony in his work as Clinical Faculty and Senior Staff for the University of Washington's School of Medicine. As professor of Psychology at Evergreen State College, he directed the Transcultural Counseling Program and was a Distinguished Scholar at Boston University's Center for the History and Philosophy of Science. He serves as consultant to the U.S. Center for Substance Abuse Prevention, is on the National Teaching Faculty for the American Psychological Association, and co-founded the National Native American AIDS Prevention Center.

Robert A.F. Thurman—Jey Tsong Khapa Professor of Indo-Tibetan Buddhist Studies at Columbia University where he also chairs the Department of Religion, Dr. Thurman is the author of numerous works, among them *Wisdom and Compassion: The Sacred Art of Tibet* and *Essential Tibetan Buddhism.* His translations include *The Holy Teaching of Vimalakirti: A Mahayana Scripture* and a new translation of *The Tibetan Book of The Dead: Liberation Through Understanding in the Between* (Bantam Books).

Carla Torres—Wife and mother.

Arthur Tsuchiya—An administrator and educator in the media arts for more than twenty years, Mr. Tsuchiya has taught at the Minneapolis College of Art and Design, and Middlebury College. He was Arts Program Analyst for the New York State Council on the Arts and assistant director of the Media Arts Program at the National Endowment for the Arts, and is now Senior Policy Advisor in the office of Policy, Research, and Technology at the NEA. As an artist, Mr. Tsuchiya has produced and exhibited photography, audio art, video, mixed-media installations, and digital works at various venues in this country and abroad.

Helen Tworkov—A student of Zen Buddhism for many years, Ms. Tworkov is the author of the book, *Zen in America,* as well as numerous articles on related subjects. She is the founder and editor-in-chief of *Tricycle: The Buddhist Review,* a contemporary Buddhist quarterly. Her father was the internationally known painter Jack Tworkov.

Rebecca Walker—Named by *Time* magazine as one of the fifty future leaders of America, Rebecca Walker, daughter of the author Alice Walker, founded Third Wave Direct Action Corporation in 1992, a multicultural organization devoted to young women's empowerment. Ms. Walker is also a writer whose work appears in *Ms.* magazine, the New York *Daily News, SPIN, Harper's,* and various women's and black studies anthologies. She has edited an anthology entitled *To Be Real: Telling the Truth and Changing the Face of Feminism* (Anchor/Doubleday).

Edith Wallace—A practicing Jungian analyst since 1951, Dr. Wallace received her M.D. and Ph.D. degrees in Europe, where she studied with C. G. Jung and Mrs. Emma Jung. She has taught workshops all over the United States and Canada as well as in England, Sweden, Italy, and Germany. Much of her work has focused on art therapy and she recently received the Creative Edge Award presented to her by the American Art Therapy Association. Dr. Wallace is also a prize-winning painter.

Andrew Weil—Director of the Program in Integrative Medicine at the University of Arizona in Tucson, Dr. Weil teaches and practices natural and preventive medicine. He is the author of six books, including *Natural Health, Natural Medicine,* and the *New York Times* best seller *Spontaneous Healing.*

Betty West—Mother of two and grandmother of two, Ms. West is a member of the Church of Christ congregation in Linton, Indiana.

Tomas Ybarra-Frausto—Associate director of the Arts and Humanities Program at the Rockefeller Foundation in New York, Dr. Ybarra-Frausto holds a doctorate from the University of Washington, Seattle, and has served as chairman of the board of the Mexican Museum in San Francisco. He has written and published extensively, focusing for the most part on Latin American cultural issues.

BIBLIOGRAPHY

⌘

A selected listing of some of the resources used to compile the chronology herein.

The African American Almanac. 6th ed. Gale Research: Detroit, Washington, London, 1994.

Ariès, Philippe. *The Hour of Our Death.* Translated by Helen Weaver. Oxford University Press: Oxford, 1991.

————. *Western Attitudes Toward Death: From the Middle Ages to the Present.* Translated by Patricia M. Ranum. Johns Hopkins University Press: Baltimore, 1975.

Ballantine, Betty, and Ian Ballantine, eds. Text by David Hurst Thomas, Jay Miller, Richard White, Peter Nabokov, and Philip J. Deloria. *The Native Americans: An Illustrated History.* Turner Publishing: Atlanta, 1993.

Becker, Ernest. *The Denial of Death.* Macmillan, Free Press: New York, 1973.

Burns, Stanley B. *Sleeping Beauty: Memorial Photography in America.* Twelvetrees Press: Altadena, CA, 1990.

Coffin, Margaret M. *Death in Early America: The History and Folklore of Customs and Superstitions of Early Medicine, Funerals, Burials, and Mourning.* Thomas Nelson: New York, 1976.

Culbertson, Judi, and Tom Randall. *Permanent Parisians: An Illustrated Guide to the Cemeteries of Paris.* Chelsea Green Publishing: Chelsea, VT, 1986.

Davis, Kenneth C. *Don't Know Much About History: Everything You Need to Know About American History but Never Learned.* Avon Books: New York, 1990.

DeSpelder, Lynne Ann, and Albert Lee Strickland. *The Last Dance: Encountering Death and Dying.* 2nd ed. Mayfield Publishing Company: Mountain View, CA, 1987.

Dychtwald, Ken, and Joe Flower. *Age Wave: The Challenges and Opportunities of an Aging America.* Jeremy Tarcher: Los Angeles, 1989.

Enright, D. J., ed. *The Oxford Book of Death.* Oxford University Press: New York, 1987.

Gorer, Geoffrey. *Death, Grief and Mourning in Contemporary Britain.* Doubleday: New York, 1965.

———. *Himalayan Village: A Study of the Lepchas of Sikkim.* 2nd ed. Basic Books: New York, 1967.

Hall, Walter Phelps, Robert Greenhalgh Albion, and Jennie Barnes Pope. *A History of England and the Empire-Commonwealth.* Blaisdell Publishing Company: London, 1965.

Kamerman, Jack B. *Death in the Midst of Life: Social and Cultural Influences on Death, Grief and Mourning.* Prentice-Hall: Englewood Cliffs, NJ, 1988.

Lifton, Robert Jay, and Eric Olson. *Living and Dying.* Praeger: New York, 1974.

Llewellyn, Nigel. *The Art of Death: Visual Culture in the English Death Ritual, c.1500–c.1800.* Reaktion Books in association with the Victoria and Albert Museum: London, 1991.

McDannell, Colleen, and Bernhard Lang. *Heaven: A History.* Yale University Press: New Haven and London, 1988.

Miller, Randall M. and John David Smith, eds., *Dictionary of Afro-American Slavery.* Greenwood Press: New York, 1988.

Mitford, Jessica. *The American Way of Death.* Fawcett Crest: New York, 1963.

Jackson, Charles O., ed. *Passing: The Vision of Death in America.* Greenwood Press: Westport, CT, 1977.

Stannard, David E. *The Puritan Way of Death: A Study in Religion, Culture, and Social Change.* Oxford University Press: New York, 1977.

———, ed. *Death in America.* University of Pennsylvania Press: Philadelphia, 1975.

Starr, Paul. *The Social Transformation of American Medicine.* Basic Books: New York, 1982.

Stillion, Judith M., Eugene E. McDowell, and Jacque H. May. *Suicide Across the Life Span: Premature Exits.* Series in Death Education, Aging, and Health Care. Hemisphere: New York, 1989.

Veatch, Robert M. *Death, Dying and the Biological Revolution: Our Last Quest for Responsibility.* Rev. ed. Yale University Press: New Haven, 1989.

ACKNOWLEDGMENTS

My first thanks must go to all the people I interviewed for this book, those whose voices appear here and those who do not. Every single one of them taught me well. I was constantly impressed and then impressed again with their generosity and openness, and with the wisdom that openness revealed. All their voices made a difference and shaped the work, whether or not they survived the limits imposed by space, time, and the relentless editorial process.

I also received a great deal of practical assistance with everything from recording equipment to room and board. Thanks to Robert James Bielecki, K. D. Kagel, the Santa Fe contingent, Mr. and Mrs. John Drimmer and the Ludwig family of purebreds plus one innocent mutt.

Transcribing assistance came from Kathleen Prata and Jane Doherty; astute and skilled editorial advice from Daia Gerson and Parvati Markus; networking leads from so many thoughtful and connected people, it's hard to count, but I must name Parvati, Johnny D., Bob Mendelson, The CityKids Foundation of New York, and that quintessential switchboard component known as Michael and Justine Toms. Thanks guys.

Also, a special thanks to Barbara Osborn for her cool head and keen eye, not to mention a veritable plethora of invaluable suggestions.

I want to express my gratitude to Heide Lange, who stepped in to help when my agent, Diane Cleaver, died. And especially to my editor at Delacorte, Jackie Cantor, a wonderful guide and helpmate for this book. An added inspirational thanks to Bob Mendelson, who thought he would be interested in reading something that showed what people really felt about death.

In the end, as always, my greatest debt is to my husband, Gregory Shifrin, whose unqualified love and support allows me to work and helps me to see.